Free speech: a philosophical enquiry

Free speech:
a philosophical enquiry

FREDERICK SCHAUER

CUTLER PROFESSOR OF LAW
COLLEGE OF WILLIAM AND MARY

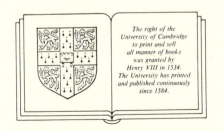

The right of the
University of Cambridge
to print and sell
all manner of books
was granted by
Henry VIII in 1534.
The University has printed
and published continuously
since 1584.

CAMBRIDGE UNIVERSITY PRESS

CAMBRIDGE

LONDON   NEW YORK   NEW ROCHELLE
MELBOURNE   SYDNEY

Published by the Press Syndicate of the University of Cambridge
The Pitt Building, Trumpington Street, Cambridge CB2 1 RP
32 East 57th Street, New York, NY 10022, USA
296 Beaconsfield Parade, Middle Park, Melbourne 3206, Australia

© Cambridge University Press 1982

First published 1982
Reprinted 1984 (twice)

Printed in the United States of America

Library of Congress catalogue card number: 82-4170

British Library Cataloguing in Publication Data
Schauer, Frederick
Free speech: a philosophical enquiry.
1. Liberty of speech – United States
I. Title
323.44'3'0973   JC591

ISBN 0 521 24340 8 hard covers
ISBN 0 521 28617 4 paperback

to Clarence's granddaughter,
with my eyes wide open

So long as there are earnest believers in the world, they will always wish to punish opinions, even if their judgment tells them it is unwise, and their conscience that it is wrong.

Walter Bagehot, *The metaphysical basis of toleration*

Contents

Preface

This book is the philosophical extension of ten years of study and writing about freedom of speech as a question of *law*. As I have written more and more about the legal aspects of free speech, I have come to look at the law relating to free speech as the specific application of a difficult problem spanning many areas of philosophical enquiry, especially epistemology, ethics, political and social philosophy, philosophy of law, and aesthetics. In recent years I have felt that I was indeed writing philosophy, albeit in a style and with examples drawn from law rather than from philosophy. In this book I have jettisoned that legal orientation to talk about freedom of speech as a philosophical question, divorcing the enquiry from questions about particular laws or about the protection of freedom of speech in particular legal systems.

Much of the motivation behind the writing of this book was my gradual realization that the legal system takes freedom of speech as a given, devoting little if any attention to the philosophical foundations of the principle it seeks to enforce. This is not only philosophically troubling, but also deficient as legal analysis. Unless we can get clear about the philosophical underpinnings of a political principle, we can hardly navigate successfully through the waters of specific application of that principle.

I view this effort as primarily an exercise in conceptual clarification. In the spirit of much of contemporary political philosophy, this book combines conceptual analysis with normative argument. But the emphasis diverges from the mode of current political philosophy, because conceptual analysis is more prominent in this book than normative argument. Perhaps that is because there has been less philosophical writing about freedom of speech than about, say, equality, or democracy, or political morality. With less having been done, more conceptual confusion remains to be cleared away. If I succeed in that task, then I am relatively unconcerned that my normative arguments may be unsuccessful.

Although this book thus adopts a philosophical rather than a legal approach, it cannot break completely from its origins. First, I come to write this book with a background as a lawyer and not as a professional philosopher. Moreover, to ignore what the law has done with respect to freedom of speech would be a mistake, because the law furnishes both doctrine and illuminating examples. The rules of law relating to freedom of speech are in many instances sources of important philosophical principles, and in many other instances illustrative of instructive mistakes. Although in this book I rarely mention specific legal rules or decided cases, much of what I have to say has its impetus in legal doctrine.

This book contains several pervasive themes. It assumes but does not argue that at the level of application there is a plurality of relatively independent principles in political philosophy. Our repeated references to freedom of speech suggest that we take it to be one of those independent principles, and much of the argument here is devoted to trying to locate the philosophical foundations for such an independent principle. My use of the plural in 'foundations' is deliberate, as another of the themes of the book is that what we normally refer to as 'freedom of speech' is in fact not one principle, but a collection of separate but interrelated principles, each more or less availing depending on the particular problem at issue.

Another important theme is the view of speech as primarily an other-regarding activity. I am not entirely sure that there can be a plausible distinction between self-regarding acts and other-regarding acts; but if there is such a distinction, then speech is more often than not other-regarding, capable of causing great harm and great good. Failure to recognize this seemingly obvious fact has led to some extraordinarily silly generalizations about freedom of speech, and setting things right in this respect is one of the foremost aims of this book.

Finally, I want to mention the close connexion between a theory of free speech and a theory of rights. I deal with this relationship throughout the book, especially in reference to what might be called the 'structure of rights'. As is true of what I say about freedom of speech, much of what I say about the structure of rights is controversial. Although developing a theory of the structure of rights has not been my main purpose, some of my discussion about rights in general may be applicable beyond the specific question of freedom of speech.

The book is divided into three parts. In the first part I try to create the framework for the analysis by setting out a somewhat artificial Free Speech Principle. I then describe and analyse those arguments that might support recognition of such an independent principle in political philosophy. In Part II I take on almost exclusively the task of conceptual clarification. What kind of right is the right to free speech? What activities does it cover, and what is the strength of its protection within the range of coverage? In Part III I deal with relatively specific applications, particularly defamation, obscenity, national security, and parades, picketing, and demonstrations. These examples are illustrative and not exhaustive, designed to show how the analysis in the first two parts is related to the kinds of free speech problems we commonly encounter.

Perhaps this book will only show the extent to which freedom of speech is like Pandora's box. To say that there is a general principle that all (or even some) linguistic and pictorial conduct should be particularly immune from governmental control is to say a great deal about an enormous range of human activity. Part of my task, as I see it, is to narrow this range to manageable proportions. When we say too much, we say as little as when we say nothing at all.

Williamsburg, Virginia   Frederick Schauer
18 April 1981

Acknowledgments

I could not have completed this book without the assistance of a great number of people. I started the book during a year when I had the privilege and honour of being a Visiting Member of the Faculty of Law at Cambridge University and a Visiting Scholar at Wolfson College, Cambridge. The opportunities for reflection and stimulating discussion during that year were indispensable, and I will always remain indebted both to the Faculty of Law and to Wolfson College for providing facilities for my work as well as an extraordinarily exciting intellectual environment. I have also been especially fortunate since then to be in the company of colleagues at the College of William and Mary with whom I could talk fruitfully about the issues dealt with in this book, and who constantly provided the support necessary to bring this project to completion.

Many of the ideas in the book have been presented earlier in papers and lectures at various universities and to numerous groups, particularly the University of Nottingham, University College Cork, the University of Pittsburgh, the Royal Institute of Philosophy, the University of Georgia, the Williams Committee on Obscenity and Film Censorship, the Faculties of both Law and Philosophy at Cambridge University, and on numerous occasions at the College of William and Mary. I am grateful to all of these institutions for giving me the opportunity to speak before them, and am even more indebted to those among my audiences whose challenging questions and comments enabled me to refine my ideas to their present state.

Thomas Barton, Harry Clor, Tom Collins, Hyman Gross, and Ian White were kind enough to read and comment upon earlier drafts of the manuscript, and the final version owes much to their penetrating observations on matters of both style and substance. I want to give special thanks to Mary Jane Morrison, who criticized the penultimate draft with great care and insight, and who vigilantly ensured that nothing I said went unchallenged.

Acknowledgments

I cannot possibly list all of the people to whom I feel indebted for valuable discussion. One of the advantages of writing about freedom of speech rather than about, for example, the Rule Against Perpetuities or the Analytic–Synthetic Distinction, is that so many people from so many different disciplines are both eager and able to provide a source for valuable learning. My failure to name everyone who has so assisted me in no way detracts from the enormous benefit I have gained from discussing these issues with them. There are some people, however, to whom I owe a particular debt. Paul O'Leary was the source of fruitful discussion about the notion of popular competence. Discussions with Alan Fuchs, John Garvey, Stanley Paulson, and Richard Tur helped me to refine my thinking about the structure of rights. And Mary Hesse demonstrated enormous patience as I speculated about the relationship between the philosophy of science and freedom of speech as a political principle. I have also profited greatly from those who have been kind enough to comment on previously published versions of the arguments presented here. Their interest has exemplified the highest ideals of academic dialogue, and has convinced me that the writing of this book was not without purpose.

PART I

THE FREE SPEECH PRINCIPLE

CHAPTER 1

The Free Speech Principle

Principles are the currency of political philosophy. In political argument we appeal to principles such as the principle of equality, the principle of liberty, the principle of democracy, and the principle of public interest. The principle of free speech is yet another principle to which we frequently appeal, and it is the principle of free speech that is the subject of this book. But before turning specifically to the principle of free speech, we need to note an important feature relevant to all principles. We can call this the *independence* of political principles, and an understanding of it will enable us to think more clearly about the specific principle of free speech.

Much talk about principles is obfuscated by a failure to distinguish between two different types of principles in political philosophy. One type is scarcely a principle at all, but is rather an *instance* of a broader principle. The other type is an *independent*, or *distinct*, principle. The former has no justification of its own, but is instead justified by the arguments supporting the broader principle, which then *subsume* the narrower principle. Independent principles, on the other hand, have their own justification. Their acceptance does not depend on the acceptance of the argument for a broader, more inclusive principle.

We can illustrate this distinction by an example about the killing of animals. Suppose someone opposes killing animals because he believes animals have rights equivalent to those of human beings, at least in terms of rights relating to life and death. Such a person might plausibly oppose any killing of animals, except in cases of self-defence. He would object to killing animals for food, for clothing, or for sport. If we were to ask this person whether he objected to hunting as a sport, he would not need and would not use an independent argument against hunting. His comprehensive principle against killing animals *includes* hunting, and his opposition

3

to hunting is but an *instance* of his broader objections to any killing of animals.

But there are many people who eat meat, and who wear leather shoes and gloves, yet who still object to hunting as a sport. For such people to make a reasoned argument against hunting, their argument cannot be an instance of a more general objection to killing animals. Acceptance of killing animals for food and clothing precludes resort to an undifferentiated principle opposing killing all animals. Instead these people would have to construct a narrower, more specific principle from a more specific argument that condemned hunting because of something peculiar to, or special about, hunting. In these circumstances it would be inconsistent to offer a general argument premised on the sanctity of animal life.

The most significant feature of a principle that is merely an instance of a broader principle is that acceptance of this narrower principle requires acceptance of the broader principle. If a person *A*, who opposes any killing of animals, wishes to persuade another person, *B*, to refrain from hunting rabbits for sport, *A* may argue that killing any animal is wrong, regardless of the reason for killing. But *B* may refuse to accept this argument, and therefore reject a principle of this breadth. For *B*, the proferred argument against hunting rabbits therefore has no persuasive force. Because he does not accept the broader principle, *B* will be persuaded only by an argument that says something specific about hunting. If *A* can say something specific about the evils of hunting for sport, then he has constructed an *independent argument* whose acceptance does not require acceptance of the broader principle that any killing of animals is wrong.

Principles may be described and deployed on different levels of particularity. A principle that is independent of other more comprehensive principles may still serve in other contexts as the broad principle that in turn subsumes other substances. If someone accepts the principle that killing animals for food and clothing is justifiable, but killing animals for sport is not, this principle will subsume the principle that hunting endangered species for sport is unjustifiable. But someone else may not accept the principle that hunting any animal for sport is without justification. That second person might still be persuaded that hunting endangered species is wrong, but only by use of an argument saying something *particular*, or *special*, about the necessity of preserving endangered species. This argument is narrower but at the same time more powerful. It is narrower in that it permits killing many types of animals for various reasons. It is more powerful because its acceptance does not require acceptance of the argument that any killing of animals is wrong, nor even of the argument that any killing of animals for sport is wrong. By requiring acceptance of fewer and narrower premises, the principle has more power to *survive*. An independent principle can survive rejection of the broader principle, but a principle that is an instance perishes when the principle of which it is an instance is rejected.

As this second example suggests, independence is relative. The independence of a principle (or an argument, reason, or theory) cannot be evaluated in isolation. Something must be independent *of* or *from* something else. We say that a principle is independent when it is independent of some other principle indicated by the context of the discussion. It is not independent of *every* other principle, for that in most cases would be impossible. Thus a principle, x, may be independent of principle y, yet still be merely an instance of principle z. We refer to x as 'independent' only if the alternative is to refer to it as an instance of y. We do not refer to x as independent if we are referring to it as an instance of the broader principle z.

I want to use the hunting example one final time to illustrate this point. Someone may object to hunting for sport because he believes in preventing waste of bullets. This reason for opposing hunting is independent of a reason based on the sanctity of animal life. At the same time, however, it could be an instance of a broader principle proscribing, for example, non-essential use of metal or tangible commodities. If an argument or reason is an instance of principle x and independent of principle y, that argument or reason survives the rejection of y, but does not survive the rejection of x.

FREE SPEECH AS AN INDEPENDENT PRINCIPLE

Many principles in political philosophy can be justified *either* as instances of broader principles *or* as independent principles.[1] Freedom of speech is a perfect example. It can be carried into acceptance as a component of a broader principle of liberty that includes the liberty to speak; or it can be justified by independent arguments, arguments derived from distinct or special characteristics of speech that justify its particular protection.

It is not difficult to justify some freedom of speech by recourse to a broader principle of liberty of which free speech is an instance. But this approach is troubling, for it seems to clash with the frequency with which we talk about 'freedom of speech' in isolation. If freedom of speech were not an independent principle there would be much less need to talk about it, and less occasion to give it a special place in legal systems or political argument. Perhaps this special place is unwarranted, and perhaps most of our talk of free speech is philosophically unsound. But our frequent references to free speech as particularly important at the very least warrant investigating a possible independent justification for a principle of free speech.

Imagine, for example, a society founded on the premise that government is illegitimate. Anarchy reigns supreme. In this society there would of course be freedom of speech (defined for now as freedom from government interference), but it would be almost incomprehensible to talk about freedom of speech as we currently understand it. Freedom of speech would be an instance of total freedom from government restraint, but it would not be a principle in its own right. Free speech would be a *fact*, but freedom of speech would not be a principle.

We rarely take seriously arguments for total anarchy. But we do frequently deploy principles of freedom and liberty. To the extent that these principles are accepted as relevant in determining the limits of state power, they will incorporate, as an instance, some amount of freedom of speech. Viewing freedom of speech in this way, however, is both uninteresting and unenlightening. This approach fails to explain why we so often refer to freedom of speech rather than the broader freedom of which free speech may be a component. We *believe* there is something special about free speech, for otherwise we would not refer to it as we do. We appear intuitively to accept free speech as an independent and distinct principle, rather than just an instance of a more general personal liberty. Our intuitions may be erroneous. They do suggest, however, that enquiring into the foundations of an independent principle of free speech would be fruitful. If such foundations exist, free speech will emerge as an independent principle, having the power and survivability to which I have referred. But if there are no sturdy foundations, if there is no principle of free speech independent of a more general liberty, then free speech is more a platitude than a principle. In order to keep this distinction to the fore, I will hereafter refer to the hypothesized independent principle as the Free Speech Principle.

The hypothesized Free Speech Principle is a principle of free speech independent of principles of general liberty. But, although independent of broader conceptions of liberty, it may still be a component of a principle of rationality, of democracy, or of equality, for example. It is tempting to say that an independent Free Speech Principle is a practical impossibility. In one sense this is correct; but in a more significant sense it is misleading. Because free speech is a liberty, it is *necessarily* part of most broader conceptions of liberty.[2] But liberty to speak has less of a logical relationship to concepts other than liberty, although such other concepts may provide powerful arguments for recognizing a principle of free speech. This distinction – between free speech as part of freedom and free speech as part of anything else – justifies reference to the hypothesized Free Speech Principle as independent, even if it is not and could not be completely independent of all other political and legal principles.

THE STRUCTURE OF A FREE SPEECH PRINCIPLE

I want to suggest by the foregoing formulation of the Free Speech Principle that the analysis of freedom of speech can and should be separated from questions about the limits of governmental authority in a broader sense. A recurrent issue in political philosophy is the scope of permissible state authority over the individual. Some argue for a minimal or negative state. Others advocate government's exercising a more positive role, or asserting more authority over the individual. But any formula for the resolution of these considerations will establish some rule, or standard, specifying the degree of legitimate state interference with the individual's freedom of action and choice. For example, one rule might confine the state to dealing exclusively with those actions causing harm to others. A modification of this standard might substitute harm to the *interests* of others, or interference with the *rights* of others.[3] A different rule might permit the state to do anything in the public interest. Under these or other rules, there is some *general rule* establishing the initial or normal standard of justification for the legitimate exercise of government power. The Free Speech Principle is an exception or qualification, of no necessary size or strength, to the general rule in force under a particular political theory. When a Free Speech Principle is accepted, there is a principle according to which speech is *less* subject to regulation (within a political theory) than other forms of conduct having the same or equivalent effects. Under a Free Speech Principle, any governmental action to achieve a goal, whether that goal be positive or negative, must provide a stronger justification when the attainment of that goal requires the restriction of speech than when no limitations on speech are employed.[4] A Free Speech Principle, properly understood, is the paradigm case of what Robert Nozick calls a 'side constraint', although it is important to note, as Nozick does not, that side constraints need not be absolute, or even close to absolute.[5]

As a standard (or threshold) of justification, the general rule prescribes the standard for limiting an individual's freedom of action. When there is a Free Speech Principle, a limitation of speech requires a stronger justification, or establishes a higher threshold, for limitations of speech than for limitations of other forms of conduct. This is so even if the consequences of the speech are as great as the consequences of other forms of conduct. If we think of the general rule as a particular point on a scale between total state control and unlimited liberty of the individual, a Free Speech Principle relocates the point on the scale when it is speech that is to be controlled.

If speech causes a harm of particular magnitude, is the power of the state to deal with that harm any less than if a harm of the same magnitude were caused by conduct other than speech? Or if the state desires to promote a positive goal, is its power to do so less if the promotion of that goal requires a limitation of speech? This can be reduced to one question: Does the presence of an actual or potential restriction on speech occasion a different method of analysis? If not, there is no Free Speech Principle. But if the answer is 'yes', a Free Speech Principle does indeed exist.

When presented in this fashion, the thesis that there might be a Free Speech Principle seems extreme. Why, after all, should the state be disabled from acting on what are stipulated to be good reasons just because the state's action involves dealing with speech? But there is no way to make the thesis less extreme. For if the state needs no stronger justification for dealing with speech than it needs for dealing with other forms of conduct, then the principle of freedom of speech is only an illusion. Formulating a reason for treating speech in this special manner is, as we shall see, no easy task, and this may show that freedom of speech is not nearly so obvious a value as is often supposed. But I see no merit in avoiding hard questions by converting them into artificially easy ones.

Formulating the enquiry in this way allows us to discuss the Free Speech Principle independent of questions about the weight or scope of the freedom involved, and independent of the relationship between free speech and other values. Acceptance of a Free Speech Principle does not entail that speech necessarily shall be free. Nor does it mandate that speech be wholly or even substantially immune from state power. And it certainly does not require that other liberties or other values be considered less important than the interests of free speech. There may be other Free . . . Principles, perhaps equal or greater in strength than the Free Speech Principle, but derived from different premises and covering different activities. My goal here is to identify *a* principle, not to identify the *only* principle, or even the most important principle. A principle that does not prevail in a particular instance is nevertheless a principle.[6] Rights need not be absolute. If we view a right as the power of the right-holder to require, for putative restrictions on the exercise of the right, a strength of justification greater than that embodied in the 'general rule', then there is nothing anomalous about the notion of a weak right. A Free Speech Principle implies only that restrictions on speech require *some* greater justification. A Free Speech Principle therefore represents a distinct restraint on government power, independent of limitations provided by other principles.

One stumbling block to clear analysis is use of the word 'freedom'. That word suggests to many people a virtually absolute immunity from restriction, yet that is not implicit in the Free Speech Principle. I would prefer to speak of 'degree of resistance to the general principles of governmental power'.[7] A Free Speech Principle would exist even if the state need only produce a *slightly* stronger justification for restricting speech than for restricting other forms of conduct not covered by a right of equivalent strength. But 'freedom of speech' is an expression too well established to be easily displaced. There will be less confusion if we rely on this explanation to distinguish the identification of the Free Speech Principle from the separate but related issue of *how much* freedom is involved. If there is a Free Speech Principle, it means that free speech is a good card to hold. It does not mean that free speech is the ace of trumps.

As a distinct limitation on government power, a Free Speech Principle is independent of, but not necessarily superior to, other limitations on state power. An independent principle of free speech survives the rejection of any other particular limitation on state authority, and survives the rejection of any broader principle of which it might coincidentally be an instance. For example, if freedom of speech is an instance of a liberty to engage in any non-violent act, then a failure to recognize that liberty extinguishes freedom of speech *pro tanto*. But if freedom of speech is an independent principle, the rejection of a liberty that might also include freedom of speech leaves freedom of speech intact.[8] An interest in free speech is not cancelled merely by an appeal to interests out-weighing a more general concept of liberty. If this were otherwise there would be little point in talking about freedom of speech.

SPEECH AS AN OTHER-REGARDING ACT

Implicit in the foregoing discussion is the assumption that speech has an effect on others. Speech is plainly not a self-regarding act, even assuming there be a category of acts that are self-regarding. Affecting others is most often the whole point of speaking. There are words, such as 'deceive', 'persuade', 'convince', and 'mis-lead', whose very logic presupposes that speech acts will affect others.

More specifically, speech clearly can and frequently does cause harm. These harms include harms to the speaker, harm to the interests and rights of individuals other than the speaker, harm to society, and harm to the governing apparatus of the state. Saying or printing something untrue (or true) about another person may damage his reputation, humiliate him, invade his privacy, offend him, or cause emotional distress. Saying something to a group of people may cause them to do something harmful to society, such as rioting or disobeying the law. Disparaging comments about my scholarship by a universally respected scholar would do me far more harm than would be done if that same person kicked me, or even broke my arm. Unfavourable reviews of a new theatrical pro-duction cause more financial damage than do most actions giving rise to legal liability.

These are examples of comparatively immediate effects of speech. There can be longer-term effects as well. What people say or pub-lish may influence widely-held views about politics or morality. The disclosure of military secrets, or the spread of lies (or truth) about government may impair the efficiency of the machinery of state. Even 'abstract' discussion can have similar effects. There is little doubt that discussion of immigration restrictions or school segregation often produces increased racial tension and reduced racial co-operation.

These examples suggest some troublesome issues in the appli-cation of a system of free speech, but I do not present them here as hard cases. Rather, I offer the examples to demonstrate the obvious – that speech has an effect on others.[9] Whatever truth there may be to the saying, 'Sticks and stones may break my bones, but names will never hurt me', it is hardly an appropriate gener-alization for the entire range of communicative conduct. I belabour this obvious and trivial point only because many arguments for freedom of speech are unfortunately intertwined with arguments about the extent to which the state should interfere with individual choice, or interfere with conduct arguably affecting only the actor. These arguments surround the discussion of such problems as distributing pornography, riding a motorcycle without a helmet or driving a car without a seat belt, smoking cigarettes or marijuana, drinking alcoholic beverages, and engaging in homosexual or other unconventional sexual conduct. Philosophical approaches to these issues are interesting and important, but have little relation to the analysis of freedom of speech.

Much of the surprising and unfortunate confusion between the principles of free speech and the principles of general personal liberty stems from the fact that one of the best-known defences of free speech, chapter 2 of Mill's *On Liberty*, is contained in the book also most commonly associated with the view that the only legitimate justification for coercion by the state is the prevention of harm to others.[10] Because of this, there are some who assume that the minimal state envisaged by Mill and advocated by others has no authority to regulate speech. But there is no necessary connexion between the two. Only when we discuss the regulation of pornography, but one small facet of the problem of free speech, do we find even a substantial overlap. A close reading of *On Liberty* reveals that, as between self-regarding and other-regarding acts, Mill treats speech as a member of the latter category. His chapter 2 is an attempt to demonstrate why speech is a special class of other-regarding acts immune, *for other reasons,* from state control. One can also read Mill as arguing that free and open discussion is the defined ultimate good in advanced societies, so that any adverse effect caused by discussion must be, *ex hypothesi,* smaller than the adverse effect of suppression. Under neither of these interpretations is there any suggestion that speech is necessarily ineffectual, or that it is incapable of causing unpleasant consequences.

If there is a Free Speech Principle, it protects certain conduct not because it is self-regarding, but *despite* the fact that it is other-regarding. Drawing this distinction between free speech theory and what might be called 'libertarian theory' is important for three reasons. First, it demonstrates that libertarian arguments do little to explain a Free Speech Principle that protects other-regarding conduct. For that we must look elsewhere, and that search will occupy the balance of the first part of this book. Second, the distinction between free speech theory and libertarian theory renders a Free Speech Principle immune from rejections of libertarianism.

If free speech is coextensive with or derived from principles of general liberty, then a rejection of such principles must be *pro tanto* a rejection of freedom of speech. Finally, recognizing that speech is protected despite the fact that speech can cause harm means that the identification of harm caused by a particular speech act does not for that reason alone justify the regulation of that speech act. If there is a Free Speech Principle, and if it covers at least some of the examples mentioned earlier (as any plausible Free Speech Principle must), then it takes more than the identification of harm to provide a sufficient reason for regulation.

The issue may be viewed in terms of *tolerance,* although that word has a distracting emotive effect because it hints at a *prima facie* right of interference to which tolerance is the exception. Still, advocates of tolerance would not approve tolerating axe-murderers and child-molesters; those most intolerant would hardly advocate not tolerating my preference for well-done meat even if they prefer it rare. The decision to tolerate that which is different is usually based on the harmlessness of the tolerated activity, the disutility of regulation, or the positive advantages of diversity and individual choice. Any principle of toleration thus includes some tolerance of speech with which we disagree. To that extent tolerance is relevant to the problem of freedom of speech. But if we are considering free speech as an independent principle, then a reason for tolerating speech must be distinct from arguments for toleration in general.

FREE SPEECH AND THE LANGUAGE OF RIGHTS

Our thinking about specific rights is frequently muddled by the *words* we commonly use to describe those rights. It is important to remember, however, that rights are far more complex (and usually more qualified) than the particular words we use to talk about those rights in everyday conversation. In this sense the language of rights is a form of technical language, providing little more than a convenient way to refer to a complex concept containing a bundle of interrelated definitions, liberties, privileges, immunities, and duties. The words we use to describe this complex concept make reference and discussion simpler, but often serve to obscure what we are in fact talking about.

Recognizing the language of rights as a form of technical language leads us to reject an ordinary language analysis of 'free speech' as a fruitful method of enquiry. Just as investigating what people ordinarily mean when they use the word 'set' tells us almost nothing about set theory, so too does investigating what people ordinarily mean when they use 'free speech' tell us little about the concept that is the focus of this book. Plainly there must be *some* connexion between the concept and the words we use to describe it. We say 'freedom of *speech*' rather than 'freedom of artichokes' or 'freedom of glimp' because communicative and linguistic conduct is in some way central. But the words provide little more than this rough, pre-theoretical guide. They tell us virtually nothing about either the dimensions of the concept or the resolution of difficult issues in its application.

This does not necessarily mean that the concept of free speech can be completely described, no matter how many volumes were available to complete that description. What is to count as speech and what is to count as *free* speech may be open-ended, continually evolving as new problems come to our attention. On the other hand, it might be possible to describe the concept at a level of abstraction sufficient to cover every conceivable application. The choice between these alternatives is not before us at this stage of the enquiry. The point is only that whatever we *can* say about free speech is not said, and not very much even suggested, by the words 'free speech' themselves.[11]

Acknowledging the relative unimportance of the words 'free speech' makes it possible to avoid two specific pitfalls. The first is the erroneous assumption that the principle of free speech covers all those activities that count as 'speech' in the ordinary language sense and none that do not. What is 'speech' in ordinary usage is not necessarily what is 'speech' for purposes of the concept of free speech. There are many forms of conduct that we do not consider in everyday talk to be speech but are within the concept of free speech, such as waving a flag, wearing a black armband or a button with a political symbol, or exhibiting an oil painting. And there are activities that are speech acts in the ordinary sense, yet have nothing whatsoever to do with freedom of speech.[12] Making a contract is a good example, and so is perjury, verbal extortion, and hiring someone to commit murder for a fee. *Why* the ordinary-language meaning of 'speech' is both underinclusive and over-inclusive for free speech purposes will be discussed later in this book. What matters now is that there is no necessary connexion between conduct that counts as speech in everyday talk and conduct that calls forth a principle of freedom of speech.

The second pitfall is embodied in the related fallacies of essentialism and reductionism. The language we use to paraphrase a more complete analysis and description of certain rights often leads people to believe that only one concept is involved, and that one concept has an essence, or central core.[13] This belief is wrong on both counts. It may turn out that free speech is not one right, or liberty, or principle, but rather a collection of distinct (although perhaps interrelated) principles. One of the goals of this book is the separation of some of these different principles, and the demonstration that not all of them will withstand close philosophical scrutiny. But even after this task is complete, we may be left with not one principle, but a group of principles. There is no reason this cannot be the case, and it is important that any analysis not be distorted by trying too hard to fit two (or more) hands into one glove. Most likely the concepts we join together under the over-simplifying rubric of 'free speech' have at best a family resemblance, and although there *may* be a closer relationship than that, there is no reason this *must* be so. Freedom of speech may have but one core, and there is nothing unseemly about looking for one. But it may instead have several cores. If this is what the analysis reveals, there is no reason to think that something is missing.

Bibliographical note to chapter 1

In addition to those sources referred to in the text and notes, general philosophical consideration of freedom of speech is found in Fred Berger, ed., *Freedom of expression* (Belmont, California: Wadsworth, 1980); Paul Freund, 'The great disorder of speech', *The American Scholar* **44** (1975), 541; Kent Greenawalt, 'Speech and crime', *American Bar Foundation Research Journal* (1980), 645; Geoffrey Harrison, 'Relativism and tolerance', in *Philosophy, politics and society (fifth series)*, P. Laslett and Fishkin, J., eds. (Oxford: Basil Blackwell, 1979), 273; John Bruce Moore, 'On philosophizing about freedom of speech', *Southwestern Journal of Philosophy* **6** (1975), 47; Joseph Tussman, *Government and the mind* (New York: Oxford University Press, 1977). John Locke's *A letter concerning toleration*, J. W. Gough, ed. (Oxford: Basil Blackwell, 1948), is focused on the issue of religious tolerance, but remains an essential source for those interested in the roots of free speech theory.

CHAPTER 2

The argument from truth

THE VALUE OF TRUTH

Throughout the ages many diverse arguments have been employed to attempt to justify a principle of freedom of speech. Of all these, the predominant and most persevering has been the argument that free speech is particularly valuable because it leads to the discovery of truth. Open discussion, free exchange of ideas, freedom of enquiry, and freedom to criticize, so the argument goes, are necessary conditions for the effective functioning of the process of searching for truth. Without this freedom we are said to be destined to stumble blindly between truth and falsehood. With it we can identify truth and reject falsity in any area of human enquiry.

This argument from truth dominates the literature of free speech. Milton's *Areopagitica,* the earliest comprehensive defence of freedom of speech, is based substantially on the premise that the absence of government restrictions on publishing (particularly the absence of licensing) will enable society to locate truth and reject error. More than two hundred years later, Mill employed the quest for truth as the expressed keystone of his plea for liberty of thought and discussion. Starting from the premise that the opinion we suppress on account of its supposed falsity may turn out to be true, or that the suppressed falsehood may contain a 'portion of truth', he argued that the elimination of suppression would consequently increase the likelihood of exchanging error for truth. More recently, this theme has surfaced in the judicial and extra-judicial writings of those American judges who have been most influential in moulding the theoretical foundations of the First Amendment to the United States Constitution, in particular Holmes, Brandeis, Frankfurter, and Hand.[1] Holmes, for example, argued that 'the best test of truth is the power of the thought to get itself accepted in the competition of the market'; and Frankfurter observed that 'the history of civilization is in considerable measure the displacement of error which once held sway as official truth by beliefs which in turn have yielded to other truths. Therefore the liberty of man to search for truth ought not to be fettered, no matter what orthodoxies he may challenge'.

These statements are but a small sample of what has been throughout modern history the ruling theory in respect of the philosophical underpinnings of the principle of freedom of speech. Under this theory, often characterized as the 'marketplace of ideas', truth will most likely surface when all opinions may freely be expressed, when there is an open and unregulated market for the trade in ideas. By relying on the operation of the market to evaluate any opinion, we subject opinions to a test more reliable than the appraisal of any one individual or government.

The theory can be said to rest in part on the value of an adversary process as a means of discovering truth. The Anglo-American legal system uses the adversary system to determine the facts in a court of law. So also, according to the argument from truth, should society enshrine the adversary system as the method of determining truth in any field of enquiry.[2] Freedom of speech can be likened to the process of cross-examination. As we use cross-examination to test the truth of direct evidence in a court of law, so should we allow (and encourage) freedom to criticize in order to test and evaluate accepted facts and received opinion. Undergirding the analogy to cross-examination is an additional analogy to economic theory. Just as Adam Smith's 'invisible hand' will ensure that the best products emerge from free competition, so too will an invisible hand ensure that the best ideas emerge when all opinions are permitted freely to compete.

No one formulation of the argument from truth is authoritative. The numerous characterizations differ from one another just as they differ in detail from the over-simplified version of the theory just presented. Still, certain core principles are found in all expressions of the doctrine. They all share a belief that freedom of speech is not an end but a means, a means of identifying and accepting truth. Further, they have a common faith in the power of truth to prevail in the adversary process, to emerge victorious from the competition among ideas. Finally, they share a deep scepticism with respect to accepted beliefs and widely acknowledged truth, logically coupled with a keen recognition of the possibility that the opinion we reject as false may in fact be true. A heavy dose of fallibilism is implicit in the view that freedom of speech is a necessary condition to the rational search for truth.

This general characterization of the argument from truth ignores many variations and refinements added by contemporary theorists. At this point, however, these relatively minor differences are less important than the validity of the fundamental assumptions shared by all formulations of the argument from truth, and upon which any version of the argument must rest.

The validity of the argument from truth turns initially on the legitimacy and importance of its goal. Only if truth is worth pursuing can a method of identifying truth claim recognition as a principle of political theory. The argument from truth is premised on the initial assumption that the quest for truth is a desirable aim.

In the context of a discussion of freedom of speech, I have no cause to question the assumption that truth is valuable. Whether one adopts a Platonic or Aristotelian position that truth is intrinsically and self-evidently good, or a Millian argument for truth on the basis of the principle of utility, or any of the more contemporary arguments for the value of truth,[3] the advantages of truth are almost universally accepted. To evaluate and contrast the various arguments for the value of truth would take me too far afield from the subject of free speech. Here I take truth as an autonomous value, requiring no further justification.

Holding truth to be an autonomous value is not equivalent to holding it to be the only value. Neither is it the same as saying that the search for truth must prevail in any case of conflict with other values, nor that truth and knowledge are always good and falsity and ignorance always bad. Identification of a goal as valuable does not entail accepting that goal as the only value. Of course it is possible to assert that truth (and the knowledge of it) is the pre-eminent value in any rational society. Indeed, such a view is implicit in some strong versions of the argument from truth. But it is unnecessary to exalt truth to such a position in order to take truth to be a valuable objective. At this point in the analysis we need not fetter the argument from truth with needless force. I maintain here only that truth is very important; that the search for truth is therefore a desirable goal; and that a society with more knowledge is better off than one with less knowledge, *ceteris paribus*. The argument from truth, and with it the vision of the marketplace of ideas, is premised on the belief that an open market in argument and opinion leads to increased knowledge. The argument therefore presupposes that the advance of knowledge is good for society, a presupposition I see no reason to challenge.

Although the argument is most commonly described as a search for *truth*, that word has the potential for introducing unnecessary complications. I wish to disencumber the argument from truth of most of the epistemological baggage carried by the concept of truth and by the word 'truth' in the limited context of the 'argument from truth' as an argument for accepting a principle of freedom of speech.

For one thing, the argument from truth is not inconsistent with any plausible form of scepticism. That is, it does not require accepting the possibility of acquiring knowledge with *certainty*. More than in most other areas of enquiry, it is crucial here to distinguish knowledge from certainty. We can approach a standard measure, such as the standard metre, by narrowing the range of tolerance (increasing the degree of accuracy) even if we can never exactly duplicate the standard metre. So too can we approach truth, or acquire knowledge, despite the lack of absolute certainty.[4] The lack of certainty does not, as some have mistakenly argued, mean that no uncertain belief is preferable to any other. Even if we can never achieve 100 per cent certainty, we can still prefer 99 per cent assurance to 55 per cent assurance, which in turn is better than 6 per cent assurance. In this context we can describe the search for truth, or the search for knowledge, as the search for beliefs of which we are more confident, rather than as the search for beliefs of which we are absolutely certain. It may or may not be that there *are* things of which we can be absolutely certain. That epistemological controversy is not at issue here. I am suggesting only that the argument from truth is not rebutted simply by the assertion that there can be no complete assurance in some or all areas of enquiry. As long as some epistemic states are preferable to other epistemic states,[5] the argument from truth remains an important statement (but not necessarily a valid argument), because the argument holds open discussion to be *a* way, or *the* way, of approaching the preferable epistemic state.

It should now be clear that the notion of truth in the argument from truth is not dependent on any one theory of truth, and can be said to cut across any plausible theory of truth. Under any theory of truth some propositions are true and others false, or at least some propositions are more likely true than others. As long as this is the case, then we have something to aim for, regardless of whether the standard for determining truth is correspondence, coherence, pragmatism, or whatever.

This view of truth appears to collapse any distinction between fact and value, between factual statements and normative statements. Later in this chapter I will probe more deeply into the relevance of the distinction to free speech theory. But here I am unconcerned about what appears to be an egregious oversimplification. All I have said about the function of 'truth' in the argument from truth applies, *mutatis mutandis,* to any cognitivist theory of ethical or moral knowledge. Moreover, our use of descriptive language in ethical discourse presupposes that we can be wrong as well as right. And if being right is better than being wrong, then what I have said about factual knowledge applies to ethical knowledge, and applies as well to questions of social or political policy. Similar observations apply to the use of prescriptive language. If we can say 'ought', then we can say 'ought not' as well, and we presuppose that only one of these is correct with respect to a particular proposition at a particular time and place. The argument from truth can thus sensibly be interpreted to make analogous claims about moral or other prescriptive statements as it does about factual statements.

In the language of epistemic or normative appraisal, each positive word has a negative corollary. For 'true' there is 'false', for 'knowledge' there is 'ignorance', for 'good' there is 'bad' or 'evil', for 'wisdom' there is 'error' or 'stupidity', for 'sound' there is 'unsound', and so on. The argument from truth can be characterized in terms of these negative words as easily as in the positive words. In many ways the search for falsity, error, evil, or unsound policy can be as important as the search for truth, wisdom, goodness, or sound policy. In order to be fair in evaluating the argument from truth, we must acknowledge the breadth and flexibility of the claims it makes.

THE PROGRESS TOWARDS KNOWLEDGE

Stipulating that increased knowledge is a valuable end does not help to answer the central question – does granting a special liberty of discussion and communication aid us in reaching that end? Is the marketplace of ideas more likely to lead to knowledge than to error, ignorance, folly, or nonsense?

To many people this question answers itself. They assert that free and open discussion of ideas is the only rational way of achieving knowledge, and they assume that the mere assertion of this proposition is proof of its truth. This is of course unsatisfactory. Without a causal link between free speech and increased knowledge the argument from truth must fail. Examining this link is the primary purpose of this chapter.

One way of avoiding the difficult task of establishing this connexion between discussion and knowledge is by *defining* truth in terms of the process of discussion; that is, define truth as that which survives the process of open discussion. Whatever is rejected after full, open enquiry is, by definition, false, wrong, or unwise. Whatever is agreed or accepted is, conversely, true, good, or sound. One might call this a consensus theory of truth. Under this theory there is no test of truth other than the *process* by which opinions are accepted or rejected.

When truth is defined in this way, the 'marketplace of ideas' metaphor is most apt, because the economic analogy is strongest. Under the purest theory of a free market economy the worth of goods is determined solely by the value placed on them by operation of the market. The value of an object is what it will fetch in a free market at leisurely sale. Similarly, the consensus or 'survival' theory of truth holds that truth is determined solely by the value that ideas or opinions are given in the intellectual marketplace.[6] Under this view the results are defined by the process through which those results are produced. The goal is then not so much the search for knowledge as it is the search for rational thinking. Given this definition of truth, knowledge flows from rational thinking as a matter of logical necessity. The argument substitutes a tautology for the problematic causal link between discussion and knowledge. Since the result is defined by the process, it is the process and not the result that matters.

This is a consummate sceptical argument, and it is no surprise that its pardigmatic expression ('the best test of truth is the power of the thought to get itself accepted in the competition of the market') comes from Holmes, whose scepticism pervades all his writings.[7] If we reject the possibility of attaining objective knowledge, and reject as unsatisfactory any method of discovering truth, defining truth as a process rather than a standard becomes compelling.

The survival theory of truth is alluringly uncomplicated; but as the basis for the principle of free speech it suffers from crippling weaknesses. Foremost among these weaknesses is that the argument begs the question. If truth is defined by reference to and in terms of a process, then why is the process of open discussion preferable to any other process, such as random selection or authoritarian fiat? Why is open discussion taken to be the only rational method of enquiry?

The survival theory, in refusing to acknowledge independent criteria for truth, provides no guidance for preferring one method of decision to any other. The survival theory does not purport to demonstrate *why* open discussion leads to knowledge, because it rejects any objective test of truth. Moreover, the survival theory does not tell us why open discussion leads to more desirable results of any kind. Thus the theory prompts us to ask why we should prefer rational thinking to any other form of thinking. But then the theory *defines* rationality as willingness to participate in open discussion and receptiveness to a variety of ideas. The survival theory thereby skirts the entire question by assuming open enquiry as valuable *a priori*. But we are still left with no criteria for evaluating whether this method of enquiry is better than any other. By taking open enquiry as sufficient *ex hypothesi*, the survival or consensus theory provides no assistance in answering the question of why free discussion should be preferred.

In his essay *On Liberty*, Mill suggests a version of the survival theory of truth in referring to the complete liberty to contradict a proposition as 'the very condition which justifies us in assuming its truth for purposes of action'. Perhaps rational assurance flows more easily from hearing opposing views. Perhaps freedom of contradiction is an important consideration in assuming the truth of any proposition. But that does not transform freedom to contradict into a sufficient condition, or even a necessary condition, for truth. We presuppose, at the very least, independent criteria of verifiability and falsifiability. Geoffrey Marshall has noted in response to Mill's argument that we should still have rational assurance 'that the Earth is roundish' even 'if the Flat Earth Society were an illegal organization'.[8] In those circumstances we would certainly want to look closely at why the contrary view was banned, so as more carefully to scrutinize the received view. But the very fact of allowing the expression of the opposing opinion is not what provides us with our assurance about the shape of the Earth.

The consensus theory seems slightly less bizarre in the context of ethical rather than factual or scientific propositions. But even with respect to ethics, a consensus theory incorporates a strange and unacceptably extreme subjectivism. If we define moral truth as what in fact survives, then we are committed to saying that Nazism was 'right' in Germany in the 1930s, and that slavery was equally 'correct' or 'wise' in parts of the United States prior to the Civil War. Nor is it satisfactory to respond by saying that these were not fully open systems, and that only propositions arising out of open systems can properly be recognized as sound. If that were the case, then any prevailing American view on anything in the last thirty years would have been correct, because there has been virtually unlimited freedom of discussion in the United States during that time.

A form of subjectivism that defines truth solely in terms of the strength of an opinion in the marketplace of ideas is so totally at odds with the idea of truth embodied in our language of evaluation as to be virtually useless. A theory of majority rule for truth distorts out of all recognition our use of words like 'true', 'good', 'sound', or 'wise'. Subjectivism may argue for greater freedom of speech, but not in a way related to the argument from truth. I will return to this theme in later chapters, but we can confidently pass over the consensus theory here. Defining truth (and, in turn, knowledge) solely in terms of a process answers none of the important questions about free speech. If free speech is justified because it defines the process that produces knowledge, and if that knowledge is in turn defined by the very same process, we are saying nothing at all. It is entirely possible that the process of open discussion is the best way of arriving at knowledge. But this is the causal link that the survival theory of truth fails even to address.

The focus on this causal link between freedom of speech and increased knowledge is arguably the greatest contribution of Mill's *On Liberty*. Earlier writers simply assumed that truth would reveal itself in the interplay of competing belief.[9] Truth was considered self-evident, needing only to be expressed to be recognized. By contrast, Mill saw the importance of explaining the way in which error would be replaced by knowledge. A paraphrase of Mill's argument may aid in precise analysis:

The relationship between discussion and truth is a product of the uncertain status of our beliefs and the fallibility of the human mind. Because we can not be absolutely certain of any of our beliefs, it is possible that any given belief might be erroneous, no matter how firmly we may be convinced of its truth. To hold otherwise is to assume infallibility. Because any belief might be erroneous, the suppression of the contrary belief entails the risk of upholding the erroneous belief and suppressing the true belief. The risk is magnified in practice because most beliefs are neither wholly true nor wholly false, containing instead elements of both truth and falsity. Only by allowing expression of the opinion we think false do we allow for the possibility that that opinion may be true. Allowing contrary opinions to be expressed is the only way to give ourselves the opportunity to reject the received opinion when the received opinion is false. A policy of suppressing false beliefs will in fact suppress some true ones, and therefore a policy of suppression impedes the search for truth.

Although Mill did not so qualify his argument, at best it tells against suppression only when an opinion is suppressed on the grounds of its alleged falsity. There are times when opinions are suppressed precisely because they are (or are perceived to be) true.

More commonly, opinions are suppressed because their expression will or is thought to cause certain undesirable consequences unrelated to the truth or falsity of the suppressed opinion.[10] Stephen Norris offers the example of the purported scientific basis for the opinion that some racial groups are genetically intellectually inferior to other racial groups.[11] Even if this were true, he argues, it is at least plausible that we might wish to prevent its dissemination in the interests of fostering racial harmony and eliminating *excess* reliance on genetic differences. We can imagine other examples of opinions suppressed because their expression is thought to impair the authority of a lawful and effective government, interfere with the administration of justice (such as publication of a defendant's criminal record in advance of a jury trial), cause offence, invade someone's privacy, or cause a decrease in public order.

When these are the motives for suppression, the possibility of losing some truth is relevant but hardly dispositive. Most formulations of the argument from truth assume that the suppression is based solely on the truth of the received opinion and the falsity of the opinion to be suppressed. When suppression is based on some other goal, the argument from truth, even if valid, is not wholly to the point. If the argument from truth generates a Free Speech Principle, then we justify suppression based on any interest other than the search for truth by weighing the interest in discovering truth against the other interests sought to be protected.

The corollary of this is that the argument from truth, if valid, also presupposes that the search for truth is the pre-eminent value in society – when it has, in Rawlsian terms, a lexical priority over all other interests. To the extent that Mill uses the argument from truth to support an argument for liberty of discussion absolute in strength (although not unlimited in scope[12]), he makes two implicit assumptions. He assumes that all suppression is based on the asserted falsity of the suppressed view. This, however, is simply wrong. Additionally, he assumes that the search for truth is superior to any other social interest. This assumption too is, at the very least, open to question, and it presents a problem to which I shall return. Thus the argument from truth is dispositive *ex necessitate* only if these two assumptions are both true. In fact, they are most likely both false.

For now it is sufficient to note that the absolutism inherent in Mill's principle of free discussion is the weakest point of his argument. But no argument should be rejected merely because its proponent overstates the case, or attributes unnecessary force to the argument. Stripped of the unnecessary absolutism, Mill's argument demands close attention.

Mill focuses our attention on the possibility that truth may lie in the suppressed opinion. If this is so, then a general policy of prohibiting the expression of opinions thought to be false extinguishes *some* knowledge and perpetuates *some* error. As Mill recognizes, however, we can say much the same thing about *acting* on a belief. If any belief might be wrong, then so might any action be wrong. Yet we cannot and do not let recognition of our fallibility paralyse us into inaction. We can function only if we act in accordance with our strongest beliefs, while still acknowledging that we may be in error. Mill responds by assuming a fundamental distinction between holding a belief and acting on a belief, and taking complete liberty of contradiction to be the very condition that allows us to act in accordance with our uncertain beliefs. We act on a belief rationally only if we know it to be the 'best' belief available, and we know a belief to be best only if we have heard all the others.

This argument again appears to overstate the case. As Geoffrey Marshall's example of the Flat Earth Society points out, there are ways of establishing rational assurance other than by standing our beliefs next to all the other beliefs. But the more serious objection is that the distinction between holding a belief and acting on a belief is not to the point. The apt distinction is between acting on a belief and *expressing* a belief, and it is this distinction that may well not exist, because expressions of belief (speech) often affect the conduct of others. If there is a risk that people may come to believe and act on opinions thought by others to be false, then suppressing the false belief is one way of acting on the true belief.

Although Mill's argument is too strong, there is value in his observations. We achieve rational confidence in our views, confidence sufficient to justify action, in most instances by comparing those views to others already evaluated. We can sensibly prefer one view to others only by knowing what the others are. Having heard other views, we can have confidence in a view that has survived all currently available attacks. This at least increases the justification for acting on the surviving belief.

On Liberty can be read as assuming that there is some objective truth, even if we are never sure we have found it. As a result, Mill has been criticized by those who reject the notion of objective truth.[13] If we are always uncertain, they say, then we never know if we have identified truth. These critics accuse Mill of inconsistency in saying that we can never be certain, but that we can search for truth. Apart from the fact that these arguments confuse truth with certainty, confuse a state of the world with a state of mind, the arguments are largely irrelevant to the issue at hand. The question is not certainty, but epistemic advance.

This point is brought out in much of the work of Karl Popper. By stressing falsifiability rather than verifiability, and by characterizing the advance of knowledge as the continual process of exposing error, Popper frees the argument from truth from the problem of certainty. The identification of error may not bring us closer to truth, but the identification of an error is still desirable, and the rejection of an erroneous belief is still an epistemic advance.[14] Popper's argument from the identification of error thus parallels Mill's argument from truth. Both share the same core principle – allowing the expression of contrary views is the only rational way of recognizing human fallibility, and making possible the rejection or modification of those of our beliefs that are erroneous.

THE THEORY AND THE REALITY

Mill, Popper, and their followers have refined the argument from truth by explaining how knowledge is more likely to be gained in a society in which all views can be freely expressed. But they have still neglected the critical question – does truth, when articulated, make itself known? Does truth prevail when placed side-by-side with falsity? Does knowledge triumph over ignorance? Are unsound policies rejected when sound policies are presented? The question is whether the theory accurately portrays reality. It does not follow as a matter of logical entailment that truth will be accepted and falsehood rejected when both are heard. There must be some justification for assuming this to be an accurate description of the process, and such a justification is noticeably absent from all versions of the argument from truth.

The argument from truth may well be the statement of an ideal. Listening to other positions, suspending judgment (if possible) until opposing views are expressed, and considering the possibility that we might be wrong virtually defines, in many contexts, the process of rational thinking. At least it is a substantial component of the definition.[15] Rationality in this sense may not always lead to increased knowledge, and there may at times be better methods of searching for truth. But all academic disciplines presuppose that this type of rationality has value, and it would be difficult to prove this presupposition unwarranted. When such rational thinking can be assumed, maximum freedom of discussion is a desirable goal. In systems of scientific and academic discourse, the argument from truth has substantial validity. Those who occupy positions in these fields may not always think rationally, but we are at least willing to say they should, and are inclined to try to replace those who do not think rationally with those who will.

It is one thing to say that truth is likely to prevail in a select group of individuals trained to think rationally and chosen for that ability. It is quite another to say that the same process works for the public at large. Only if the process is effective throughout society can the argument from truth support a Free Speech Principle to limit government power. We must take the public as it is. A scientist who is irrational can or at least should be replaced. A population with a similar failing cannot be replaced. The extent of reason in society is a fact with which we must work, and it is a fact that a plausible theory must accommodate.

It is hardly surprising that the search for truth was so central in the writings of Milton, Locke, Voltaire, and Jefferson. They placed their faith in the ability of reason to solve problems and distinguish truth from falsehood. They had confidence in the reasoning power of *all* people, if only that power were allowed to flourish. The argument from truth is very much a child of the Enlightenment, and of the optimistic view of the rationality and perfectibility of humanity it embodied. But the naïveté of the Enlightenment has since been largely discredited by history and by contemporary insights of psychology. People are not nearly so rational as the Enlightenment assumed, and without this assumption the empirical support for the argument from truth evaporates. The most prominent weakness of Popper's *The Open Society and Its Enemies* is the assumption that the populace has the rationality Popper sees in scientific enquiry. It is no easy task to apply *The Logic of Scientific Discovery* to a public often unwilling or unable to be logical.

I do not mean to be taken as saying that falsity, ignorance, or evil have inherent power over truth, knowledge, or goodness. Rather, I mean only to deny the reverse – that truth has inherent ability to gain general acceptance.[16] The argument from truth must demonstrate either that true statements have some intrinsic property that allows their truth to be universally apparent, or that empirical evidence supports the belief that truth will prevail when matched against falsehood. The absence of such a demonstration, in the face of numerous counter-examples, is the most prominent weakness of the argument from truth. History provides too many examples of falsity triumphant over truth to justify the assertion that truth will inevitably prevail. Mill noted that 'the dictum that truth always triumphs over persecution is one of those pleasant falsehoods which men repeat after one another till they pass into commonplaces, but which all experience refutes'. My point is that, *contra* Mill, the point would be the same if we removed the persecution and instead let truth battle with falsehood rather than the forces of oppression. Mill's assumption that the removal of persecution will allow truth to triumph in all cases is every bit as much a 'pleasant falsehood'.

Of course we know that falsity at times prevailed over truth only by having finally discovered truth with respect to a particular issue. Thus discussions along this line usually distinguish between the long run and the short run. Those who reject the assumptions of the Enlightenment point to instances in which truth and reason have not prevailed. In response, those who place their faith in the power of reason observe that when erroneous views have at times been accepted they have also been discredited in the long run. But the validity of this response depends on just how long the long run is. If there is no limit to its duration, the assertion that knowledge advances in the long run is both irrefutable and meaningless. Yet if the relevant time period is discrete and observable, history furnishes far too many counter-examples for us to have much confidence in the power of truth consistently to prevail.

The elements of rational thinking that prompt and justify the argument from truth undoubtedly are present at various points in society. Although there is no indication that this capacity to separate truth from error is invariably or even consistently present in the population at large, this is not sufficient completely to reject the argument from truth. Certainly the argument retains validity for select groups in which rationality can be presumed. More importantly, the free expression of all views by the entire population, even if a less than perfectly rational population, assists those who can most effectively separate truth from error. The process of advancing knowledge by offering and evaluating challenges and alternate hypotheses depends in part for its effectiveness on the number and variety of such challenges. Although the public may not be the body to identify most effectively sound policies and true statements, its size and diversity make it the ideal body to *offer* the multitude of ideas that are the fuel of the engine for advancing knowledge.[17] By allowing the freest expression of opinion, we increase the number of alternatives and the number of challenges to received opinion. If some proportion of currently rejected ideas indeed are correct, then increasing the pool of ideas will in all probability increase the total number of correct ideas in circulation, and available to those who can identify them as correct. Any perceived inability of the population at large to discern truth does not necessarily deny to that population a valuable function in the truth-seeking process. But there is no particular reason why the group that offers the hypotheses must be the group that decides which hypotheses to accept and which to reject.

In discussing fallibilist theory, we often forget that it is only *possible* that the received opinion is erroneous, and therefore only *possible* that the rejected opinion is true.[18] When we say that all views should be permitted expression so that knowledge may advance, this necessitates being willing to achieve *some* increase in knowledge at the expense of tolerating a great deal of falsity. In order to locate all the sound ideas, we must listen to many unsound ideas. When we allow the expression of an opinion that is only possibly true, we allow the expression of an opinion that is also possibly, perhaps *probably*, false. If the expression of the opinion in question involves no unpleasant consequences even if it is false, unsound, or useless, then there is a potential benefit at no cost. But it is simply a mistake to say that the expression of false or unsound opinions can never have unpleasant consequences.

The predominant risk is that false views may, despite their falsity, be accepted by the public, who will then act in accordance with those false views. The risk is magnified in those circumstances in which people have seemed particularly disposed towards the acceptance of unsound ideas. One good example is race relations. History has shown us that people unfortunately are much more inclined to be persuaded of the rectitude of oppressing certain races or certain religions than they are likely to accept other unsound and no less palpably wrong views.

Moreover, unpleasant side effects may accompany the expression of erroneous views even when there is no risk of widespread acceptance. By side effects I mean those consequences that are not directly attributable to the *falsity* of the views expressed. People may be offended, violence or disorder may ensue, or reputations may be damaged. It is foolish to suppose that the expression of opinions never causes harm. Generally, but not always, the expression of unsound opinions causes greater harm than the expression of sound opinions. When we allow the expression of an opinion because it is possibly true, we often accept an appreciably higher probability of harm than the probability of the truth of a seemingly false opinion. As a result, the strength of protection of the right to dissent afforded by the argument from fallibilism is directly proportionate to the value placed on the goal of searching for knowledge. There is absolute protection only if the search for knowledge is the transcendent value in society. If the search for knowledge does not have a lexical priority over all other values, the possibility that the rejected view may be correct will often be insufficient to justify allowing it to be expressed – depending, of course, on the evaluation of the harm expected to flow from its dissemination.

To cut off access to possible knowledge is undoubtedly a harm. But the question to be asked is whether we should take a large risk in exchange for what may be a minute possibility of benefit. Unfortunately, we cannot be sure we have properly weighed the harms and benefits unless we know what benefits the suppressed opinion might bring. And this is impossible to assess so long as that opinion is suppressed. Therefore we are merely guessing when we suppress; but we are also guessing when we decide not to suppress. If the expression of an opinion possibly causes harm, allowing that expression involves some probability of harm. If the suppression of that opinion entails the possible suppression of truth, then suppression also entails some probability of harm. Suppression is necessarily wrong only if the former harm is ignored. Therefore a rule absolutely prohibiting suppression is justified only if speech can never cause harm, or if the search for truth is elevated to a position of priority over all other values.

Mill assumed that in all cases we could act in furtherance of the policy embodied in the received opinion, while at the same time permitting the expression of the contrary opinion. But in some cases the very act of allowing the expression of the contrary opinion is inconsistent with acting on the received opinion. For example, we prohibit slavery in part because of a received opinion that racial equality and respect for the dignity of *all* people is the morally correct position. If we allow people to argue that slavery is morally correct, many others will be offended, their dignity will be insulted, and there is likely to be increased racial disorder. The expression is thus detrimental to acting on the received opinion, to furthering racial equality and respect for the dignity of all. A strong version of the argument from truth would hold that the possibility, however infinitesimal, that slavery is good makes tolerating the harm that will flow from the expression of that opinion worthwhile. But the size of that possibility and the extent of the potential harm are irrelevant only if the search for knowledge must always prevail over other values.

29

The argument from truth presupposes a process of rational thinking. Indeed, one of its virtues may be that it encourages this process. Yet because the process of rational thinking is the foundation of the theory, the theory weakens or dissolves when the process does not obtain. Even if we assume that rational thinking is the norm, there may be times when the process does not function properly. When, because of emergency, passion, or anger, there is no opportunity to reflect on the wisdom of an expressed opinion, and there is no opportunity for counter-argument, there is no reason to rely on the argument from truth. Those chiefly responsible for engrafting the argument from truth to American constitutional doctrine were also those who recognized that when there was a 'clear and present danger' there would be no opportunity for rational consideration of various arguments.[19] At such times there is less justification for allowing expression of the apparently false opinion. Take Holmes' classic example of a man's falsely shouting 'Fire!' in a crowded theatre. It would be most unreasonable to say that such expression should be permitted because others have the opportunity to express the opinion that there is no fire, followed by discussion and investigation to determine which of the two opinions was correct. The 'clear and present danger' test has implications far beyond American constitutional doctrine. Neither the argument from truth nor any other argument can be applied when the conditions for its validity are not present.

CATEGORIES OF KNOWLEDGE

In my discussion of the argument from truth thus far, I have treated truth as if its evaluation and identification were wholly independent of the nature of the proposition asserted. Clearly this is a gross over-simplification, albeit one prompted by the usual statement of the argument from truth. That argument hinges in large part on the lack of certainty in the received opinion. To this extent the validity of the argument varies in direct proportion to the degree of uncertainty inherent in the *category* of proposition involved. Comte argued for censorship of certain normative ethical opinions by saying that no one could reasonably demand freedom to disagree with the truths of mathematics. Even accepting his questionable premise about truth in mathematics, his conclusion follows only if all knowledge is in the same epistemic category. This is plainly unjustified. Knowledge in mathematics and logic is more certainly attainable than is knowledge in many other areas, and an argument based on the possibility of error cannot fail to recognize the difference.

The argument from truth may easily be characterized as an argument from uncertainty. Uncertain of our beliefs, we allow, perhaps even encourage, the expression of opposing views in order to have the opportunity of rejecting or modifying our erroneous beliefs. The more (properly) certain we are of our beliefs, the less likely we are to advance knowledge by the expression of opposing views. The more certain we are, the less telling is the uncertainty we may sometimes have about our opinions. And then, the less is the force of this reason for the argument for freedom of speech. Matters of taste present the paradigmatic example. If the state were to propose suppressing bad literature or bad art,[20] we would be quick to argue against this on the ground that judgments about artistic matters are ones of which there is little certainty and little agreement about what is good and what is bad. We could consistently still hold that there are objective standards for aesthetic evaluation, for that means saying some things *are* good and others *are* bad. But this is a far cry from reaching agreement as to what is good and what is bad. Standards in aesthetics are more highly variable than are standards in most other subjects. Here the danger of suppressing that which may at some future time be considered good or valuable presents a powerful argument for allowing the expression of the currently unacceptable opinion. (I do not claim this to be the only argument, nor do I claim this to be the strongest argument. I shall discuss other arguments relating to artistic freedom in chapters 4 and 7.)

Similar considerations apply to religious, political, or moral views. One of the reasons that the traditional expositions of the argument from truth have gained such great acceptance is that those expositions were directed primarily at the expression of normative propositions in ethics, politics and religion. In these fields there is quite little consensus; consequently there is a large risk of suppressing an opinion that may subsequently be taken to be correct.

Thus, even within a category of propositions, such as within the category of political and moral propositions, there are differing degrees of uncertainty. Although neither Mill nor any modern moral sceptic would be willing to say that we can be absolutely certain that the torture of innocent children is bad, or that respect for others is good, these plainly are beliefs in which we can have more confidence than in the belief that the Labour Party ought to be in power in Great Britain, or the belief that affirmative action to remedy past racial discrimination is a salutary policy. The argument from truth in its strongest form would apply with equal force in all of these instances. Yet at first sight it seems more reasonable to say that the strength of the argument from truth should be evaluated in reference to the certainty we have in the particular proposition at issue. If the degree of the state's interest in suppressing the advocacy of slavery is the same as the degree of its interest in suppressing the advocacy of a socialist economy, a logical application of the argument from truth would be more likely to support the act of suppression in the former case than in the latter, because we are more certain of the falsity of the good of slavery.

To make such a claim, however, would be to deny the usefulness of *categories* of propositions, and to look instead to particular propositions. Categorization in free speech theory is in one sense a compromise. It is a compromise between two competing insights. One insight is that it is over-simplified and erroneous to treat all propositions in the same way, especially in light of the varying degrees of certainty that attach to different propositions. The other insight is that we are reluctant to allow any governmental body with power to suppress to make decisions concerning suppression on the basis of *its* certainty of the falsity of the opinion to be suppressed. We attempt to reconcile these competing considerations by creating categories of expression. There is nothing unseemly about categorizing here, but we must realize that the process of categorization is rather more artificial than natural, and that the forces leading us to categorize might also lead us to make those categories ever smaller, ultimately denying the existence of categories altogether.

If we accept the validity of categorization, it follows that freedom of speech (for the population at large) as a method of gaining knowledge may be least persuasive in the realm of factual or scientific propositions. In this area we have the greatest amount of verifiable confidence in received opinions. There may be many good reasons for permitting people to argue that the moon is made of green cheese, but the possibility that that proposition may be true is hardly the most important of these reasons. The very fact that we usually consider the laws relating to defamation and misrepresentation as outside the scope of many of the principles of freedom of speech demonstrates that intuitively we make the distinctions I am suggesting here. If I am prosecuted for selling as 'Pure Orange Juice' a liquid containing only water, sugar, and artificial flavouring and colouring, it is not and should not be a defence that some extreme sceptics would be reluctant to exclude completely the possibility that we could be mistaken about when a liquid is orange juice and when it is something else.[21]

Many factual propositions are of course less certain than the proposition that there are five fingers on my left hand. Because of errors in observation, interpretation and description, the factual statement we accept as true may be false, and the statement we reject as erroneous may be true, just as such possibilities exist for statements about ethics, religion or politics. But in the majority of instances involving factual or otherwise verifiable propositions the possibility of error is miniscule, and the risks of assuming our infallibility are consequently smaller. When this is the case, the argument from truth is of quite limited assistance to an argument for freedom of speech.

A LIMITED JUSTIFICATION

The argument from truth is plagued by two major flaws. Most fundamentally, the argument from truth, as an argument for general freedom of speech throughout society, rests on an assumption about the prevalence of reason, for which the argument offers no evidence at all, in the face of numerous counter-examples from history. It may be correct to say that decisions ought to be made by those who will rationally consider all arguments, and that those in such a position ought to tolerate or encourage the widest range of opinion and disagreement. It is quite something else to say that society at large is in fact such a group, at least without more in the way of empirical support. Knowledge is not necessarily a one-way process. Additional propositions can retard knowledge as well as advance it. Truth can be lost just as it can be attained. Unless knowledge can be shown to have some inherent power, or unless truth is self-evident, there is no reason to assume that open debate and discussion will automatically and in every case be beneficial.

Moreover, any strong version of the argument from truth must elevate the search for knowledge to a position of absolute priority over other values. In this form the argument is so powerful as to be unworkable. If we weaken the argument to take account of other interests that may at times predominate, we find the argument from truth to say little more than that the quest for knowledge is a value that ought to be considered. In such a form the argument from truth says very little.

Although the argument from truth fails to provide the doctrinal support claimed by its advocates, it is nevertheless useful. It does

33

focus our attention on fallibility, on the possibility that 'we' may be wrong and that 'they' may be right. To the extent that suppression of opinion may be inconsistent with this understanding of our fallibility, the argument from truth at least gives us pause before we so quickly assume the truth of received opinion. It gives us one reason for treating the suppression of opinion differently from the way we treat other governmental action.

More importantly, this focus on the possibility and history of error makes us properly wary of entrusting to any governmental body the authority to decide what is true and what is false, what is right and what is wrong, or what is sound and what is foolish. As individuals are fallible, so too are governments fallible and prone to error. Just as we are properly sceptical about our own power always to distinguish truth from falsity, so should we be even more sceptical of the power of any governmental authority to do it for us. It is a wise caution to heed when we must decide how much authority we will give to those in power to determine what is right and to suppress what is wrong.

The argument from truth may be based not only on its inherent scepticism about human judgment, but also on a more profound scepticism about the motives and abilities of those to whom we grant political power. The reason for preferring the marketplace of ideas to the selection of truth by government may be less the proven ability of the former than it is the often evidenced inability of the latter. To the extent that this is implicit in the argument from truth, there is a strong link between the argument from truth and the argument from democracy, which is the subject of the next chapter.

Bibliographical note to chapter 2

Consideration of Mill should also refer to the criticism in Maurice Cowling, *Mill and liberalism* (Cambridge: Cambridge University Press, 1963); Willmoore Kendall, 'The "Open Society" and its fallacies', *American Political Science Review* 54 (1960), 972. Also questioning the assumptions about the power of truth is Yves Simon, 'A comment on censorship', *International Philosophical Quarterly* 17 (1977), 33. Also useful are Francis Canavan, 'John Milton and freedom of expression', *Interpretation* 7 (1978), 50; Francis Canavan, 'Freedom of speech and press: for what purpose?', *American Journal of Jurisprudence* 16 (1971), 95. A more recent work by Zecheriah Chafee, including commentary on the judicial opinions of Holmes and others, is *Free speech in the United States* (Cambridge: Harvard University Press, 1941). Karl Popper's views on freedom of enquiry pervade most of his work, but the major source is *The open society and its enemies*, fifth edition (London: Routledge and Kegan Paul, 1966).

CHAPTER 3

The argument from democracy

A CONDITIONAL ARGUMENT

The argument from truth can be characterized, following Thomas Scanlon, as a 'natural' argument.[1] It proceeds directly from what Scanlon perceives as natural moral principles (for example, the desirability of truth), rather than being instrumental to any particular theory of the design of political institutions. By contrast, the argument from democracy is characterized by Scanlon as 'artificial', because it is derived from and is contingent upon one particular theory of government, a theory by no means universally accepted. I find the distinction somewhat tenuous, because we can give natural moral arguments for democratic processes, which in turn would include those principles necessary for democracy to operate. Still, the distinction is useful here, because it highlights at the outset the conditional nature of the argument that is the subject of this chapter.

The argument from democracy, as its name indicates, requires for its deployment the *a priori* acceptance of democratic principles as proper guidelines for the organization and governance of the state. To the extent that the argument from truth is valid, its validity applies to any form of social organization. But the argument from democracy is wholly inapplicable to autocracies, oligarchies, or theocracies. Such forms of government are less frequently advocated today than in the past, but they certainly are not extinct. The argument from democracy, in presupposing certain principles of governmental structure to be discussed presently, is an argument relevant to a narrower range of societies than most other arguments for freedom of speech.

The argument from democracy views freedom of speech as a necessary component of a society premised on the assumption that the population at large is sovereign. This *political* basis for a principle of freedom of speech leads to a position of prominence under the argument for speech relating to public affairs, and even more prominence for criticism of governmental officials and policies.

35

Such freedom is held to be necessary for two purposes. First, freedom of speech is crucial in providing the sovereign electorate with the information it needs to exercise its sovereign power, and to engage in the deliberative process requisite to the intelligent use of that power. Second, freedom to criticize makes possible holding governmental officials, as public servants, properly accountable to their masters, the population at large.

The argument from democracy has been most carefully articulated by the American political philosopher Alexander Meiklejohn, although we can see similar ideas in the writings of Spinoza, Hume and Kant.[2] Freedom of speech is most commonly associated with liberalism, but the argument from democracy has found some appeal among those who reject the fundamental tenets of liberalism. By emphasizing the ultimate power of the people as a group and the relationships among people, the argument from democracy avoids the (perceived) atomistic and elitist character of liberalism in general and of the argument from truth in particular. For example, Robert Paul Wolff, although holding the position indicated by the title of his book *The Poverty of Liberalism*, remains sympathetic towards a version of the argument from democracy.

I have already delayed too long in defining what I mean here by 'democracy'. This is a word that has come to mean all things to all people. The word 'democracy' has gained so much emotive force as to lose virtually all meaning it ever had. Its descriptive content is minimal and it is now a term of almost pure political approval. Democracy is today so commonly accepted as the proper way of organizing a state that all governments feel the necessity of describing themselves as 'democratic', regardless of how autocratic they may be. All entrenched governments are 'democracies', and all revolutionary movements against those governments are 'democratic'. More than almost any other word in common use in political discourse, 'democracy' has come to have so many meanings as to be totally useless as a word of description.

For the purposes of this chapter, I feel obligated by tradition to continue to use the word 'democracy', but I will use it in a much stricter sense. I take democracy to mean a system that acknowledges that ultimate political power resides in the population at large, that the people as a body are sovereign, and that they, either directly or through their elected representatives, in a significant sense actually control the operation of government. I do not use the word 'democracy' as synonymous with any system that provides for peaceful change (Russell and Popper), with any system designed for the benefit of the people (Bentham, James Mill, and many Marxists), with any system providing a maximum amount of equality (some Marxists), or with any system evidencing great respect for the interests of individuals (de Tocqueville, J. S. Mill, and many modern theorists of pluralistic democracy). Although all of these factors may be and frequently are to some extent present in societies based on popular sovereignty actually exercised, they need not be. Such factors do not define democracy. 'Democracy' as I use it here is not defined as rule *for* the people, but as rule *by* the people. The latter may entail the former, but the reverse is clearly not true.

It is not significant in the context of this chapter whether any of the alternative formulations of a theory of democracy is in some way more 'correct', or whether any of these formulations are more desirable political theories. All I am maintaining here is that the argument from democracy, the subject of this chapter, is an argument that derives its force from the initial supposition that governments ought to be structured to provide, usually through a system of frequent and open elections with universal suffrage and with some principle of majority rule, a state in which the population at large has sovereignty in theory and in practice. It is a system that embodies the very idea of self-government. Most significantly in this context, it is a system of government that gives the people the right to be wrong.

THE ARGUMENT EXPLAINED

The argument from democracy as understood today was most prominently articulated by Alexander Meiklejohn. Although he presented his argument as a theory of interpretation of the United States Constitution, the constitutional basis for his position is tenuous. His rigid distinction between public and private speech is unsupported by constitutional text or doctrine, and is unworkable in practice. Nor is there any indication that the First Amendment was ever intended to or could in fact be given the absolute force he ascribes to it. But as a matter of political philosophy, his arguments are important and worthy of close scrutiny, especially in this part of the book, where I am concerned more with the foundations of a principle of free speech than with its strength.

Meiklejohn was much taken with the notion of self-government, and consequently was strongly influenced by the institution of the town meeting, a form of government prevalent in small towns in New England. Under a town meeting form of government, all major decisions are taken by the entire adult population assembled together. It is self-government in the purest form. A key feature of the town meeting is that there are no government officials in the sense of political leaders; there is only a moderator whose sole function is to organize the meeting and enforce the rules of order. Members of the population propose ideas, debate those ideas, and then adopt or reject them by vote of all the people.

Meiklejohn saw all democracies as New England town meetings writ large. His thesis extended the ideal of popular sovereignty embodied in the town meeting to the larger and more complex republic. To Meiklejohn the size and complexity of the modern state did not diminish the theoretical absolute sovereignty of the populace. As final decision-making authority rests in the people who attend the town meeting, so does that same authority rest in the people who populate the more cumbersome modern state. As the essential feature of the town meeting is the open debate and public deliberation that precedes any decision, so also is open debate and public deliberation an intrinsic and indispensable feature of any society premised on the principle of self-government.

The argument from democracy is composed of two critical elements that support a principle of free speech. The first is the necessity of making all relevant information available to the sovereign electorate so that they, in the exercise of their sovereign powers, can decide which proposals to accept and which proposals to reject. Because the people are the ones who make the decisions, the people are the ones who need to receive all material information before making any decision. Although a restriction on the general liberty of the individual would not necessarily affect the democratic governmental process, a circumscription of speech would limit the information available to those making the decisions, impair the deliberative process, and thereby directly erode the mechanism of self-government. Because we cannot vote intelligently without full information, it is argued, denying access to that information is as serious an infringement of the fundamental tenets of democracy as would be denying the right to vote.

Second, freedom of speech is perceived as the necessary consequence of the truism that if the people as a whole are sovereign, then governmental officials must be servants rather than rulers. This in turn generates several more specific foundations for freedom of speech. It reminds us that, in a democracy, our leaders are in office to serve the wishes of the people. Freedom of speech is a way for the people to communicate those wishes to the government, and any suppression of the public's stated demands is inconsistent with the notion of government's existing for the precise purpose of responding to the demands of the population. It is noteworthy that petitioning for the redress of grievances, closely connected with freedom of speech, is the basis both of Magna Carta and the Bill of Rights of 1689. Petitioning for the redress of grievances is also conjoined with freedom of speech in the First Amendment to the United States Constitution.

Additionally, if the government is the servant, censorship by government is anomalous. It results in the servants pre-selecting the information available to the sovereign, although, argued Meiklejohn, logic would suggest precisely the opposite.

Finally, and probably of the greatest importance, the role of government as servant compels a recognition of the right to reject and criticize our leaders. Under a theory of self-government, this lies at the very core of democracy. Criticism of public officials and public policy is a direct offshoot of the principles of democracy. In 1720 John Trenchard and Thomas Gordon, writing under the pseudonym 'Cato', argued for the right publicly to examine and criticize our rulers as a principle divorced from more individualistic or libertarian notions of free speech.[3] The argument from democracy re-establishes this independent basis for the freedom to criticize governmental policy and governmental officials.

In some respects the argument from democracy is related to the survival theory of truth discussed in the previous chapter. By placing ultimate power in the people, this version of democracy, characterized by popular sovereignty and majority rule, implicitly embodies the view that political truths are, by definition, those that are accepted by the majority of the people. If the people are sovereign it is not for governments to decide what is true and what is false, especially in matters political, because as servant the government has an institutional role of trust based on and requiring impartiality or neutrality towards the people, and therefore towards the various ideas held by the people.[4] Inherent in the ideal of self-government is the proposition that it is for the people alone to distinguish between truth and falsity in matters relating to broad questions of governmental policy.

The survival theory of truth seems more plausible for questions of political policy than for most other categories of human knowledge. It is not unreasonable to argue that we are further from certainty regarding questions of political theory and policy than we are in other categories of thought, and that even if some objective test is conceivable, we are a long way either from finding it or from agreeing on what it might look like. In view of the rampant disagreement existing over issues of public policy, perhaps here, and here alone, majority rule is the best available test of truth. Alternatively, truth may not be the issue. Popular sovereignty incorporates a majority's right to be wrong. Where democracy is accepted, popular will is taken to prevail over any other method of arriving at knowledge, no matter how much better these other methods may seem. And accepting that the people have a right to be wrong entails accepting that wrongness can hardly be the criterion for denying the people access to information and opinions that may bear upon their decisions.

A PARADOX OF POWER

The argument from democracy pivots on the particular conception of democracy from which it was spawned. The entire argument is generated by the single principle of a sovereign electorate. Paradoxically, the same concept of sovereignty that provides the foundation for the argument from democracy also exposes the argument's most prominent weaknesses.

If the people collectively are in fact the sovereign, and if that sovereign has the unlimited powers normally associated with sovereignty, then acceptance of this view of democracy compels acceptance of the power of the sovereign to restrict the liberty of speech just as that sovereign may restrict any other liberty. Moreover, there is no reason to say that the sovereign may not entrust certain individuals with certain powers. The power to delegate authority is implicit in the unlimited power that sovereignty connotes. But if the people may entrust Jones with the exclusive obligation and authority to round up all stray dogs, why may it not entrust Brown with the exclusive obligation and authority to determine truth or falsity, or to exercise a power of censorship over publications?

Recall from chapter 1 the implications of recognizing a Free Speech Principle. The Free Speech Principle functions as a distinct restraint on governmental power, as a specific limitation on what as a general rule are accepted to be the powers of a sovereign majority. If we accept that the majority may legislate by itself, or through representatives, on anything, then a Free Speech Principle exists only if it is an exception to the general rule of majority sovereignty; only if it is a right, of indeterminate strength, against the majority. Any distinct restraint on majority power, such as a principle of freedom of speech, is by its nature anti-democratic, anti-majoritarian. If this were not the case, then the majority would be no more restrained in dealing with speech than in dealing with any other form of conduct, and free speech would be little more than a platitude.[5]

Thus, the very notion of popular sovereignty supporting the argument from democracy argues against any limitation on that sovereignty, and thereby argues against recognition of an independent principle of freedom of speech. To the extent that we support individual rights of expression, argument and criticism, we make claims inconsistent with a view of democracy founded on the absolute sovereignty of the people as a whole. Even viewing freedom of speech not so much as an individual right but as a social interest in individual expression,[6] the application of that view still entails granting the individual a right to speak when in some instances the majority might want to restrict that speech. The more we accept the premise of the argument from democracy, the less can we impinge on the right of self-government by restricting the power of the majority. If the argument from democracy would allow to be said things that the 'people' do not want to hear, it is not so much an argument based on popular will as it is an argument against it.

My argument may prove too much. By the same token the 'people' by majority vote could withdraw from the minority the right to vote, an action fundamentally opposed to any plausible conception of self-government. This paradox is resolved by looking to the idea of equality. Equal participation by all people in the process of government is even more fundamental to the ideal of self-government than is the idea of majority power. Indeed, given the foregoing paradox, equal participation most commends the argument from democracy. If everyone is to participate equally, then everyone must have the information necessary to make that participation meaningful. The argument from democracy thus transformed still argues powerfully for broad freedom to communicate ideas and information relevant to the processes of government. But as we shift from a sterile notion of democracy as majority rule to democracy as equal participation, free access to information becomes more a matter of respect for individual dignity, individual choice, and equal treatment of all individuals, and less an idea grounded in notions of sovereignty.

If equal participation in government is premised on an assumption of equal competence and universal rationality, the theory lacks both intuitive and empirical support. A plausible theory of equal participation must rest not on an assumption of competence, but on the view that equality is an independent and autonomous value. I discuss these individualistic conceptions of freedom of speech in the following two chapters; but it is worthwhile here to observe that, viewed as a form of equal respect for individuals, the argument from democracy does not give an independent argument for a Free Speech Principle. It is, however, a reminder that the *issues* relevant to self-government are especially important, and that individual interests and dignity are almost always implicated by decisions relating to the exercise of political power. The argument from democracy may constitute, then, a principled reason for giving pride of place to political speech, but only as part of a Free Speech Principle derived from sounder independent principles.

The argument from democracy generates yet another argument related more to the equality aspects of democracy than to the concept of popular sovereignty. Predominant among the problems that have concerned political theorists throughout modern history is that of the legitimacy of majority rule. What is the moral obligation of the minority to obey a particular law enacted by the majority over the objections of the minority? I do not wish here to rehearse the abundant answers that have been given to this question. One answer, however, is particularly relevant to this aspect of the problem of free speech. One reason for precluding the majority from withdrawing the minority's freedom to dissent is that the minority's right to object, to attempt to influence the majority, to have some say in the formulation of final policy, provides the moral basis for binding everyone to the rule ultimately adopted. This final rule, the 'law of the land', then is seen not so much as the work only of the majority but as the work of everyone who did or could participate in its formulation. Speaking, attempting to influence others to your point of view, is one way, perhaps *the* way, of so participating.

The argument has in one sense gone full circle. Under many formulations of the argument from democracy, freedom of speech is valuable because it allows *listeners* to receive all information material to the exercise of voting rights by members of a sovereign electorate. Indeed, the emphasis on the rights of the listener rather than on the rights of the speaker is one of the most important contributions of the argument from democracy. But now the focus instead is on the *speaker*. Especially when we look upon freedom of speech as a speaker's interest, the core of the theory has much more to do with individual dignity and equality, the moral right of equal participation, than it does with any notion of electoral sovereignty, or even with any pragmatic or utilitarian calculation of how government may function most effectively.

Upon closer analysis the argument from democracy moves further and further away from its source in the theories of sovereignty and self-government. This is not at all startling. The paradox presented at the beginning of this section merely illustrates that the conception of sovereignty supporting the argument from democracy is itself fundamentally flawed, not only as the foundation for a principle of free speech, but also as a more general theory of democracy. This point has been exhaustively treated by others, and I need not recapitulate those arguments here. Popper's discussion of the 'paradox of sovereignty' is a particularly effective attack on over-simplified views of popular sovereignty, and the limitations he and others have exposed both weaken and narrow the argument from democracy.[7] That argument is not merely restricted to democratic societies, but it is premised on and to some extent restricted to a particular conception of democracy that otherwise commands little serious attention. Just as the emphasis on popular sovereignty leads to such paradoxical conclusions as the right of the people to alienate that sovereignty by electing an absolute despot, so does the emphasis on electoral sovereignty in the argument from democracy help very little in explaining why rights of free speech are rights against a majority, why they are in any way immune from the principles of majority rule. An argument that cannot explain these matters is not an argument for a Free Speech Principle.

The complexity of modern societies further narrows the range of application of the argument from democracy. The more a governmental structure is removed from the paradigm of the New England town meeting, the less applicable becomes Meiklejohn's sterile formulation of the argument from democracy. But this distance between reality and the town-meeting model suggests an alternative formulation of the argument from democracy. As our leaders become elected rulers rather than servants, governmental superstructures are more likely to become as concerned with perpetuation of their own power as with acting in what they perceive to be the public interest. I do not mean to offer propaganda for the minimal state, or a testimonial to the ideas of Robert Nozick. I am making the much more modest observation that the same motivations that lead people to aspire to governmental office also lead those people to want to retain those positions. Freedom to criticize the government is a check on the survival instincts of self-perpetuating governmental organizations.[8] Freedom of speech, and perhaps more particularly freedom of the press, can be an integral part of a system of government based on separation of powers and checks and balances. The extraordinary immunity of the American press from actions for defamation, invasion of privacy, or contempt, an immunity grounded in large part on the writings of Meiklejohn, is due in part to a view of the press in an institutional context, as a check on governmental power. By contrast, the severe contempt and defamation sanctions that exist in Great Britain may be explained in part as the failure to accept such an institutional role for the press.

The process of communication is the principal way, and perhaps the only way, in which a mass of atomic individuals can join as the independent force envisaged by the model of pure self-government. The public may appear to have little power, but public opinion can have a great deal of power, and the process of communication enables the former to be converted into the latter.

Nothing in what I have said just now is necessarily inconsistent with the earlier formulations of the argument from democracy. By recasting the argument in this way, however, I have stressed the most important feature of the argument, the role of public officials as responsible and responsive to the people. I have concurrently de-emphasized the conception of the electorate as a national debating society. The two notions are not unrelated, but it is the former that has more direct contemporary application.

Even when reconstituted in this way, the argument that emerges remains narrow, because of its almost exclusive emphasis on public or political matters. We could argue, of course, that all subjects are indirectly related to the governmental process, or that a more complete view of democracy includes a broader range of issues.[9] At this point, however, the argument becomes quite attenuated. I can make little sense of a notion of self-government in art, literature, or science. But there is no reason to stretch the argument beyond its breaking point. The narrowness of the argument from democracy is also its greatest strength. The argument fails to provide a justification for a broad Free Speech Principle, but it does furnish several strong reasons for giving special attention and protection to political speech and criticism of government.

A RETURN TO FALLIBILITY

I have been treating the argument from democracy as if it were wholly distinct from the argument from truth. There is nothing in the origins of the argument from democracy to suggest any close relationship. Meiklejohn himself mocked the argument from truth as primarily a game for 'intellectual aristocrats' (such as Holmes) who were seen by him as remarkably unconcerned with issues of self-government. Yet the arguments are not nearly so distinct. An examination of the paradoxes and other weaknesses of the argument from democracy reveals that much of its strength derives not from its independent force, but from the extent to which it is a discrete and important subset of the argument from truth.

Almost as an offhand remark, Meiklejohn observed that the body politic 'must recognize its own limitations of wisdom and of temper and of circumstance, and must, therefore, make adequate provision for self-criticism and self-restraint'.[10] This seems crucial because it is the only plausible and useful explanation of why a sovereign electorate should place limits on its own sovereign power. Meiklejohn did not think this particularly important, which is not surprising, because it is largely unrelated to and surely inconsistent with his argument from popular sovereignty. What it is is the same lesson about caution in the face of uncertainty that emerged from the discussion of the argument from truth. It is fallibility writ large, a restatement of what both de Tocqueville and Mill saw as the tyranny of the majority. Far from being an argument from majoritarian democracy, it is an argument against majoritarian democracy.

The power of the majority, and especially an erring majority, was recognized even in classical times. Horace described '*civium ardor prava jubentium*', usually translated as 'the frenzy of the citizens bidding what is wrong'.[11] It is not so much that protection is needed particularly against a majority, as opposed to other forms of leadership. As majorities are not of unlimited wisdom, temper, or prudence, neither are other types of rulers immune from these weaknesses of humanity. One of the reasons we prefer democracy, so we think, is that these weaknesses are less prevalent in majorities than in individual tyrants. Moreover, majorities have fewer potential victims of their tyranny than do individual despots. But the weaknesses of the majority still exist. Just as individual tyrants can be wrong, so too with large groups, such as majorities. We wish to preserve the freedom to criticize the policies of the majority because those policies may be wrong, just as any other judgment may be wrong. Criticism may help the majority or its designates see error, and recognize their fallibility.

The argument from democracy does not dissolve completely into the argument from truth. The self-government model reminds us that when we are dealing with governmental policies, and with the performance and qualifications of our leaders, we are playing for higher stakes. By virtue of the power we grant to government, the effects of its fallibility are magnified by the importance of the decisions it makes. The special concern for freedom to discuss public issues and freedom to criticize governmental officials is a form of the argument from truth, because the necessity for rational thinking and the possibility of error in governmental policy are both large and serious. There is little certainty in questions of governmental policy, and the consequences are particularly serious when the chosen policies turn out to have been mistaken. If the expected harm is the product of the degree of uncertainty and the extent of damage should the chosen policy be erroneous, the risk of harm in governmental policy is enormous, and therefore the risk in assuming infallibility is equally enormous. The argument from democracy adds the lesson that political speech is different in kind as well as in degree. No facet of the argument from democracy is conclusive, but it provides several reasons for treating political speech as a wholly different creature. It thus gives added force to the argument from uncertainty, when that argument is applied to questions of governmental policy, power, and control.

Bibliographical note to chapter 3

Theories of free speech grounded in the functioning of the political process are also explored in Lillian BeVier, 'The First Amendment and political speech: an inquiry into the substance and limits of principle', *Stanford Law Review* **30** (1978), 299; William Brennan, 'The Supreme Court and the Meiklejohn interpretation of the First Amendment', *Harvard Law Review* **79** (1965), 1; Frank Morrow, 'Speech, expression, and the constitution', *Ethics* **85** (1975), 235. On the relationship between political process and individual rights theories of free speech, see Ronald Dworkin, 'Is the press losing the First Amendment?', *New York Review of Books* (December 4, 1980), 49. And on the relation between political speech and the forum in which it occurs, see Frederick Schauer, ' "Private" speech and the "private" forum: *Givhan* v. *Western Line School District*', *The Supreme Court Review* (1979), 217; Steven Shiffrin, 'Defamatory non-media speech and First Amendment methodology', *UCLA Law Review* **25** (1978), 915.

CHAPTER 4

Free speech and the good life

MUST FREE SPEECH BE INSTRUMENTAL?

The arguments discussed in the preceding chapters hold in common a consequentialist approach to freedom of speech. Both the argument from truth and the argument from democracy treat free speech not as an end but as a means. In the former argument free speech is a means of increasing knowledge, discovering error, and identifying truth; in the latter it is a means of ensuring the proper functioning of a state based on the principles of self-government. Each of these arguments values open communication for what it does, not for what it is.

The argument from truth and the argument from democracy also have a common emphasis on the interests of society at large rather than on the interests of the individual. Freedom of speech is most commonly conceived to be an individual interest; but there are two types of individual interests, and they must be distinguished. Some individual interests are valuable by virtue of the benefits derived by the persons exercising the interests. Other individual interests are recognized not primarily because of their ultimate value for the individual, but because the value to the person exercising them is instrumental to the value that accrues to society from the widespread exercise of individual interests. Both the argument from truth and the argument from democracy are examples of this latter variety of individual interests. The individual rights they generate are but a mediate step towards maximizing the goals of society at large. These individual rights are grounded in the societal interests in the exercise of individual rights, a relationship recognized and described most clearly by Roscoe Pound.[1]

From this perspective the arguments treated in the preceding chapters all derive their strength from some conception of what is good for society as a whole, rather than from any concern with the well-being of individuals in a narrower sense. There are those who criticize liberalism for being excessively individualistic, or for failing to recognize the importance of relationships among individu-

47

als. These criticisms may be correct, but they are incomplete unless they recognize that much of liberal doctrine is premised on the benefits to society as a whole that come from individual choice and diversity. But although the concepts of social and individual interests are useful tools for looking at rights in general, they are just two sides of the same coin, at least for any arguments that view the interests of society as the composite of the interests of the individuals who comprise society.

In contrast to this social side of individual interests, both this chapter and the next focus on freedom of speech as an individual interest in a narrower (and stronger) sense. Here the ultimate point of reference is the individual, not the state, or society at large. Although society may benefit from the satisfaction of individual interests, the arguments discussed here treat such benefits as incidental to a primary focus on individual well-being. An individual interest in this strong sense remains important even if society might in some way, or on balance, be worse off for recognizing it.[2] Here individual well-being is an end in itself.

The arguments discussed in this and the next chapter are interrelated, and the division is neither wholly distinct nor wholly satisfactory. But individual autonomy and choice is sufficiently important that it seems right to treat it as separate from a discussion of individual development. The latter will be treated now; the former is the subject of the next chapter.

The question is whether free speech is a component of the 'good life'. Is free speech an integral part of human nature, or self-realization? The emphasis is on free speech as an autonomous value, not a value instrumental to some social objective. Free speech has at times been suggested to be a good in itself, without need of further justification. This hypothesis is the point of departure for this chapter.

Some would find it sufficient to stop at this point, contending that freedom to say what you wish is of course good, not needing further argument or analysis. These people claim to intuit the intrinsic goodness of free speech. But recognition of a Free Speech Principle requires more. There may be value in intuitionist thinking in social and political philosophy, but almost any activity with which governments normally interfere can be maintained under some theory to be inherently good. To say merely that free speech is inherently good is insufficient to establish a Free Speech Principle, because it does not distinguish speech from a wide range of other voluntary actions. Here intuitions are insufficient. A Free

Speech Principle requires that speech be treated differently, and only if a reason for such differential treatment exists can we say there is a Free Speech Principle.

The view of freedom of speech as an intrinsic good is most commonly articulated in terms of a particular perception of human nature, and a particular perception of the ideal aspirations of mankind.[3] This approach sees man as continually striving for improvement and self-development, and it sees free communication as an integral part of this objective.

But this argument is fundamentally misguided. Equating freedom of speech with happiness, or holding it essential to pleasure, is simply false. Many people indeed believe that freedom to express their opinions is a primary component of their happiness. But others are as likely to be satisfied with other freedoms, or prefer the security or intellectual anaesthesia that accompanies rigid controls on expression. The warning of the Grand Inquisitor in *The Brothers Karamazov* demands respect. It is not a necessary truth that people equate happiness with freedom in a broad sense. To equate happiness with a particular type of freedom is even less warranted.[4] Moreover, there are numerous interests to consider – the interests of speakers, the interests of listeners, and the interests of third parties affected by the consequences of speech. An attempt to justify free speech purely in terms of happiness is met by the often-conflicting pleasures involved, as well as by the argument's tenuous empirical assumptions.

Aristotelian conceptions of happiness present a stronger argument for freedom of speech as an intrinsic good. The argument is then grounded not so much on what man is as on what man ought to be. This conception of the rich life is derived from ideas of personal growth, self-fulfilment, and development of the rational faculties. Under this conception, one who is enjoying the good life may be neither content nor euphoric in the ordinary sense. He may not even be happy in the ordinary sense, for his happiness resides not in, for example, sensual satisfaction, but in knowing that he has maximally developed all the *potential* that distinguishes man *qua* man from all other creatures. He should feel satisfied in the knowledge that he is realizing his full potential. If it is the power of reason that distinguishes man from other forms of animal life, then only by fully exploiting this power can one be said to enjoy a full life. Because the basis of this conception of the full life is complete use and development of the mind and thinking process, speech is said to be an integral component of self-fulfilment, the one being inseparable from the other. Free speech is thus said to be justified not because it provides a benefit to society, but because it is a primary good.

In this form the argument is freed from most of its *obvious* weaknesses. The argument demands close attention, and a discussion of the argument will occupy the balance of this chapter.

SPEECH AS EXPRESSION

Treating freedom of speech as a primary good suggests that we should be looking not at freedom of speech but rather at freedom of *expression*. References to 'freedom of expression' are as common as references to 'freedom of speech'. 'Freedom of expression' is protected by the European Convention on Human Rights, and 'freedom of expression' is the term most commonly used in academic writing about the subject. 'Expression' avoids the strictly oral connotations of 'speech', and thus 'expression' may be preferable because it more clearly includes writing and pictures. Or, the preference may be explained solely by the fact that 'expression' is the longer word. But if 'expression' is anything more than a synonym for 'communication', a view of speech as expression must be derived chiefly from the naturalistic concepts that constitute the subject of this chapter. We must consider whether freedom of speech is something more than the freedom to communicate.

Much of the unfortunate confusion of freedom of speech with freedom of expression can be traced to the fact that 'expression' can have two quite different meanings, meanings that are often uncritically interchanged in this context.[5]

First, 'expression' can mean communication, requiring both a communicator and a recipient of the communication. For example, if my new colour television set insists on presenting its offerings solely in black and white, it would be quite natural to say that I would *express* my dissatisfaction to the manager of the store where I bought the television set. If someone is a good public speaker, we may say that he *expresses* himself well. If someone's prose style is ambiguous and ungrammatical, we are likely to say that he cannot *express* himself in writing. In this sense the word 'expression' could easily be replaced by the word 'communication' without any significant change in meaning (except to the extent that to express oneself well in speaking or writing implies a certain elegance of style that is not suggested by the word 'communication').

On the other hand, the word 'expression' can also be used to describe certain activities not involving communication. This is the other meaning of 'expressing', or 'expressing oneself', a meaning that generates the locution 'self-expression'. For example, my reaction to the absence of colour on my new colour television set might be to throw a paperweight at the television screen. In that case I could be said to be *expressing* anger, or *expressing* hostility. I would be *expressing myself*, although there was no communication. 'Expression', on the one hand, can refer to communication, and, on the other hand, it can refer to any external manifestation of inner feeling. The existence of these two senses of the word 'expression' has created confusion about just what it is that freedom of speech is intended to protect.

The confusion is compounded because communicating, the first sense of 'expression', is one very important way of 'expressing oneself' in the second sense of 'expression'. Artists, poets and novelists, for example, are expressing themselves in the sense that they are doing something that is an extension of their emotions, and at the same time they are expressing their ideas and their emotions *to* viewers and readers. One who protested against the war in Vietnam by shouting obscene epithets at public officials might both have been expressing his own anger (which does not require a listener), and at the same time have been communicating a message of objection to government policy. Although in this book I am (I hope) expressing my ideas to the reader, I am also expressing myself in the second sense by choosing to write it. Moreover, I am expressing myself in this second sense by choosing to be an academic rather than a farmer, a postman, or a neurosurgeon, and by choosing to reside in Williamsburg rather than in Rangoon. Some choices, of course, are consequent upon (or derivative from) other choices and may therefore be less expressive or not expressive at all. My choice of residence may be a primary choice, in which case it would be a form of expression, or it may on the other hand be the only place in which I can practise my chosen profession, in which case it would be derivative from a form of expression. I am not arguing that every intentional act is necessarily a form of expression (although that is not an implausible position), but only that the range of expressive activity is broad, and that 'expression' in this sense is very different from 'expression' in the communicative sense. The problem occurs when we try to separate these meanings of 'expression', and when we look at the relation of the two meanings to the principle of freedom of speech.

It is certainly possible to argue that a free speech principle is in fact a free expression principle, encompassing other forms of self-expression as well as communication. But if we look closely at this argument, we discover that there emerges no Free Speech Principle at all, because we must conclude that there is nothing special about speech. My mode of dress is usually a form of self-expression, as is the length of my hair and the style in which I wear it. Both my choice of occupation and residence are frequently ways of expressing myself. Choosing to drive a Ford or a Mini might not be an obvious form of self-expression, but choosing a Ferrari or an Hispano-Suiza most certainly is. If I have beaten this point beyond submission, it is only to emphasize that self-expression is an unworkably amorphous concept, subtracting far more than it adds to any sensible view of what free speech means.

Speech as communication is of course a method of self-expression, but the concept of self-expression is not helpful to an analysis of free speech. When speech is considered merely as one form of self-expression, nothing special is said about speech. Because virtually any activity may be a form of self-expression, a theory that does not isolate speech from this vast range of other conduct causes freedom of speech to collapse into a principle of general liberty. If the Free Speech Principle is derived from the value of self-expression, then any of the foregoing examples would be included within the Free Speech Principle. Any form of voluntary conduct may be to the actor a form of self-expression, and we are left with only a justification for a broad and undifferentiated principle of general liberty. Unless we can derive an argument for freedom of speech that is independent of the arguments for general personal freedom, there is little need to emphasize free speech. True, we might refer to free speech as a more concrete example of an abstract principle, but if that is all we are doing we have lost the special force of a Free Speech Principle. We might reject the existence of a Free Speech Principle, but accepting it is inconsistent with treating free speech merely as an instance of freedom of self-expression. If, as in the self-expression model, freedom of speech is coextensive with freedom of action, the state is no less constrained in dealing with speech than it is in dealing with any other form of human activity. In Robert Nozick's utopia this might be of little consequence, but existing states assert and exercise greater authority over the individual than Nozick would concede to be legitimate. Real states restrict action quite frequently, and often quite legitimately. If freedom of speech is freedom of self-expression, anyone who has conceded some of his freedom of action must, *pro tanto,* have conceded his freedom of speech. If there is an independent principle of free speech, this is an unnecessary concession.

Free speech and the good life

Rejecting a theory that equates freedom of speech with freedom of self-expression forces us to return to freedom of speech as freedom to communicate.[6] If there is a natural right to communicate, apart from any natural right to general liberty, it is most sensibly derived from the idea of freedom of thought. Freedom of thought (or its synonyms freedom of belief and freedom of conscience) seems particularly amenable to a naturalistic justification, because few things can more easily be perceived as inherently good than the independent use of one's mind to come to such conclusions as it wishes. However, the very value of freedom of thought points up the futility of considering freedom of thought to be an important principle of political theory. We can think silently. It is not necessary to speak or write in order to think. And when we think silently, our thoughts are beyond the reach of government sanction. Obviously thoughts can be *influenced* by government. Propaganda is an example, and so is a system of explicit or implicit rewards. But a silent thought *qua* thought is immune from punishment, and to that extent is discretely different from outward expression or communication. Prisoners in some of the Nazi concentration camps supposedly sang a song entitled 'Meine Gedänke Sind Frei' (My Thoughts Are Free). The intended meaning is particularly relevant – whatever you may do to me, whatever you may physically compel me to do *or say*, my thoughts are still free because they remain beyond the reach of your powers.

Government sanctions may penalize belief to the extent of driving it deeply underground. Punishing those known to hold certain beliefs, compelling the affirmation of belief, requiring the disclosure of belief, and precluding people with certain beliefs from holding government positions are all restrictions on freedom of thought. But they are restrictions only on *expressed* thought. These restrictions operate against overt manifestations of thought, and against those who are unwilling to lie for their beliefs, but this is not the same as punishing the thought alone. The largely internal nature of what we ordinarily call a thought puts that thought to a great extent beyond the power of governmental punishment.

Thoughts and beliefs, however, are not static. They develop, they change, they are embellished or combined, and at times they are rejected. The argument for a natural right to free speech is premised on the assumption that this process operates effectively only when there is communication. Reading, writing, speaking and exchanging ideas with others is perceived to be of critical importance if thoughts are to develop and grow in the human mind. The theory aims to protect not *a* thought, but the process of thinking.

Here it is important to remember that language is not only the medium of communication, it is also the medium of thinking. We think not in complete abstractions, but (most commonly) in words. Our ability to think creatively, therefore, is to a great degree dependent upon our language. If communication is stifled, the development of language is restricted. To the extent, therefore, that we curtail the development of linguistic tools, we chill the thought process that utilizes those very same tools. Although Waismann and others have emphasized that language must follow our thoughts, it is in many respects equally true that thoughts follow our language. Each is a cutting edge for the further development of the other.

The theory that communication and personal relationships are central features of human development has roots in the writings of Aristotle. If man is a political and social animal, then communication and the use of language are vital components of humanity, because we relate to other people predominantly by linguistic communication. This argument is not that communication facilitates certain types of relationships (although of course it does). Rather it is that communication is an integral part of human nature, at least when human beings are viewed in this social and political way. If communication is that basic to mankind, it is argued, then its special protection is easily justified.

At the heart of this argument, whether characterized in terms of individual values or in terms of social and political values, is the concept of self-development. The argument is based on the proposition that a person who uses his faculties to their fullest extent, who is all that it is possible to be, is in some sense better off, and in an Aristotelian sense happier, than those whose development is stultified. And because it is thinking, reasoning, rationality, and complex interrelationships with others that distinguish humanity from other forms of animal life, then it is the faculties of reason and thinking that are at the core of self-development. What is seen as the ultimate goal for man is the fullest use of the capacity to think, the greatest degree of mental exertion, the exploration of the limits of the mind.

But minds do not grow in a vacuum. Intellectual isolationism is almost wholly inconsistent with intellectual development. The image of the mountaintop guru, developing great ideas in a sublime and isolated existence, is far more myth than reality. For one thing, we learn to think as we are taught language. Further intellectual self-development comes from communication of our ideas to others. Our thoughts are refined when we communicate them. Often we have an idea in some amorphous and incipient stage, but see it develop or see its weaknesses for the first time when the idea must be specifically articulated in a form intelligible to some other person.

Seen in this light, communication is an integral part of the self-development of the speaker, because it enables him to clarify and better understand his own thoughts. Communication may also be inseparable from the self-realization of the hearers, the recipients of communication. Mill (whose disclaimer of making appeals to natural rights should not be taken too seriously) was concerned both with the development of the mind and with the values of choice and diversity. He saw reason and intellect as faculties that improved with exercise, and in his view the greatest practice came from exercising the powers of choice, of intellectual discrimination. Communication makes an individual aware of choices he may not be able to imagine or formulate alone, and thereby furthers the self-development of the recipient of a wide variety of different ideas and opinions. As we hear more ideas, then we have more ideas to evaluate. And as we are compelled to evaluate more ideas, then we have more opportunity to practise the important skill of evaluating and choosing among ideas.

If we accept the premise that mental self-fulfilment is a primary good, then the way in which the communication of ideas is related to intellectual development provides an apparently sound argument for a special freedom to communicate, and a correlative freedom to be the object of communication. But the superior (compared to other forms of animal life) rationality of human beings does not necessarily lead to the conclusion that the development of this particular faculty is more important than the development or satisfaction of other desires or needs less peculiarly human. Other characteristics not exclusive to humanity also profit from development and fulfilment. Our physical well-being, our non-intellectual pleasures, our need for food and shelter, and our desire for security are also important, although these are wants we share with the rest of the animal world. Because any governmental or private action to restrict communication is usually justified in the name of one of these or other similar wants of all or part of humanity, a particular protection of communication under this version of a natural rights theory must assume that communication is *prima facie* more important than these other interests. This priority is often justified by reference to the unique characteristics of the species *homo sapiens*. But it is equally plausible to conclude that the needs and wants that man *shares* with other animals are, for that reason, more basic and therefore more important.

Those sympathetic towards natural rights arguments in moral and political philosophy will find the argument for freedom to communicate appealing because that argument attempts to demonstrate that communication is indeed an important interest. But the argument does not demonstrate why freedom to communicate is more important than other well-recognized interests, and thus it does not show why freedom to communicate should be an independent principle of political philosophy.

The argument from self-fulfilment underscores the importance of communication, but the argument can be deployed with equal force in reference to most human needs or desires. If an argument from inherent goodness supports a right to free speech, so too can it support a right to eat, a right to sleep, a right to shelter, a right to a decent wage, a right to interesting employment, a right to sexual satisfaction, and so on *ad infinitum*. But when a list of rights becomes coextensive with the list of wants, or even with the list of fundamental needs, we lose any strong sense of having a right. Because governmental action of any kind almost always is directed towards satisfaction of some important need or want of the population, a right to free speech that rests on the same footing can no longer sensibly operate as a side constraint against such action in furtherance of the public interest. The Free Speech Principle, if it exists, operates as a side constraint, or trump. But if all of the suits are trumps, we are in effect playing at no trumps.

FREEDOM OR FREEDOM OF SPEECH?

The argument from self-fulfilment suffers from a failure to distinguish intellectual self-fulfilment from other wants and needs, and thus fails to support a distinct principle of free speech. But the same conclusion follows even if we accept the primacy of intellectual self-fulfilment. For the sake of argument, let us assume that there is something special about the power of reason that commends the development of its particular faculties to special treatment. Let us assume further that intellectual development occurs primarily, as many have argued, through a process of mental exploration, a process by which a range of alternatives gives the mind room in which to expand and the challenge with which to develop.

Under these assumptions, communication does seem rather

important. Communication informs us of the choices and hypotheses made or suggested by others while also allowing us to refine our own thoughts through the necessity of articulating them. But once again the connexion between communication and the realization of human potential is, although seductively appealing at first glance, still logically incapable of generating a true Free Speech Principle. The fact that A may cause B, or even that A must cause B, does not entail the proposition that only A can cause B. There is no reason X, Y or Z cannot also cause B. Even if communication is a sufficient condition for intellectual self-fulfilment, it does not follow that it is a necessary condition. The fact that communication will produce the desired result does not mean that that same result cannot also be produced by *experiences*. It seems as likely that intellectual self-realization can be fostered by world travel, by keen observation, or by changing employment every year, to give just a few examples. These and many other experiences can open one's eyes, triggering deeper thought and consequent development of the intellect. There is nothing in the argument that shows communication to be necessarily better than any of these other methods of mental development.

Moreover, even if communication is a necessary condition for intellectual advancement, that does not make it a sufficient condition. The value of communication in the process of intellectual development is of necessity limited by the range of experiences that are the subjects of the communication. F. A. Hayek, in *The Constitution of Liberty*, argues that we over-estimate the importance of freedom of thought and ideas at the expense of underestimating the value of actually *doing* things. He argues that speech follows experience, and therefore that freedom of speech is meaningful only when there is freedom of action, because new ideas spring from new environments and additional experiences. Hayek's argument is not without flaws, but it is particularly apt here. If we are concerned with the development of the mind, then choice, diversity, individuality and novelty are every bit as important in the entire range of human conduct as in the particular segment of man's activities that we call 'communication'.[7] If we take Hayek's point that the value of communication is dependent upon what it is that can be communicated, then the other forms of conduct are logically prior to and therefore possibly more important than communication.

I do not mean to be taken as saying that communication is not valuable. I am only arguing that it is but one aspect of an Aristotelian argument for an extremely wide-ranging freedom to engage

57

in multitudinous varieties of conduct. The argument from self-fulfilment can be a powerful argument for freedom in a very broad sense, but it tells us nothing in particular about freedom of speech. Freedom of speech under such a theory is merely a component part (or an instance) of that general Good that we often call 'freedom' or 'liberty'. Therefore, to the extent that we support or provide for freedom in this general sense, we find that freedom of speech is included *pro tanto*. Conversely, and more significantly, to the extent that a given society or government has for some reason elected to limit individual liberty in the broad sense, there remains no reason freedom of speech should not be subject to equivalent limitations.

This conclusion is virtually identical to the conclusion I reached about the natural rights argument for speech as self-expression. In both cases it may be possible to generate an argument for individual freedom in a broad sense, but in neither case is there an argument that is directed towards showing why freedom of speech is any more valuable than anything else we may be or should be free to do. Without this distinction, most talk of a right to free speech is at best misleading.

The importance of these distinctions is highlighted when we realize that this and most other discussions of freedom of speech are exercises in what Rawls calls 'nonideal theory'. It may be (although I do not wish to argue the point here) that an ideal society would in fact grant rights in a strong sense to engage in a very wide range of conduct. If this were the case, freedom of speech would to some extent be subsumed within this broad freedom, rendering an independent Free Speech Principle less important. But existing societies, often for very powerful reasons, do not grant strong rights of general liberty. As long as this is the case, the search for a Free Speech Principle remains important. Moreover, any plausible principle of general liberty will be subject to an exception for exercises of liberty that cause harm to others. Yet, as the examples in chapter 1 were designed to demonstrate, our pre-theoretical understanding of freedom of speech assumes that many speech acts that do cause harm to others will be protected despite the harm they cause. But if freedom of speech is merely a component of general liberty, the principle of free speech will not protect the speech in these and many other examples. Only by divorcing a theory of free speech from a theory of general liberty will a principle of free speech of any strength emerge.

Bibliographical note to chapter 4

Self-expression and self-fulfilment are the basis of theories in Edwin Baker, 'Scope of the First Amendment freedom of speech', *UCLA Law Review* **25** (1978), 964; Edwin Baker, 'Commercial speech: a problem in the theory of freedom', *Iowa Law Review* **62** (1976), 1; Kenneth Karst, 'The freedom of intimate association', *Yale Law Journal* **89** (1980), 624; David A. J. Richards, 'Free speech and obscenity law: toward a moral theory of the First Amendment', *University of Pennsylvania Law Review* **123** (1974), 45. An interesting variation is Allen Buchanan, 'Revisability and rational choice', *Canadian Journal of Philosophy* **5** (1975), 395. For an imaginative effort to ground freedom of speech in the use and development of language, see Paul Chevigny, 'Philosophy of language and free expression', *New York University Law Review* **55** (1980), 157.

CHAPTER 5

Individuality and free speech

THE LIBERAL IDEOLOGY

Freedom of speech is commonly thought of as a liberal doctrine. Freedom of speech, freedom of religion and some freedom in personal way of life are usually considered to be among the primary components of that amorphous credo that is commonly called 'liberalism'.[1] Liberalism is frequently characterized by a particular preoccupation with individualism and individual rights, especially as against the state or against the majority. Liberalism places great stock in personal choice, personal freedom, and the value of variety, or diversity. It is concerned with the interests of the individual, and is often accused of being less aware of and less concerned with social interaction and communal values.

The arguments I have discussed in this book, particularly the arguments in chapters 2 and 3, in large part belie this reflexive association of freedom of speech with liberalism. Upon closer analysis both the argument from truth and the argument from democracy emerged in a form that does not look especially liberal. I do not mean that anything presented so far is necessarily inconsistent with liberalism. Rather, the arguments have not been notably concerned with the individualism and choice that constitute the foundations of liberal ideology. The values underlying the arguments from truth and democracy are more social than individual. In the previous chapter, however, the liberal flavour of the concept of free speech began to appear. Yet in the context of the specific purpose here, the result was a dead end. The arguments from self-fulfilment appeared under critical scrutiny to be little more than arguments for general liberty. We learned little in particular about free speech except that free speech can be subsumed under some broad notions of personal freedom. The arguments provided scant assistance in justifying a Free Speech Principle.

When we speak of liberalism, or for that matter when we speak of liberty, we suggest principles based on individuality. Although we may argue that respect for individuals is the keystone of the best society, our primary concern is less for social benefits than it is for the good of individuals *qua* individuals, and not individuals *qua* members of a social group. Liberalism embodies a profound respect for individual differences, and as a consequence places great emphasis on individual choice. By respecting freedom as choice, liberalism recognizes (as it must) that freedom is hardly a worthwhile topic of consideration if everyone's freedom is directed toward the same desires, the same choices and the same actions. Freedom that does not produce diversity when that freedom is exercised is psychologically unrealistic as well as fundamentally inconsistent with the liberal creed. Diversity of action is not merely a result of liberalism. It lies at the core of liberalism. A theory of government represented by a presumption in favour of freedom is grounded on the disutility of conformity, or at least on the conscious refusal to regard conformity or uniformity as important primary goods. By encouraging diversity and individual choice, and by raising barriers to governmental or social interference with those goals, liberalism sees itself as especially concerned with human dignity, a dignity that is insulted when there is insufficient respect for personal choice.

These ideas can often turn into platitudes, as they may have in the previous paragraph. But because such ideas appear so often in various explications or applications of liberalism it is worthwhile to repeat these ideas in a way that ties them together. I do this so that it becomes easier to analyse and evaluate the position of free speech within the particular liberal conception of freedom.

IS THERE A RIGHT TO DIGNITY?

What is at the core of these appeals to individuality, individual freedom and individual choice? We may take two tacks in responding to this question. First, we may look at the *results* of respecting, permitting, and even encouraging individual choice. I am referring not to the psychological effects on the person exercising the choice, but to the products of the process of choosing, the choices actually made. From this perspective the diversity occasioned by individual choice may be most important. I consider this alternative in the next section of this chapter, in evaluating the premise that variety is the ultimate goal of liberalism.

But looking at the products of choice is not the only alternative. We may look instead not at what is chosen but at the act of permitting the choice to be made. What interests do we acknowledge when we permit people to exercise their free will?[2] What are the harms of *not* permitting individual choice? Here we see liberalism as grounded in notions of dignity, self-respect, equality and independence of personality. Liberalism in this form is prominent in the work of Ronald Dworkin.[3] If we accept the importance of treating each person with *equal* respect, and of treating each person as independently valuable, then, the argument goes, we must treat each person's choices with equal respect as well. To deny a person his right to choose, especially as to what Dworkin calls 'internal' preferences, is to deprive him of his dignity by denying the respect that comes from acknowledging his choices to be as worthy as the choices of anyone else.

I have yet to say anything specific about speech. But it should by now be apparent that an argument for freedom of speech is easily extracted from the premises of dignity I have just described. On this conception of individuality the act of suppression provides the cornerstone of the argument for freedom of speech. When the state suppresses a person's ideas, or when the state suppresses that person's expression of those ideas, the state is insulting that person and affronting his dignity. There is a close link here with the concept of equality. When we suppress a person's ideas, we are in effect saying that although he may think his ideas to be as good as (or better than) the next person's, society feels otherwise. By the act of suppression, society and its government are saying his thoughts and beliefs are not as good as those of most other people. Society is saying that his ideas, and by implication he himself, are not worthy. He is not deserving of treatment as an equal member of society.

The easy criticism of this view is to point out that it is just not true that anyone's ideas are as good as anyone else's. Such an extreme form of relativism or subjectivism is scarcely comprehensible. We do not need a particularly strong commitment to certainty or objectivity to take some ideas to be better than others, and some propositions to be more likely true than others. A theory resting on a bizarre subjectivism is on a shaky foundation. When we say that some actions, such as helping injured people or contributing to charity, are better than other actions, such as polluting rivers or torturing cats, we make evaluations and condemn certain choices. Yet we scarcely think of insult or dignity in this context. Nor does it do to say that the latter examples are different because they involve harm. That begs the question, because the argument from dignity as an argument for free speech is useful only if it holds that insult and indignity caused by suppression are more serious than harm caused by the speech at issue, an analogue of a point I stressed in chapter 1. A Free Speech Principle based on the premise that speech causes no harm is a Free Speech Principle of very narrow range.

We must look closer at the concept of equality. The argument from human dignity is based largely on the view that failing to treat A's ideas as being of equal value with everyone else's ideas is like treating A as an unequal member of society. It is not sufficient to answer that A's ideas may not be as good as B's, C's, or D's. A person would not forfeit his general right to equality by being less good in some respects than the norm in society. If A is stupid, clumsy, rude, inconsiderate, loud, boring and dirty, he is still entitled to equal treatment by the governing authorities. Why not the same for A's ideas when they are wrong, offensive and ill-conceived?

But society does not treat everyone the same. Even those societies with the strongest egalitarian aspirations make distinctions among people on the basis of ability, industry, or other criteria ideally related to the reasons for requiring a distinction. Equality is much less an idea of sameness than it is the limitation of the criteria of selection to differences relevant to some legitimate purpose. The evil of racial and religious discrimination, for example, lies not in the fact of making distinctions, but in the reasons for making the distinctions. We object to distinctions that either do not relate to requiring a choice (as in discrimination in employment) or that distinguish when there is no reason to make a choice at all (as in requiring certain races to sit in the back of the bus). But we would not object to distinguishing along racial lines in calculating the level of lighting at a television station.

If we look at distinctions in the speech arena, to distinctions among ideas, we find the concept of equality to be of little independent assistance.[4] It is both true and trivial that a governing authority should avoid meaningless distinctions among utterances. But a principle of free speech operating as a side constraint is useful only if some distinctions among speech are plausibly advantageous to the public interest. That does not mean such distinctions necessarily should be made. If that were so, there would be no point in discussing a Free Speech Principle. But if some distinctions among utterances are related to legitimate ends of government, as surely they are, then a principle of equality no more tells us to ignore these distinctions than it tells us to refrain from making relevant distinctions in any other area of conduct.

If dignity and equality do justify some immunity of speech from the principles of government action that would otherwise prevail, it must be that people are insulted or deprived of their dignity when there is excess intrusion into their personal affairs. When one with justification could say 'That's none of your business!', it is possible that government control is morally precluded. While I am not sure that this is correct as a general principle, it is at least a plausible reflection of one of the fundamental tenets of liberalism. But with respect to speech one would be justified in saying 'That's none of your business!' only if the speech can be said to cause no harm to others, i.e. if the speech can be taken as primarily self-regarding. But when words are other-regarding, whatever the precise definition of that term, the ideas of dignity and insult are no more dispositive than they would be if someone claimed his dignity to be insulted by restrictions on his freedom to pollute the atmosphere, commit assault, play the saxophone in church, or practice cardio-vascular surgery without a medical degree or licence. Dignity relates closely to self-regarding actions. In reference to other-regarding actions it seems out of place; and but a small group of utterances are self-regarding. Even if many utterances were self-regarding, this would not help. For if the dignity principle relates only to self-regarding speech, however much there may be, the principle offers no justification for a Free Speech Principle that protects speech with possibly unpleasant consequences.

Dworkin argues that expressions of adherence to the Communist Party are not subject to regulation because the desire to regulate those utterances is an external rather than internal preference. But that misses the point. The desire to limit such expression is not based on the position that such views (and those who express them) are less worthy than others. It is based primarily on the perception that such words constitute a threat to national security, public order and the chosen way of life of the majority. They are regulated on the same theory that regulates *actions* thought to threaten these same interests.[5] We make a strong statement about freedom of speech only if the burden of proof to justify restrictions on speech that may harm the national interest is greater than the burden of proof necessary to justify restrictions on other action also thought to harm the national interest. Here the argument from dignity is of little assistance. My dignity may be affronted equally by restrictions on my other-regarding conduct as by restrictions on my other-regarding speech, yet we do not think of dignity when we regulate other-regarding conduct. Personal dignity is at the core of freedom of speech if speech is taken to be self-regarding, or if a Free Speech Principle includes only self-regarding speech. Neither view is acceptable.

Even if we accept the dubious premise that dignity and respect are at the heart of the special protection of speech, the other activities within the same principle expose the principle's weakness. Dworkin puts 'expressions of adherence to the Communist Party' in the same analytic pigeonhole as private homosexuality, contraception and pornography.[6] In so doing he lays bare that he is not referring to any particular protection for speech beyond that available to activities he treats as self-regarding. He is thus forced to accept the legitimacy of restrictions on speech when the speech can be shown to cause harm, when the justification for its regulation is no greater than the justification for regulating factories that emit distasteful aromas.

The issue may be viewed in more practical terms. One who advocates free speech on the basis of a broad and undifferentiated Millian freedom has no arrows left in his quiver if and when his arguments for this broad Millian freedom are rejected. Many countries recognize a strong Free Speech Principle but regulate on the basis of moral and paternalistic principles. If the only argument for free speech must argue against such other bases of regulation as well, then freedom of speech has no power to survive a rejection of the premises of a broadly libertarian state.

The problem here, as with the argument from self-fulfilment discussed in the previous chapter, is that the argument from dignity is an argument for personal liberty, not an argument for a special liberty of speech. Freedom of speech may, as in Dworkin's version of the argument, be an instance of a concept of liberty smaller than total liberty of action, but it is still no argument against the vast number of putative restrictions on speech based on some specific other-regarding feature of the intended expression.

I have not completely rejected the equality aspects of the argument from equal dignity and respect. Equality has a place, as I argued in chapter 3, in a concept of democracy. Equal participation in the process of government is properly regarded as one of the most important features of what we call 'democracy'. Because argument and deliberation are as much a part of the political process as the casting of a ballot, then to that extent equal participation in the deliberative process is supported by arguments independent of arguments for general liberty, and a Free Speech Principle in democratic societies for speech related to matters of public concern finds a place in the reconstituted argument from democracy. Equality remains an important concept, and the notion of dignity is not wholly unrelated, but in the context of an argument for a specific freedom of speech the important arguments relate to the theory of the governmental process, rather than to largely irrelevant (for this purpose) general theories about dignity and equality.

THE ARGUMENT FROM DIVERSITY

I suggested at the beginning of the previous section that the value of individuality and independence may lie not in the process of exercising choice, but in the results of the choices made. Because people differ in attitudes, desires, motivations and abilities, we can expect that the free play of individual choice will produce great variety in opinions expressed and choices made. The liberal tradition has emphasized the inherent value of the diversity resulting from deference to individual differences. Mill is frequently said to have made, beneath the epistemic trappings of his argument, an argument in favour of variety for variety's sake, making diversity an end in itself.

An argument for the autonomous value of variety can take two forms. First, a multiplicity of options may be valuable in sometimes enabling us to reject established doctrines or expand beyond traditional orthodoxies. In its extreme form this can be a strongly relativist position, seeing variety as a good because nothing is better than anything else. But a moderated form of this position avoids this weakness. Variety is good not because everything is as good as everything else, but only because the majority or received view might be wrong. Divergence from accepted attitudes may demonstrate the advantages of the alternatives and the weaknesses in received views. This appears to be a powerful argument for diversity of opinion as a valuable goal, because that diversity places before us for consideration a wide range of what may turn out to be more advantageous alternatives.

In this form, however, the argument is virtually identical to the precipitate that remained after distilling off all that was superfluous or erroneous from the argument from truth. Diversity is valuable in this respect, but talk of diversity is merely an alternative way of saying that all of the advantages of the fallibilist approach to the argument from truth are increased by multiplying the number of available alternatives and challenges. There is hardly anything revolutionary in this observation, especially to students of the philosophy of science. By encouraging variety for its own sake, we recognize the significant role of chance in the advancement of knowledge, a role that is evidenced, for example, by the importance that some people place on guessing in the growth of scientific knowledge.[7] There is no reason to suppose that such perceptions are less apt to other areas of knowledge.

Variety is advantageous not only in allowing us to explore various alternative hypotheses, but also in encouraging experimentation with alternative policies, alternative styles of life, alternative governmental organizations, and so on. Here again diversity is almost an end in itself, because it encourages the trial and error process, another way of rejecting inadequate ideas and replacing them with superior ones. But when variety is viewed in this light, speech has no special claim to protection. We can as easily argue from this premise for freedom of *action* in any other field. Indeed, because in most instances speech is but a preliminary step to action, this type of argument from diversity tells much more for freedom of conduct than it tells for freedom of speech.

In the context of freedom of speech, a special emphasis on diversity is valuable in enabling us to see and therefore to evaluate a wider range of alternatives. Although this position overlaps with the argument from truth, it adds an important embellishment by reminding us that, in most instances, an increased number of alternatives and challenges raises the probability of recognizing error and thereby advancing the state of knowledge. As I mentioned earlier, the validity of this aspect of the argument is not a function of the identity of the decision-maker, and thus is not diminished by the possibility that it ought to be a smaller and more select group that evaluates the alternatives and makes the choices. Still, individual choice is not wholly unrelated. The relationship between individual choice and freedom of speech derives in part from the variety of choices available to the individual, and the process of choice may suggest an independent argument for a Free Speech Principle. This is an argument I will describe and evaluate in the following section.

THE ARGUMENT FROM AUTONOMY

In the *Crito* Socrates acknowledges the 'right' of the state to punish him, and therefore refuses to escape to the safe shores of Thessaly. Yet in the *Apology* he has just said 'that I shall never alter my ways, not even if I have to die many times'. On the face of it the two dialogues present an inconsistency. If there is a duty of obedience to the state, then why does Socrates refuse to change his ways? One answer, suggested in the *Apology* itself, is that although the state may legitimately exercise power within its domain, there is an area of choice that belongs to Socrates himself. Perhaps, then,

Socrates is asserting a claim of sovereignty, or autonomy, over his own mind, an autonomy that leaves to him the final choice on any matter, even if by choosing one alternative rather than another he must accept some physical punishment inflicted by the state. This notion of individual sovereignty, or individual autonomy, now associated with Kant, provides the foundation for a theory of freedom of speech premised on the ultimate sanctity of individual choice.

My earlier treatment of freedom of conscience is relevant here. When we refer to freedom of conscience, we ordinarily mean some sort of private domain of the mind, some area that is under the exclusive control of the individual. This domain is off limits to the state, not only as a matter of moral right, but also as a matter of necessity.[8] If I say that I am following my conscience, I mean that I am retreating into that portion of my personality that is an exclusive preserve against governmental interference. Similarly, references to freedom of thought mark off an area of exclusive control by the individual, an area that simultaneously sets the outer boundaries of permissible (and practical) state intrusion. The concept is not altogether unlike the distinction between self-regarding and other-regarding actions, or Dworkin's distinction between personal and external preferences, or the arguments of those who seek to limit governmental power by resort to appeals to notions of personal dignity. Human dignity or human personality may be perceived as inherently personal. It is *mine*, intrinsically and morally beyond the force of government coercion. The argument I am outlining here makes an analogous distinction. The distinction is easier to accept, however, because it employs a much narrower conception of the area that is under exclusive individual control. Because thought may be inherently as well as morally beyond the reach of state power, it is plausible to suggest that the province of thought and individual decision-making is an area, or the only area, in which the individual is truly autonomous. As a narrower conception of the range of autonomy, this formulation is largely immune from many of the attacks on theories that postulate substantially larger areas of self-regarding actions.

From this conception of individual autonomy Thomas Scanlon, in a very important article, constructs an impressive argument for freedom of expression.[9] Beginning with the premise that the 'powers of the state are limited to those that citizens could recognize while still regarding themselves as equal, autonomous, rational agents', Scanlon seizes on the autonomy component of that premise to argue that 'a person must see himself as sovereign in deciding what to believe and in weighing competing reasons for action'. '[A]n autonomous person cannot accept without independent consideration the judgment of others as to what he should believe or what he should do'. Thus Scanlon's argument hinges on the fact that the ultimate choice as to any question, whether of belief or of action, rests with the individual. Even when an act is prohibited by law, even properly, the autonomous individual retains the choice whether to obey the law or to violate the law and take the consequences. These are decisions that government cannot and must not make, as they are wholly within the boundaries of individual sovereignty.

Scanlon derives the substance of his argument for freedom of speech from this notion of absolute individual sovereignty in matters of choice. If the final decision is properly for the individual, then that individual's decision ought to be as informed and intelligent as possible. Thus the information material to this individual decision ought not to be restricted. Scanlon's argument touches Meiklejohn's point that the government cannot pre-select the information available to the sovereign electorate. Scanlon makes essentially the same argument, but he sees the issue from the perspective of individual rather than electoral sovereignty. Thus Scanlon argues that no government has the authority to distort the individual's ultimate choice by preventing him from hearing any argument solely because it is on one side of an issue rather than another. He focuses not so much on what is restricted but on the reasons for the restriction. 'Those justifications [for restricting speech] are illegitimate which appeal to the fact that it would be a bad thing if the view communicated by certain acts of expression were to become generally believed.' Scanlon's theory, therefore, is best characterized not as a right to speech, but rather as a right to receive information and, more importantly, a right to be free from governmental intrusion into the ultimate process of individual choice. It is a right to be free from an assault on what Felix Frankfurter called the 'citadel of the person'.[10]

Scanlon's argument, although couched in the style of Kant and of the *Apology*, also has a strong contractarian basis. Individual autonomy is closely related to the concept of a state with limited powers. Indeed, they are opposite sides of the same coin. The individual is sovereign and autonomous because, quite simply, this area of ultimate choice has not been ceded to the state. Writing in a more recent article, Scanlon associates his theory with the writings of Rawls, designating the argument for freedom of speech as the Principle of Limited Authority.[11] Because the state has no authority ultimately 'to decide matters of moral, religious or philosophic doctrine (or of scientific truth)', because those in the Original Position would not grant that authority,[12] the state therefore has no mandate to limit the information upon which this choice may be made by the individual for the individual. In this form the argument is hardly novel. Locke, in the *Letter Concerning Toleration*, grounds much of his argument on the premise that solely the individual is authorized to decide questions of faith. 'The care of souls is not committed to the civil magistrate, any more than to other men'. Even earlier Spinoza drew the connexion between mental autonomy and freedom of speech in his *Tractatus Theologico-Politicus*.[13] These are all variations on the theme that places reliance on a division of authority between state and individual, a division that may be based on notions of inherent autonomy, or on the terms of a social contract, or, as suggested by Charles Fried, on ideas of comparative institutional competence.[14]

In any form, the argument is not without flaws. The so-called 'right' of civil disobedience is to a great extent the foundation of the theory, because the right of access to persuasion (whether from factual information or normative arguments) is in turn grounded on a right to disobey even those laws that are just and that are in the interests of society. Perhaps the individual does retain this degree of autonomy. And probably an individual who chose to act autonomously in the most informed and intelligent manner would, if rational, seek out many opinions before making a decision. But there is a difference between what the rational individual would do and what the state should do. A limitation on the state's power to interfere with the information available makes sense only if the state must recognize the right of civil disobedience. The argument from autonomy is plausible only if the state can be deemed to say, 'You can obey, or you can pay the penalty; it makes no difference to us.' But this seems odd. It seems more reasonable to hold that if a law is indeed just, then the state is politically and morally authorized to enforce compliance, not merely collect penalties for non-compliance. We do not expect the state, having enacted a law, to be neutral on the issue of whether it is obeyed. The conclusion from this is not that there is no such thing as individual autonomy or individual sovereignty. Rather it is that it would be anomalous for the state to recognize that autonomy, at least in respect to areas in which the state validly may regulate. Personal moral philosophy cannot always be congruent with political philosophy. If a law is just, then a state is neither morally nor politically precluded from attempting to ensure compliance. Limiting that information that might produce non-compliance is not the only means at the state's disposal in attempting to ensure compliance, but there is no reason given in the argument from autonomy that compels us to prohibit the state from using this tool.

Moreover, because the argument from autonomy 'rests on a limitation of the authority of states to command their subjects rather than on a right of individuals', it is much more adaptable to governments on the authoritarian model than a democratically conceived society. For if it is applied to the democratic model, then presumably the people could change the rules of the game, a fact that Scanlon himself recognizes. But this seems to be what takes place in any case of suppression. Suppression in a democratic society is most commonly suppression in the name of the people. The suppression is never based on unanimous consent of the population, but neither is any other governmental action. In order for the argument from autonomy to hold up, it must be rooted in social contract theory, in some original position of unanimity. But if this is the case, the argument fails to tell us why the state's authority is more limited in dealing with speech than it is in dealing with other forms of conduct. It is circular to answer that individual autonomy supplies the reason, because what is missing is some reason why a group of individuals in the original position would choose to recognize some sort of 'right' to disobey just laws.

These difficulties notwithstanding, the argument from autonomy represents a significant contribution to free speech theory. It shares a natural rights foundation with some of the other ideas discussed in this and the preceding chapters, and like other arguments it relies on concepts of individuality and dignity. The value of the argument from autonomy is that it is an argument that is directed at *speech*, rather than at the entire range of interests that might with some minimal plausibility be designated 'individual'. The argument from autonomy stresses the motives of those who would suppress *arguments*, not the motives of those who suppress individuality. It is an argument for freedom of communication in a limited sense, and that is its greatest strength. As an argument for freedom of speech, rather than merely a particularized application of an argument for freedom in a broad and abstract sense, the argument from autonomy employs broadly liberal principles to address specifically the problem of free speech.

The natural rights underpinnings of the argument from autonomy are not universally appealing. But even from a positivist or utilitarian perspective the argument from autonomy is important because it emphasizes freedom of speech as a principle embedded in a line of demarcation between the individual and government. That line may neither be straight, distinct or easy to locate, but it represents a division nevertheless. In relying on this separation between the individual and the organization of government, the argument from autonomy shares numerous characteristics with the most valuable features of both the argument from truth and the argument from democracy. I will return to this relationship in the concluding section of the following chapter, because the values represented by the various arguments for freedom of speech share more in common than the original formulations of those arguments may have suggested.

Bibliographical note to chapter 5

Arguments from individual autonomy are found as well in Glenn Tinder, 'Freedom of expression: the strange imperative', *Yale Review* **69** (1980), 162; Irving Younger, 'The idea of sanctuary', *Gonzaga Law Review* **14** (1979), 761. For commentary on Scanlon, see Robert Amdur, 'Scanlon on freedom of expression', *Philosophy and Public Affairs* **9** (1980), 287; Allen Buchanan, 'Autonomy and categories of expression: a reply to Professor Scanlon', *University of Pittsburgh Law Review* **40** (1979), 551.

CHAPTER 6

The utility of suppression

In 'The Theory of Persecution', Frederick Pollock observed that 'It is not the demonstration of abstract right, but the experience of inutility, that has made governments leave off persecuting.' Such appeals to utility are still widely accepted. Arguments from natural right are not universally attractive, and the consequentialist arguments from truth and democracy have significant flaws. Part of the magnetism of arguments from utility is that utilitarian considerations are relevant even in deontological systems.[1] Even if utilitarian considerations do not solve *all* problems, they may still be quite useful.

The pervasive appeal of utilitarian arguments has produced many diverse arguments supporting a principle of freedom of speech. The most important of these are discussed in this chapter, although the diversity in arguments produces some looseness of structure.

A shared feature of utilitarian arguments for free speech is a highly psychological orientation. The arguments depend upon hypotheses about the way in which individuals and groups actually deal with certain forms of discourse. To that extent the arguments cry out for empirical support for their psychological and sociological assumptions. Regrettably the empirical research to support or refute these arguments has not been undertaken in a systematic way. Thus the arguments treated here share a weakness as well, in depending for their validity on untested empirical assumptions.

THE CHALLENGE OF ERROR

In *Liberty, Equality, Fraternity* James Fitzjames Stephen assumed that *if* we could be absolutely certain that a proposition were true and its negation false, there would be no reason not to suppress the negation. Some contemporary writers have made the same assumption.[2] Although at times conceding the value of a healthy scepticism, proponents of this view look upon a demonstrably false proposition as having no value, and therefore no claim to any further hearing.

This view has some superficial appeal. If we are searching for truth, plain error does nothing to help the process. It reduces the proportion of true propositions among all propositions expressed, thereby diluting the frequency of truth and making it harder to locate. A needle is harder to find in a haystack than in two pieces of hay.

Yet many have taken issue with the surface logic of denying value to falsity. Most of these arguments have focused on the valuable by-products of false statements. In the *Areopagitica* Milton argued that awareness of error is necessary for 'confirmation of truth', and that truth will be healthier when forced to meet and conquer its opponents. 'I cannot praise a fugitive and cloistered virtue, unexercised and unbreathed, that never sallies out and sees her adversary, but slinks out of the race, where that immortal garland is to be run for, not without dust and heat'. And in the third part of Mill's argument for liberty of thought and discussion he claims that if people fail to understand why the true opinion is true and the false opinion false, they will acquire knowledge by mere rote, and not understand the 'real' truth. Should this continue, truth will turn into 'dead dogma', lacking the power to survive new attacks. Only by the continuing fight with error, Mill argued, does truth legitimately become accepted. What distinguishes knowledge from superstition was the *understanding* acceptance of truth. Thus falsehood should be allowed to circulate in order to give truth the force with which to endure.

Mill was concerned as well with the benefits to the individual of going through the mental exercise of justifying truth and rejecting falsity, an exercise that could not take place without some falsity to reject. To the same effect is the statement of Justice Jackson of the United States Supreme Court. 'The danger that citizens will think wrongly is serious, but less dangerous than atrophy from not thinking at all'.[3]

The argument looks upon false doctrine as a gymnasium for intellectual exercise to produce stronger minds. But the argument is premised on an optimistic view of how people react to falsity. Like any strong rationalist version of the argument from truth, the argument from intellectual exercise supposes that people have the capacity to reject falsehood consistently, and will do so when falsity is encountered. As with the argument from truth, this argument is only as strong as the rationalist assumptions on which it is premised. But unfortunately falsity is often to many people more appealing than truth, especially when accepting falsity requires less effort than identifying truth. There is a valuable lesson here in the metaphor of the path of least resistance.[4] The argument from intellectual exercise is premised on the value of challenge, but this value is illusory if it turns out that false views are accepted. Gymnastics on the parallel bars is superb exercise for those who can do it, but no exercise at all for those who fall off and injure themselves.

The argument from intellectual challenge thus suffers from the same problems as the argument from truth. The benefits of the challenge must be weighed against the harms that would flow from acceptance of error. Because in many cases the expected harm may outweigh the expected benefit, the argument from intellectual challenge provides a justification no stronger than that provided by the argument from truth.

IS SUPPRESSION COUNTERPRODUCTIVE?

Some have argued that suppression is counterproductive, not serving the goals that give rise to the desire to suppress. Many acts of suppression are based on the desirability of promoting true beliefs and eliminating false ones. In this sense censorship is an attempt to promote the received view and extinguish its negation. Presumably, then, any particular act of suppression is premised on the assumption that it will be effective; that as to the opinion suppressed, this opinion will be less accepted after the suppression than before. Conversely, the received opinion will be more accepted after the suppression than earlier. Although no act of government is guaranteed effective, an act of suppression presumes at the very least that the probability of effectiveness, if not necessarily greater than .50, is at least greater than the probability of its having the opposite effect.

It is this presumption that has frequently been challenged, the argument being that the act of suppression is often at least as likely to foster acceptance of the erroneous view as it is to promote its rejection. The argument is supported by several behavioural hypotheses, the first of which is aptly summarized by William Haley:[5]

Mankind is so constituted, moreover, that if, where expression and discussion are concerned, the enemies of liberty are met with a denial of liberty, many men of goodwill will come to suspect there is something in the proscribed doctrine after all. Erroneous doctrines thrive on being expunged. They die if exposed.

I am not now concerned with the last sentence of the quoted paragraph, for I have discussed that problematic claim in the context of the argument from truth. But the sentiments preceding make an interesting point. Is it possible that the act of suppression fuels the fire of noxious doctrine?

Part of the argument is based on the assumption that we make a mistake when we take too seriously what seems to be an erroneous belief. But this seems peculiar. Why does it follow that taking a belief or a group seriously heightens its credibility? We take polio, smallpox, tidal waves, earthquakes, burglary and rape very seriously without anyone suggesting that any of these events are beneficial or would be thought to be so merely because we treat them as grave dangers. Why is the National Front, for example, any different? A possible answer is that by taking them seriously, by bothering to suppress them, we acknowledge that they have enough strength and popularity to constitute a danger. Therefore, it can be argued, we admit their presence as a substantial force by the act of suppression, providing an aura of respectability and thus increasing the probability of their gaining new adherents. People are more likely to side with a large group holding extremist views than they are willing to be a lone voice crying out in the wilderness. There is still safety in numbers.

This argument has an intuitive plausibility, but these intuitions seem grounded in the *motives* of suppression, or, more precisely, in distrust of those motives. Milton, for example, contended that when the state suppresses an opinion people are likely to wonder why the state does not let the opinion be expressed and then show why and how it is false. Is the state afraid that the opinion is true and therefore will prevail? In a similar vein, Bagehot suggested that an imposed conformity of opinion produces an unacceptable quantity of doubt.

Even without this suspicion, people are naturally curious. If the doctor instructs me not to remove a bandage for three weeks, I am likely to disobey and peek before ten days are gone. People are equally likely to be curious about the opinions they cannot hear, perhaps to the point of being substantially more interested or susceptible to persuasion than if the opinion were not suppressed. In addition to this natural curiosity, people are inclined to suspect the motives of a suppressing government. They are likely to feel that that which is kept from them might be true, by virtue of the very fact that it is kept from them. Why, they might wonder, can we not hear this? Maybe there is something to it?

The argument assumes first that suppression will be less than fully effective. It assumes that the curious and suspicious can learn in some way about the opinion they are not permitted to hear. This assumption seems well-founded, but there is no way in which the assumption can be tested, because an effective act of suppression would be effective against my discovery of the suppressed opinion. Still, there seems something to the hypothesis that suppression is rarely completely effective. Machiavelli's observation in *The Prince* that enemies must either be caressed or totally annihilated seems especially apt here.

Moreover, we encounter here an assumption of rationality similar to that discussed in the context of the argument from truth. If people are suspicious of suppressed opinions, it is largely based on their belief that opinions that really are false can be allowed expression without danger. Although, as I have mentioned earlier, this view seems largely unjustified, it still commands much popular support. That is especially important here, because the issue now is not whether people are rational, but whether people *think* they are rational. If people believe that false opinions will invariably be rejected, then it is not surprising that they will distrust the motives of a suppressing government, and this will contribute to the disutility of suppression.

In addition to relying on some questionable behavioural assumptions, the argument that suppression is counterproductive is of limited application. It presupposes that the goal of suppression is preventing people from coming to believe the erroneous opinion. Although this is indeed the aim of many acts of suppression, there are other objectives as well.[6] When the harm at which suppression is directed is not the possibility that the suppressed view will be accepted, but rather some more direct result of a particular instance of expression, then the argument is unavailing. For example, it was argued in the United States that the American Nazi Party should be prevented from marching in areas with concentrated Jewish populations because those Jews would be offended, arguably to the point of physical illness, by seeing, hearing, or even knowing about the march. In this situation it is unlikely that the act of suppression would cause American Jews, or others, to be more receptive to the opinions of the American Nazi Party. The primary purpose of suppression in this instance would not be the fear that the views of the Nazis would be accepted; hence here there could be no suggestion that the state was concealing an argument. As a result, there would be no particular occasion for curiosity or suspicion, and the argument from counterproductiveness seems inapplicable.[7] There are arguments for permitting such a march, arguments I touch on in the concluding section of this chapter and elaborate in Part III of this book, but the argument that the suppression will be counterproductive does not appear to be one of them.

THE FORCE OF ARGUMENT OR THE ARGUMENT OF FORCE?[8]

I do not hesitate to take as true the assertion that in general it is better to settle disputes by discussion than by force and violence, that decision-making by rational means is preferable to decision-making with fists, knives, guns or bombs. I do not mean that a particular decision to resort to force may not be a rational choice. I am not ready to concede, for example, that the American Revolution was an irrational act. Nor am I saying that everyone is rational, only that it would be nice if people were, and any policy conducive to rational discussion and prejudicial to decision by force is probably worth pursuing, or at least considering, for those reasons alone. Thus, what I mean is that as an ideal a decision procured by reason, discussion and argument will be more likely to produce satisfactory results and will have fewer unpleasant side effects (such as death or dismemberment) than a decision procured by force of arms.

From this assumption it is plausible to argue that suppression is an unwise policy because it increases the likelihood that the initial use or threat of force (here, the act of suppression) will produce further resort to forcible means of making decisions. This argument is based not on the actual existence of an ideal state of rational deliberation, but on the belief that suppression will foster irrationality and use of force, and that freedom of argument and discussion will promote calm and reasoned deliberation.

More specifically, this argument has been presented as part of a broader theory of the advantages of peaceful change. Certainly peaceful change is itself a desirable goal, so much so that for many, including Popper and Russell, the capacity of a society to allow for peaceful change is a defining feature of the concept of democratic government. Russell defined democracy as 'a method of settling internal disputes without violence'.[9] Within the framework of this ideal, it is possible to see freedom of speech as a way of substituting logical persuasion for force, or, in the words of Thomas Emerson, of achieving a desirable 'balance between stability and change'.[10] If people have the opportunity of debating all issues, so the argument holds, then they will be more likely to rely on this process and less likely to resort to violence. Conversely, if there is a prohibition on criticism of official policy, then those who strongly object to official policy will be more prone to violence, because they will then see violence as the best way of achieving their objective.

Under this view freedom of speech will produce more stability and less violence in two ways. First, people may place greater trust in a government that is willing to hear and consider a wide range of arguments. But if they see government as irrational, or arbitrary, or closed, then faith in government generally and governmental leaders in particular will diminish, and respect for the rule of law will decrease commensurately.

Second, individuals who have an opportunity to object to governmental policy during and after the process of its becoming law are likely to feel that they have participated in the process of making laws, and may be therefore more inclined to obey even those laws with which they disagree. This is the 'legitimization' argument I discussed in the context of the argument from democracy.

We can look at this issue not just from the perspective of the individual, but also from the perspective of the government. Freedom to challenge may provide advantages to government by furnishing an imperfect but inexpensive method of testing putative governmental policies. Clearly not all proposed governmental action will be successful. The state may err in choosing its goals, and, more likely, it may err in choosing the means for the pursuit of those goals. If the only way to test these means is by trial and error, then the costs of implementing the policy, as well as the harms caused when the trial turns out to be an error, are substantial costs to society. To the extent that policies may be evaluated, challenged, and criticized before being put in effect, then some error in policy may be exposed without the costs of actually implementing the proposed policy.

Finally, there is what is variously referred to as the 'safety-valve', 'letting off steam', or 'catharsis' argument.[11] This argument maintains that there will always be in a society those who so strongly object to governmental policy that they will be inclined towards violent acts unless we let them 'blow off steam' by objecting, however heatedly, in words. Otherwise they will be inclined to object violently with guns or bombs. The argument parallels one frequently heard in reference to the United Nations, an argument I can paraphrase as follows: 'Yes, the United Nations is an ineffectual organization, but it is better to have people yelling at each other in New York than shooting at each other somewhere else.'

The 'letting off steam' argument, by metaphorically equating the personality of the angry citizen with the boiler of a steam engine or the respiratory tract of a sperm whale, again indulges in some questionable behavioural speculation. Like the other arguments discussed in this section, it assumes that more argument will produce less violence, as if every human being were granted a fixed quantum of anti-governmental energy. If some of the allotment is used for argument, there supposedly remains less for violence. But this is not the only possible theory. It is equally plausible to suggest that disagreement and argument would increase anger, thereby increasing the possibility of violence.

Although I have no strong empirical evidence to support either proposition, I intuitively still have sympathy with the argument from catharsis. Violent rebellions and civil disobedience seem all too often the result of frustration. If there is a sense of participation, a feeling that someone is listening, a belief that there remains a chance to change things by words alone, then it is likely that there would be less frustration. Freedom to challenge authority with words will not be totally effective in defusing violence, in part because the words are not always effective. But even if freedom to criticize produces only slightly more reason and slightly less force, there is still much to be said for it.

THE ARGUMENT FROM NEGATIVE IMPLICATION

Most rights, in the sense that I am talking about rights, can be justified in either a positive or a negative way. When we provide a positive justification for a right, we offer reasons why the activity covered by the particular right is especially valuable, and therefore deserving of special protection. The process of offering a negative justification is somewhat different. Here we do not focus on the special value of the activity covered by the right, but rather focus on the special dangers of treating that activity in the same way that we treat other activity. A negative justification, therefore, concentrates on the special dangers of regulation, rather than on the special place the particular activity occupies within the realm of all activity. The argument is negative in the sense that it highlights evils rather than goods. Where a negative argument is valid, the resultant right may look quite similar to that produced by a positive argument. But a right is created from a negative justification only to ensure that the particular activity is ultimately treated no less favourably than activity of equivalent value. We add special protection just to even things out, just to counteract the harmful tendencies that provide the basis of a negative justification.

In terms of this distinction, most of the justifications for recognizing a Free Speech Principle that I have discussed so far have been of the positive variety. These justifications have attempted to identify some way in which speech is particularly valuable, compared to other forms of conduct, such that it has a claim to special immunity from the general principles of governmental action. But it is possible also to offer a negative justification for a Free Speech Principle. Even if there is nothing especially good about speech compared to other conduct, the state may have less ability to regulate speech than it has to regulate other forms of conduct, or the attempt to regulate speech may entail special harms or special dangers not present in regulation of other conduct. If this is the case, if the regulation of speech is either less efficient or more likely to produce unpleasant side-effects than the regulation of other forms of conduct, then a Free Speech Principle will emerge by negative implication.

Throughout history the process of regulating speech has been marked with what we now see to be fairly plain errors. Whether it be the condemnation of Galileo, religious persecution in the sixteenth and seventeenth centuries, the extensive history of prosecution for expressing seditious views of those now regarded as patriots, or the banning of numerous admittedly great works of art because someone thought them obscene, acts of suppression that have been proved erroneous seem to represent a disproportionate percentage of the governmental mistakes of the past. Similar examples from contemporary times are scarcely more difficult to locate. Experience arguably shows that governments are particularly bad at censorship, that they are less capable of regulating speech than they are of regulating other forms of conduct. These superficial intuitions inspire a search for a deeper reason.

If such a reason exists, it would, as with the other arguments discussed in this chapter, be grounded on some psychological aspect of the process of regulating speech that makes it particularly inefficient. One reason may be the bias or self-interest of those entrusted with the task of regulating speech. In particular, the regulation of speech on grounds of interference with government, such as by treason, sedition and so on, is entrusted to those very people who, as governmental officials, have the most to lose from arguments against their authority. Reasons of power, prestige, mission, or money inspire in people the desire to attain government office, and those same reasons also inspire in them the want to retain those positions.

Yet any system of regulating political speech puts in control those with the most to lose from the activities they are regulating. There is a maxim of natural justice, *nemo debet esse judex in sua propria causa* (no man to be judge of his own cause), which is directly applicable here. Most systems of regulating speech involve just this problem. Even the intervention of a jury, which was thought so important in eighteenth and nineteenth century arguments about free speech, because the jury represents the people, is of little importance when much censorship is administrative, and when in addition administrators, legislators, executives and prosecutors, who make and enforce law, have a personal interest in the preservation of existing governmental structure.[12]

It is true that there is no hard empirical support for the proposition that governmental officials are likely to be over-aggressive censors for reasons of self-interest. And it is equally true that this argument sounds uncomfortably like a naïve conspiracy theory. I do not intend to take that position. But we routinely exclude the relatives of the parties of a lawsuit from serving on a jury without any empirical evidence that they would in fact be biased.[13] We also prohibit any beneficiary from being a witness to a will. It is the nature of the relationship that justifies the assumption of bias, and so too may similar assumptions apply to the regulation of speech, especially political speech.

It has been suggested that there exists in people a desire for unanimity, an urge to suppress that with which they may disagree even if there seems no harm to that expression. Justice Holmes is often quoted on this point.[14]

Persecution for the expression of opinions seems to be perfectly logical. If you have no doubt of your premises or your power and want a certain result with all your heart you naturally express your wishes in law and sweep away all opposition. To allow opposition by speech seems to indicate that you think the speech impotent, as when a man says that he has squared the circle, or that you do not care wholeheartedly for the result, or that you doubt either your power or your premises.

This desire to suppress, this longing for a consensus, may be stronger in reference to speech than in reference to other forms of conduct. There is something particularly public about speech. People speak with the intention and usually the result that other people hear their words. Conduct that is not communicative may be more easily avoidable. We may advocate freedom for others because in many cases we need not confront the exercise of that freedom. We know it exists, but we do not have to see it existing. But speech may be different, with the consequence that the desire to enforce unanimity may be strongest with respect to speech. If some of these conjectures are correct, if the impulse to make speech conform is especially great, if the urge towards intolerance is greater with respect to speech than with respect to other actions, then the power to suppress may be over-used when that power is available. If there is this special urge to suppress, then a Free Speech Principle may be necessary merely to counter the tendency towards over-regulation.

Moreover, the distinctions necessary in any form of government regulation might be harder to draw when it is speech rather than other forms of conduct that is the subject of the regulation. Any exercise of state power involves an attempted 'fit' at two levels. The specific mode of regulation must fit the goals that provide the reason for regulating, and the actual conduct regulated must fit the particular regulating rule chosen. If distinctions are especially difficult to draw, the fit may be loose at both levels, creating a greater than normal risk of over-inclusive regulation.

The hypothesis here is that 'slippery slope' and 'where do you draw the line?' arguments may have special relevance with respect to regulating speech. This suggestion is hardly novel. Lord Chesterfield, speaking against the Theatres Act of 1737, remarked that:[15]

There is such a connection between licentiousness and Liberty, that it is not easy to correct the one, without dangerously wounding the other. It is extremely hard to distinguish the true limit between them; like a changeable silk, we can easily see there are two different colors, but we cannot easily discover where the one ends, or where the other begins.

Censorship is a double futility. It cannot prevent any single intended criticism; and it is bound to suspect a theoretically infinite number of unintended ones.

More recently, Joel Feinberg has expressed similar sentiments.[16]

There are serious risks involved in granting any mere man or group of men the power to draw the line between those opinions that are known infallibly to be true and those not so known, in order to ban expression of the former. Surely, if there is one thing that is *not* infallibly known, it is how to draw *that* line.

Now it is true that the regulation of any form of conduct involves drawing lines, making distinctions, and granting power to make those distinctions to human beings who are far from infallible. It is equally true that 'slippery slope' and 'where do you draw the line?' arguments are in most instances either invalid or greatly exaggerated. If an argument from the slippery slope is to succeed, there must be some reason why the slope is likely to be especially slippery in this area.

When we make a slippery-slope argument, we presuppose that there is something that is properly subject to restriction. At the heart of a slippery-slope claim is the belief that although it is permissible to regulate x, attempting to do so in practice will result as well in the regulation of y, where y is something that as a matter of the ideal theory cannot be regulated. A slippery-slope argument maintains that the attempt to regulate what can be regulated will have the effect of regulating something else that *cannot* be regulated. The question, then, is how this might occur. *When* do we slide down the slippery slope? Why is it not possible to stop? In looking for an answer, we see that slippery-slope claims can be divided into two different major types, and that both of these types have particular relevance to the question of freedom of speech.

The first type of slippery-slope argument, or the first source of a slippery-slope effect, is the phenomenon of conceptual vagueness, or, more precisely, linguistic over-inclusiveness. Thus, assume that x is that which can be regulated, and that y is that which, although it cannot permissibly be regulated, is nevertheless the source of our slippery-slope fear. Slippery-slope effects from linguistic over-inclusiveness occur when the *term* we use to describe x may also include y as well. It is quite possible that the infinite variety of linguistic and pictorial expression makes it impossible, given the current tools of our language, to specify with precision the utterances that are to be prohibited. If our descriptive language about speech is less refined or less precise than our descriptive language about other forms of conduct – and this seems by no means an implausible hypothesis – then any regulating rule may be particularly vulnerable to the vice of linguistic over-inclusiveness. And if this is so, then there is some validity to the claim that slippery-slope fears are more well-founded in reference to regulation of speech than in reference to other forms of conduct. Such a conclusion would support recognition of a Free Speech Principle solely to counteract the special slipperiness of this particular slope.

An alternative source of a slippery-slope effect is what might be characterized as the phenomenon of limited learnability.[17] Human beings have only so much mental space, and there is a practical limit on the complexity of the concepts that we can reasonably expect people to understand. Although it might be possible for a group of lawyers, philosophers, or whatever to formulate a carefully delimited and highly complex code that would regulate all that can be regulated and nothing that cannot, it might very well be impossible to teach this code to all of the judges, jurors, prosecutors, and administrators who are part of the process of regulation. A code, or a definition of the object of regulation, may be only as complex as the understanding of the least teachable member of the enforcement chain. It is a fact of life that 'certain very complex codes break down because ordinary people can't keep all the distinctions, caveats, and exceptions straight in their heads.'[18] Unlike the case of linguistic over-inclusiveness, we assume here that it is possible in theory to formulate a precise definition. But if that definition requires for its application the understanding and internalizing of a corpus of theory beyond the capacities of the administrators, then each instance of lack of understanding increases the slippery-slope risk. If, as seems quite likely, the values of disagreement and challenge are especially counterintuitive, then the slippery-slope risk here is once again greater than normal, and there is again justification for employing the argument from negative implication to generate a Free Speech Principle that serves to counteract the special problems of learnability involved in the regulation of speech.

SOME TRANSITIONAL CONCLUSIONS

The divergent nature of the arguments in this chapter reflects to some extent the loose connexion among all the arguments presented in this entire Part. This approach has not been unintentional. Although I have criticized many arguments, supported others, and offered some of my own, I am less concerned with particular conclusions than I am with overall method. What is important is the exploration of the philosophical, psychological, and political assumptions supporting any argument for freedom of speech. Demonstrating the necessity of exploring to this depth is more important than what any individual explorer, including myself, may find.

Nevertheless, I do find some consistency in the arguments that tend to support a distinct Free Speech Principle. It is not imperative that all of the arguments for freedom of speech relate closely to each other, or that they be distillable into one principle or argument. One of the problems of much theorizing about freedom of speech is that there has been too much distillation and not enough dissection.

The arguments for freedom of speech are to some extent distinct. They may apply in different circumstances, and in conflicting ways. I do not consider this a failure. Too much synthesis may result in a principle so abstract as to be useless or trivial, or a principle so qualified as to be hardly a principle at all.

But the arguments I have found to have some validity do have in common an emphasis on the separation between individual and government, a demarcation of not wholly congruent areas of authority. Freedom of speech is based in large part on a distrust of the ability of government to make the necessary distinctions, a distrust of governmental determinations of truth and falsity, an appreciation of the fallibility of political leaders, and a somewhat deeper distrust of governmental power in a more general sense. It is possible to use such arguments to justify a general limitation of government, but I make no such argument here. I am arguing only that the power of government to regulate speech should, for a number of reasons, be more limited than are its powers in other areas of governance.

Looking at all of the arguments presented in this Part, we can see that the determinative question is whether to grant to government the power to determine what shall be suppressed and what shall not. The question is one of justifying a practice.[19] Thus in any case the issue is not whether the suppression was proper, but whether the exercise of authority was valid. These are different questions, and they may at times yield different answers.

I might summarize the foregoing paragraphs by saying that the most persuasive argument for a Free Speech Principle is what may be characterized as the argument from governmental incompetence. This characterization is in part a transition to the remainder of this book, in which I attempt first to clarify and then to apply the Free Speech Principle. But clarification and application occur in the context of the reasons for recognizing a Free Speech Principle in the first instance. Development of a deep theory (or theories) must precede clarification and application of that theory. If the foundation is a weak assembly of platitudes, then the superstructure above it is highly vulnerable and of little value.

Bibliographical note to chapter 6

Works not previously cited that treat the relation between freedom of speech and the actual practice of governments include C. Hyneman, 'Free speech at what price?', *American Political Science Review* **57** (1962), 847; Peter Ingram, 'Principle and practice in censorship', *Social Theory and Practice* **4** (1977), 315.

PART II

EXPLICATION

CHAPTER 7

The meaning of 'speech'

THE COVERAGE–PROTECTION DISTINCTION

Many discussions of rights make the unfortunate mistake of masking the important distinction between the coverage of a right and the protection of a right. Unless we get clear about this distinction as it applies to all rights, we cannot get clear about specific rights, such as a right to free speech.

Rights of course are not unlimited in scope. A right to free speech does not include the 'right' to commit murder, to drive a car in a pedestrian zone, or to sell heroin. Nor does a right to free speech include a 'right' to commit perjury, or to extort, or to threaten bodily harm, although all of these are speech acts. But a right to free speech is generally taken to include the right to criticize public officials. Yet even this conduct is without legal protection if found to be defamatory and factually false. We could say that such defamatory utterances too are outside the scope of the right, but this is unduly crude. Perjury and extortion have nothing to do with what free speech is all about. Criticism of public officials most certainly does have something to do with freedom of speech, although under some circumstances the protection is lost.

If I am wearing a suit of armour, I am *covered* by the armour. This will *protect* me against rocks, but *not* against artillery fire. I can be wounded by artillery fire despite the fact that I am covered by the armour. But this does not make the armour useless. The armour does not protect against everything; but it serves a purpose because with it only a greater force will injure me.

So also with rights. They may cover certain conduct, by requiring greater persuasive force in order to restrict that conduct. If a particular act is covered by a right to engage in acts of that general type, it takes a better reason to restrict that act than would be the case if the act were not covered by a right. But some reasons may be sufficiently powerful to penetrate the coverage of a right, just as artillery fire may be sufficiently powerful to penetrate the coverage of the armour.[1]

89

Thus, when we say that certain acts, or a certain class of acts, are covered by a right, we are not necessarily saying that those acts will always be protected. We are saying only that these acts have a facial claim to be considered with reference to the reasons underlying the decision to put those acts within the coverage of a right.

We may wish to structure our rights such that protection is always absolute. The decision on coverage would be dispositive of protection, because no reason for restriction could outweigh the protection of the right. But it is not necessary that protection be absolute within the coverage of the right. As long as the burden of justification (for restriction) is greater within the coverage of the right than it is outside that coverage, a right exists, even though the right is less than absolute in strength.

If our talk about rights were purely descriptive, we would have no need to draw the distinction between coverage and protection. We could merely describe the limits of the existing right, incorporating within that description all existing exceptions and qualifications. But in fact we talk about rights in a prescriptive sense as well. We describe as an existing right what ought to be recognized and applied in the future. Were we omniscient we could once again define a right limited in scope but absolute in strength, building into the defined boundary all of the exceptions and qualifications to be applied. The difficulty of this is that we simply do not know what all of the exceptions and qualifications might be. Lacking omniscience we can at best imperfectly predict the future. Rights whose shape incorporates all exceptions and qualifications would be extremely rough tools for dealing with the uncertainties of the future. Instead we wisely achieve finer tools for future use by combining a relatively vague definition of the coverage of the right with a relatively vague specification of the weight of the right. We employ vagueness to give us finer tools for dealing with the uncertainties that exist at the margin of indeterminacy of any right. As Quine, incorporating the thinking of I. A. Richards, has noted, 'a painter with a limited palette can achieve more precise representations by thinning and combining his colors than a mosaic worker can achieve with his limited variety of tiles, and the skillful superimposing of vaguenesses has similar advantages over the fitting together of precise technical terms'. If we could specify in advance what will happen in the future and how we wish to deal with those circumstances, we would have no need for the distinction between coverage and protection. But we cannot hope to specify everything in advance, so we properly distinguish between coverage and protection in order to maintain the necessary flexibility.

The distinction between coverage and protection suggests both the structure and the order with which to clarify the concept of free speech. It is necessary first to determine what activities are covered, and then determine how and to what extent those activities are protected.

The goal of this chapter, then, is to examine the question of coverage. I want to see what activities are covered by the concept of free speech, what activities are to be, to some extent, 'free'. In effect I am looking for a definition, in this context, of the word 'speech'.

In the first part of this book I implicitly assumed a coarse preliminary definition of the 'speech' component of freedom of speech. The 'speech' I have been discussing could be defined as the communication of ideas, information, and artistic sentiment through means that are either linguistic, pictorial, or traditionally artistic. Although this definition adequately supported the largely abstract examination of the foundations of the Free Speech Principle, it is not sufficiently precise to serve in the application of that principle.

It is not possible to offer any simple definition of 'speech' in terms of equivalent words or of concrete things to which it refers. The concept of free speech is far too complex for that, and at too many points the definition depends upon the resolution of undetermined behavioural, ethical and empirical issues from which any justification for freedom of speech must be resolved.

Moreover, any attempt at this simple type of definition is fundamentally unsound. In defining 'speech' we are not just attempting to describe something. Rather we are trying to carve out categories of activity and give to the activities thus circumscribed a particular degree of protection. In this sense 'speech' is a functional term. It must be defined by the purpose of a deep theory of freedom of speech, and not by anything the word 'speech' might mean in ordinary talk. We must remember that 'free speech' is defined not by what it is, but by what it does.[2]

We are attempting to identify those things that one is free (or at least more free) to do when a Free Speech Principle is accepted. What activities justify an appeal to the concept of freedom of speech? These activities are clearly something less than the totality of human conduct and, as shall appear, something more than merely moving one's tongue, mouth and vocal chords to make linguistic noises. As I discussed briefly in chapter 1, 'speech' functions as a term of art in the phrase 'freedom of speech'. An activity is not within the coverage of the Free Speech Principle merely because that activity is described as 'speech' in ordinary language. Conspiracy, perjury, fraud and extortion, for example, are all 'speech' in the ordinary sense, yet are not 'speech' under *any* conception of freedom of speech. It is not that regulation of such acts meets the heightened burden of justification implicit in the Free Speech Principle. Rather, such acts are not within the scope of the Principle at all. In order to define 'speech', we must look at the deep theory (or theories) of the doctrine of freedom of speech, for without such enquiry we are merely stumbling in the dark.

SPEECH AS COMMUNICATION

Although I have until now been using the preliminary definition of speech as communication, this is not the only plausible conception. I wish to consider some other definitions of 'speech', and only if these prove unsatisfactory can speech as communication be accepted for more than preliminary purposes.

I have already rejected for these purposes the ordinary language definition of the word 'speech'. For reasons previously explained in chapter 4, we must reject as well any attempt to define speech as expression, at least where 'expression' is in turn defined as self-expression, or some type of external manifestation of inner feelings.

I recognize that the concept of expression is under some aesthetic theories central to the identification of 'art'. Certainly an adequate theory of freedom of speech must in some manner deal with protection of art, because censorship of the visual and literary arts has been pervasive in modern history. Indeed, so prevalent has been artistic censorship that many people equate freedom of speech with an immunity from the suppression of art. But because the problem of what art is or what art does is in some ways *sui generis,* it seems best to discuss artistic censorship separately. I will therefore return to the question of art later in this chapter, but for now I wish to put aesthetic issues aside.

With art temporarily out of the way, speech as self-expression remains an unacceptable interpretation of freedom of speech. Because a person can express himself through virtually any form of voluntary conduct, defining speech as self-expression would fail to excise any particular portion of the totality of human conduct for the distinct protection that is inherent in the concept of a Free Speech Principle.

I suppose it would be possible to say that only conduct *intended* as self-expression should be within the scope of freedom of speech. We manage with at least some success to determine intent in many areas of law, and the absence of a clear line of demarcation between two concepts does not render those concepts indistinguishable.[3] But the question is not whether we can identify self-expression within the totality of voluntary conduct. The problem is that all voluntary conduct *is* self-expression. A self-expression subset of voluntary conduct is not merely hard to find – it does not exist.

The most prominent defect of the self-expression theory is that it does not identify a *class* of conduct with some degree of immunity to the general principles of governmental control. If we recognize a distinct right to free speech, the definition of 'speech' must serve to delimit an area smaller than the universe of intentional actions, and thus smaller than the universe of actions that in some way manifest the inner feelings of the actor. Because speech as self-expression fails to accomplish this purpose it must be rejected.

Freedom of speech is often suggested to be related or identical to freedom of thought. But as the self-expression theory fails because it is over-inclusive, the freedom of thought theory fails because it is under-inclusive. Immunity from punishment is one aspect of that amorphous notion we call 'freedom'. There is more to freedom than immunity from punishment, but a person who is free from being punished for engaging in certain conduct is in one sense 'free'.

In this sense of freedom, thought is intrinsically free. The internal nature of the thought process erects a barrier between thought and the power of governmental sanction. Not everyone has the ability or desire to keep his thoughts to himself. But the person who can keep his thoughts to himself is thereby able to immunize himself from punishment. To say that thought is free is to make a statement about the nature of the mind rather than about political philosophy. There is thus a danger that excess attention to freedom of thought (or its equivalents freedom of belief and freedom of conscience) will blind us to important questions about the proper limits of governmental power.

When we raise freedom of thought as an issue, we must consider the ways in which thought could not be free.[4] When we examine these various ways of limiting freedom of thought, we expose the limited utility of a principle of free thought.

One way that thought would not be free is when we are not free to *act* in accordance with our beliefs. But this is not helpful, because we are again left with only an undifferentiated principle of general liberty, and an implausible one at that.

It is possible the state could penalize us directly for our unexpressed thoughts, if it were to use polygraphs, truth serum or whatever, in order to examine the thoughts of each of us. Such a possibility is indeed frightening, but the outrage we feel is based on the assault on our personality, or on our privacy. At this point the connexion with the kinds of problems to which a theory of free *speech* is directed is tenuous.

Our thought is also less free when we are prevented from expressing our thoughts in language. But then we are talking about freedom to communicate rather than freedom to think. Under some versions of the arguments from individuality and autonomy, freedom of thought justifies a principle of free speech. Freedom of speech is recognized because it leads to a wider range of alternatives and to less restricted choice among alternatives. But it is the *speech* that needs protection, although freedom of thought may provide the justification. In describing the scope of the principle, we look at what is to be protected and not the reasons for protection. The scope is determined by the reasons, but is not identical to them.

There are many ways in which thought can be influenced by governmental action. Propaganda is an obvious example, and points up the fact that a whole system of punishment, reward, praise, and condemnation exercises influence over what we think. Any form of government action has potential for influencing thought, and to say that government may not attempt to influence our thoughts would be to deny all power to government. In this sense freedom of thought is an impossibility.

It is also impossible to equate freedom of speech with individuality. The problem here is the same as with freedom of expression – it is merely a principle of general liberty. If the concept of free speech has the independent significance I suggested in Part I, the distinction between freedom of speech and freedom of choice must be preserved.

What remains is the relation between the communicative aspect of speech and its claim to special protection. Communication dominates all the arguments that would with any plausibility generate a Free Speech Principle. For example, any version of the argument from truth relies on the fact that dissenting views are placed in contact with received opinion. If views other than the received view should receive special protection, it is because those views may persuade those who hold the received view, or those who remain undecided. The value of criticism lies in some one or some view being criticized. The value of free speech under the argument from truth is not that dissenting views are held, but that dissenting views are disseminated. Without communication the argument from truth is nonsensical.

Similarly, the argument from democracy derives its force from the significance of the deliberative process. If the argument from democracy were dependent solely on personally held views, then it would constitute no more than an argument for free elections. The emphasis on the deliberative process, and on the accountability of governmental officials through criticism and examination of their official acts, is tied to communication. What is important is the interaction among citizens, and the interaction between citizens and officials. Communication is the distinguishing feature that justifies including freedom of speech among the principles that together form what we call 'democracy' or 'free institutions'.

Communication is equally central to the more individualistic arguments, the argument from dignity and the argument from autonomy. Under some versions, such as Scanlon's, the key feature is the ability to receive communication unimpeded by state interference. Other versions of the argument stress the importance to the individual not only of holding views but also of transmitting those views to others. From either perspective communication is central.

The various arguments from utility are linked to communication as well, but I will belabour the point no further, for *any* particularized argument for freedom of speech focuses on the communicative aspects of speech, although the various arguments differ in the way they value communication. When freedom of speech is not treated as an independent principle, speech can be defined in numerous ways. This is not surprising, because an undifferentiated principle has little need for a precise definition of its boundaries. But if freedom of speech is a principle independent of other principles of political philosophy, then it is the special virtue of communication that supports the principle.

MUST COMMUNICATION BE LINGUISTIC?

Locating communicative activity at the core of the principle of free speech is only the first step in clarifying the 'speech' component of freedom of speech. This is an important first step, as it identifies

the interpersonal or interactional nature of what is being protected. But people can communicate in various ways. It is necessary to see what methods of communication are within the scope
of the Free Speech Principle.

There is little point here into delving deeply into the variety of
linguistic communication. If it is communication that is to be protected, then linguistic communication, spoken and written words
(generally formed into sentences) comprises the largest proportion
of what we are protecting. Language developed from the need to
communicate. Language is separate from communication only in
the exceptional instance. In the standard case one is inseparable
from the other. There are instances in which the use of language
is not communicative, such as the shrill utterance of a single word
in order to prevent someone else from being heard. But by and
large if we are to protect communication, then we cannot go very
far wrong by treating linguistic communication as at least presumptively within the range of the principle of freedom of speech.
It seems useful, therefore, to treat language as a core and move
outwards in the analysis to discuss the fringes of communicative
methods.

If language in the narrow sense is plainly within the scope of
the concept of communication, then so must be those signs or
symbols that denote particular words, phrases or sentences; those
symbols that serve as virtually exact linguistic equivalents. This
includes any form of code, such as semaphore signals, Morse code
or Braille, and any other symbol that has a one-to-one correlation
with a letter, word, phrase or sentence in some recognized language. Red and green to stand for 'stop' and 'go' would be an
example, as would the use of the extended middle finger to convey
(at least in America) a particular two-word message. Whether that
gesture is 'worthy' of protection is another matter, but nothing can
come of trying to make a distinction between the gesture and the
words that it denotes. In all of these cases, and many more, a distinction between symbols and speech in the strictest sense would
be artificial and, for these purposes, erroneous.

Slightly more difficult are those symbols that convey a commonly understood message, but which do not have exact linguistic equivalents. These symbols convey a message that could be
expressed linguistically, but the exact words of the linguistic
equivalent are less clear. For example, the gesture known to Amer-
icans as a 'Bronx cheer' has no one 'translation'. This noise-making
gesture, usually used in reference to athletes, entertainers, or
political figures, may be translated as 'You're a bum!' or 'Your

performance on this occasion is not up to the standards I expect from someone in your position.' But there is still a commonly recognized meaning of general disapproval. Similarly, a flag of a certain colour or pattern often conveys a particular message of national reference, loyalty or patriotism, although there can be gradations in interpretation. A black armband is sometimes used to show mourning, and sometimes used to object to the death caused by wars or a particular war, but the message is inferable from the context. The peace symbol (☮) is another such example. In each of these cases there is no exact linguistic analogue, but there is a message that could have been expressed in words. Moreover, the message is one easily understood by an observer without need of additional amplification, and the message perceived by the observer is at least broadly similar to that intended by the communicator. Because there is an intent to transmit a message through the use of a commonly understood symbolic convention, because the existence of that convention insures that in the large majority of cases the recipient will understand the speaker's intention and message, and because the method of transmission contains virtually no non-communicative component, there is no valid reason for distinguishing such communication from speech in the ordinary language sense for purposes of application of the principle of freedom of speech. We may not protect all of these utterances in all contexts, but they are at least covered by the Free Speech Principle to the same extent as if they were translated into words.[5]

A similar conclusion is mandated where pictures are the medium of communication, as with, for example, photographs, drawings, paintings, charts, graphs or diagrams. Where the intent is to communicate particular ideas, information or relationships (excluding for the moment artistic depiction), these methods of communication are indistinguishable from linguistic speech. It is not always true that 'one picture is worth a thousand words', but the fact that this ancient proverb treats the two as different denominations of the same currency suggests that words and pictures have similarities particularly relevant in the context of the principle of freedom of speech. The conventions of pictorial representation are so widely shared that the message intended by the communicator is most often that that is perceived by the recipient. Again, no meaningful distinction can be drawn between pictorial representation and linguistic representation.

If an observer may understand a non-linguistic symbol to convey a message, it is entirely possible that an observer may receive a 'message' even where there is neither intent nor ability to communicate. I can be awed by the Matterhorn, amused by a hippopotamus, pacified by waves, frightened by the traffic in Paris, and mystified by a chambered nautilus. If I may perceive a message of opposition to war by seeing a black armband, so may I perceive a similar message from war itself. But of course it is bizarre to suppose that freedom of speech can encompass any stimulus that evokes a mental response. Any coherent formulation of a Free Speech Principle requires communicative intent as well as a perceived message. Communication is a joint enterprise, and only that joint enterprise triggers the principle of free speech. Without communicative intent, a communicated message, and a recipient of the communication there is no complete communicative act, and no occasion to talk about freedom of speech.

When we communicate with non-linguistic symbols, there is greater variability in the extent to which those symbols are understood than there is with the use of language. Just as there is more descriptive content in 'cat', 'dog', 'petunia' and 'throw' than there is in 'democracy', 'liberty', 'thing' and 'nice', so is there more descriptive content in some non-linguistic symbols than in others, but the problems are compounded. For example, there is more of a settled meaning surrounding the wearing of a black armband than there is, to take a recent American case, surrounding the display of a demolished automobile on one's lawn to communicate a message about the consequences of a high-speed police chase.[6] It is tempting to say that where a method of communication is so unconventional as to be incapable of understanding by recipients of that communication, then there is no communicative content and thus no justification for deploying the Free Speech Principle. But this involves two problems. First, if one of the justifications for a Free Speech Principle is the perceived inability of the state to regulate communication as effectively as it regulates other forms of conduct, then it is unlikely that there will be substantially greater ability to identify those attempted communications in fact lacking communicative content. Although recognition of a Free Speech Principle must involve drawing a line between what is included within the principle and what is not, a Free Speech Principle derived from the concept of governmental inability must insure that this line is not subject to the same infirmities. To avoid this problem a margin of error must be created, thus including within the Free Speech Principle any method of communication even remotely capable of transmitting a message. The demolished automobile may properly be excluded, but the reason is not simply that it is not communicative, but that it is not even remotely communicative.

The other problem is that the exclusion of all non-traditional methods of communication may impair the development of novel communicative tools. There are many instances in which ordinary language is not all right as it is.[7] As J. L. Austin said, 'There may be plenty that might happen and does happen which would need new and better language to describe it in.'[8] In these circumstances we must often break the rules of language in order to convey new ideas and new experiences. We see this in the use of metaphor, and in much that we call creative writing – breaking the rules of language in order to penetrate through the structural constraints on thought imposed by ordinary language. We can expand this to include methods of communication as well. To the extent that we restrict non-traditional methods of communication we restrict communication to the traditional. In some respects this may be good. New methods of communication are not necessarily superior. But neither are standard methods of communication necessarily satisfactory. If development of the tools of communication is seen as one of the goals of a principle of freedom of speech, then communicative intent has independent significance regardless of communicative content. As long as the method is solely communicative, a focus on communicative intent brings an advantage at minimal cost. The cost is that encouraging new methods of communication may also impede our ability to communicate. We see this with words as well. Breaking the rules of language may enable us to convey new thoughts and emotions, but often at the expense of clarity and precision. This, however, seems a risk inherent in any progress, communicative or otherwise. We can only realize the advantages of progress if we are willing to accept the risks involved in searching for it.

The most difficult problems occur when communication is coupled with non-communicative conduct. This happens with picketing and demonstrating, where the message is linked to the pure physical mass of the demonstrators. It happens as well with electronically amplified speech, where communicative content is coupled with the non-communicative unpleasantness of the noise itself. I deal specifically with these problems in the final chapter of this book. But in the context of this discussion of non-linguistic modes of communication, it is important to deal with those forms of communication that are non-linguistic, that do convey a message to others, but that contain significant non-communicative elements. For example, I may destroy government property in protest of official policy. The destruction causes damage unrelated to the message sought to be conveyed, but the destruction also communicates in vivid fashion my protest to any observer. If I believe that someone has been unjustly convicted of a crime, I might chain myself to the wheel of the vehicle that is to take him to prison. I may do this solely to make it more difficult for the vehicle to get to the prison. Or I may do it in order vigorously to communicate my concerns to the government and to any spectators. But if I have the latter motive, I also achieve the former result. The communicative and non-communicative elements are combined in the same act. We see the same phenomenon where picketing around an official building conveys a message but also obstructs the operation of the department housed in the building.

If freedom of speech is a positive good, as it is under the argument from democracy, some versions of the argument from truth, and the arguments from autonomy and individuality, then the problem is significant. The pursuit of a valid governmental interest has the effect of inhibiting something (communication) thought to be positively and distinctively valuable. In these circumstances an application of the Free Speech Principle requires balancing those governmental interests not related to the suppression of communication against the positive advantages of allowing communication to flourish, a balance that must at least take account of the heightened free speech interest. The result of that balance need not in all cases accede to that heightened interest, but recognition of the interest in freedom of speech mandates that there be less governmental power to protect valid governmental interests when that power is exercised in a way that has the effect of restraining or inhibiting the process of communication. This could be done by requiring a higher showing of governmental necessity in such a case, either as to ends or as to means. We might, for example, require that the state show that no method exists for protecting the governmental interest that has less of an effect on communication.[9] I discuss this and other techniques in more detail in chapter 9, but it is worthwhile here to note that treating communication as a positive good requires that we look at the effect of governmental action as well as its intent.

If, on the other hand, the Free Speech Principle is derived from the more negative considerations I discussed in chapter 6, then the problem seems to dissolve. If the danger lies in governmental regulation of communication, then so long as the sanctions are directed solely at the non-communicative elements of the conduct,

100

there is no call to subject the governmental action to a higher standard of justification. Governmental action not directed at the communicative impact of the conduct may in many instances have incidental effect on communication, but a negative justification for freedom of speech will not consider this effect to be particularly pernicious. Where the danger lies in the process of regulating communication, rather than in the fact that communication is impaired, then a process not directed at communicative impact does not implicate the Free Speech Principle.[10] Thus the scope of the principle may be determined not by the effects of the governmental action, but by its purpose. There may of course be questions of motive and intent, especially if the governmental action seems selective. But in the pure case, if it is the danger of governmental regulation that supports the Free Speech Principle, then the regulation of non-communicative effect does not implicate the Free Speech Principle even if communication is incidentally affected.

THE CONTENT OF THE COMMUNICATION

It would be alluringly uncomplicated to hold the principle of freedom of speech to cover (but not necessarily protect) all communication, regardless of its content. Indeed, if the arguments for a Free Speech Principle coalesce around the separation between the individual and government, as well as a special distrust of the government's ability to regulate speech, then an absence of discrimination on the basis of content must be considered central to the concept of free speech. It is the state's inability to make the necessary distinctions that causes us to suspect that the state cannot regulate speech as effectively or as efficiently as it regulates other forms of conduct.

The aversion to regulation on the basis of the content of the communication, therefore, stems from our distrust of the ability of government to distinguish between the true and the false, the useful and the useless, the valuable and the worthless. But if the inability to distinguish *within* the Free Speech Principle is especially troublesome, then so too must be any attempt to set the boundaries of the principle itself. Mistakes can be made at the edges as well as at the centre. This may provide added justification for including all communication within the scope of the principle of freedom of speech.

Such a solution, however, sacrifices principle to the goal of simplicity. There are many acts of communication that simply have

101

nothing to do with what the concept of free speech is all about. To include them for the sake of safety or simplicity is likely to so distort the principle of freedom of speech that it will be of little utility. We may wish to add a margin for error, but that is not the same as abandoning the search for a principled delineation of the scope of the concept. Ideally we are looking for a principled definition of the Free Speech Principle, a definition that incorporates only those forms of communication that in some way relate to the reasons for recognizing such a principle in the first place. Definition is parasitic on justification. As is apparent from Part I, various justifications can support a Free Speech Principle, and the definition of that principle will turn on just which of those justifications are thought to be controlling. Nevertheless, some general observations may be made.

Initially, we can easily exclude most performative uses of language. The concept of free speech does not limit the state in regulating verbal betting, in determining the rules of the law of contract, in establishing the circumstances in which saying 'I give' does or does not constitute a legally enforceable gift, or in laying down the rules that govern a wide range of commercial dealing that may necessarily involve the use of written or spoken words. Although threats and extortion are not as clearly performative, these as well seem safely outside the scope of the Free Speech Principle.

Things get slightly more difficult when we are dealing with what might be called 'propositional wrongs', such as perjury, fraud or larceny by false pretences, for such statements, although propositional, hardly seem likely candidates for inclusion within the principles of freedom of speech. The problems are illuminated by the following example. Adam stands on a podium in Hyde Park and advocates to whomever is listening that military secrets be given to the enemy because the enemy is just and this nation is wicked. Bruce, having heard Adam, goes to Charles and encourages Charles to deliver military secrets to the enemy. Charles, who works in a defence plant, tells his colleague Daniel that an enemy agent will be standing on the corner of High Street and Blossom Court at 6:00 p.m. on Thursday with £1000 to pay for military secrets. Daniel goes to meet the enemy agent at the appointed place and time and describes the plans for a top-secret missile. Everything that has occurred in this scenario has been oral communication, and it may be that in time of war all four should be and would be prosecuted. Yet clearly the case of Adam and perhaps the case of Bruce are ones in which freedom of speech seems at least a relevant consideration, but the cases of Charles and Daniel are ones in which we would intuitively laugh if someone claimed that free speech were material to the issue. What, then, are the differences among the cases?

Several distinctions are pertinent to the foregoing example. First, there is the distinction between advocacy and action. Some words advocate conduct. Others are closer to the conduct itself, or are the conduct itself. Second, some speech is public in two important senses. It is addressed to a public audience, and it is relevant to some issue of public importance. Other speech has no public significance, relating only to the particular transaction in which the participants are involved. Finally, some words attempt to influence belief; they are normative or persuasive. At times this normative communication may be supported by a factual proposition, such as, 'You should not vote for Smith because he was convicted of embezzlement in 1968.' But other forms of communication neither convey nor support normative messages.

I am not saying that any of these factors is dispositive, either separately or in conjunction with the others. Nor am I suggesting that any amount of free speech protection for perjury or extortion is now or is likely to become a significant problem in free speech theory. But these factors, all of which seem helpful in analysing the example given, are important in helping to explain why only some types of communication are thought to be within the coverage of a Free Speech Principle, others being treated as wholly unrelated to the concept of free speech. None of these factors is crystal clear, but all relate to the justifications for free speech discussed in Part I. It is inevitable that many forms of communication, those having no relationship to the reasons for recognizing a Free Speech Principle, are properly excluded from the coverage of that principle. In this context 'communication', like 'speech', is a term of art, a term of technical language, whose definition cannot be derived solely from ordinary usage.

It should be clear that many, perhaps even most, forms of communication will be outside the coverage of a Free Speech Principle. I cannot answer definitively what is inside, because that will turn on particular justifications for the Free Speech Principle. But we must recognize the relation between justification and definition, because failure to do so leads to numerous mistakes, such as, *pace* recent decisions of the United States Supreme Court,[11] including commercial advertising of products and services within the concept of free speech. Some justifications will of course produce broader areas of coverage than others. The argument from democracy, for example, might restrict the Free Speech Principle to the political, and so might a narrow version of the argument from government incompetence. Most versions of the argument from truth would generate much broader areas of coverage. And, of course, there is no reason that there need be only one acceptable justification. Thus the area of coverage may be produced from a number of overlapping justifications. In most cases normative and related factual statements will constitute the core of the Free Speech Principle, but the subjects covered will also depend on justification.

An area of interest concerns those statements that convey nothing but information about the speaker's feelings – statements of pure emotive content. Does the Free Speech Principle cover those communications in which the speaker says nothing except that he feels positively or negatively about something? For example, when a person utters a four letter word at another, or screams an unintelligible noise at a speaker to voice disapproval, or cries at a public gathering, are these free speech cases? When a member of an audience shouts 'Hear! Hear!' or 'Rubbish!', something is being communicated, but it is little more than emotion. This communication, although not explicitly propositional, is still susceptible of interpretation in propositional form. The speaker is asserting a proposition about his own feelings, a statement of approval or disapproval that may be especially relevant in this context. The utterances become important in the context of a comment on some activity, or on some other proposition.

If the relevant interest is that of the speaker, as it is under some of the arguments for freedom of speech, then utterances such as this seem plainly included. If what we are protecting is the interest of a person in articulating an opinion, in making his views known to others, then communications of this sort are as germane to the justifications for freedom of speech as are those expressed in more moderate, sophisticated, or content-laden form. But if the relevant interests are those of the listeners, or of society at large, as under most versions of the arguments from democracy, truth and autonomy, then it becomes easier to say that communications with no substantive content are outside the range of the principle. It can be argued that a pure expression of emotion adds little if anything to the search for truth, or to the process of rational deliberation about matters of public importance. Moreover, discourse of this type often *detracts* from the ideal of the process of rational deliberation. Perhaps we should exclude the irrelevant and the irrational from the public forum, just as we exclude the irrelevant and the irrational from learned journals, so that we can focus our attention on that which is relevant and enlightening?[12]

There are two major flaws in this conclusion. First, the strength and extent of agreement or disagreement, even standing alone, may indeed be relevant in the deliberative process. If one is uncertain of one's views, it may be material that many people agree or disagree with those views, or that people feel quite strongly one way or another. By protecting emotive utterances we can learn the extent of such feelings. There is, as discussed in chapter 3, special importance attached to the discussion of public issues. If one of the purposes of freedom of speech is to facilitate the process by which errors in or disagreement with governmental policy are pointed out, then the extent and depth of that disagreement has particular relevance, even if the reasons for the disagreement are not stated, or are stated by someone else. And if, as perhaps with many questions of public policy, truth is measured in terms of a consensus, then the expression of emotion alone would fall within the scope of the Free Speech Principle.

Moreover, a negative argument for freedom of speech, focusing on the denial to government of the authority to decide which speech is valuable and which speech is not, highlights the difficulty in entrusting to any one person or government the power to determine the point at which factual or normative content *coupled* with emotive content shades into emotive content alone. The oath 'Damn!' uttered alone may be devoid of substantial content, but 'Damn the army!' has more substantive content, and 'Damn those who put national power ahead of human life!' even more still. Yet depending on the context, all three may be intended to impart and be taken as imparting exactly the same message. The line between pure emotion and substantive content is difficult to draw, and if distrust of governmental power to deal with speech is part of the justification of a Free Speech Principle, then the fact that communication *seems* worthless is insufficient warrant to place that speech outside the range of the Principle.

The foregoing discussion illustrates, among other things, that the analysis and at times the result may vary with whether it is the interest of the speaker, the interest of the listener, or the interest of society as a whole that is the significant point of reference.[13] These interests are of course interrelated. If we desire to protect the interests of hearers, then we must in practice grant rights to speakers. Similar considerations apply when we are concerned with the interests of society as a whole. Ideas and information do not come from Aladdin's lamp; they come from people. If we wish to have ideas expressed, we must protect those who would express them, even if those people are not the primary object of our concern. In application, therefore, we will in most instances apply the Free Speech Principle to protect speakers, even though that protection is only instrumental to the protection of some other interest. In this regard protection of the speaker may be said to be a derivative right.[14] There will be instances in which the scope and strength of the right will vary with the identity of the primary interest, and there are instances in which it is possible to make free speech claims directly on behalf of listeners. Cases of this type will be discussed in later chapters, but it is important to note here that the identity of the interest – speaker, listener, society or some combination of these – must always figure in a complete analysis of any free speech problem.

FREEDOM OF THE PRESS

The modern conception of freedom of speech has roots in two distinct strands of thought. One of these is the theory of religious toleration, as exemplified in Locke's *Letter Concerning Toleration,* Bayle's *Treatise on Universal Toleration,* and Turgot's *Memoire to the King on Tolerance.* The other strand is freedom of the press, the subject of, for example, Milton's *Areopagitica,* the tracts of the Levellers, and many of the pamphlets surreptitiously circulated in pre-Revolutionary America. Although religious toleration provides the fallibilistic and individualistic roots for modern free speech doctrine, the concept of freedom of the press furnishes the notion that freedom of speech is related to the operation of government, and to the demarcation between citizen and government.

We talk frequently about freedom of the press, and the use of that phrase suggests three alternatives. Is freedom of the press an independent principle, is it coextensive with freedom of speech, or is it a distinguishable subset of freedom of speech?

The word 'press' has undergone a transformation in meaning. In the earlier literature on the subject, particularly that of the seventeenth and eighteenth centuries, 'press' was used to refer to any form of printing, as distinguished from oral speech or handwritten letters. Thus 'press' would include not only newspapers and magazines, but books and pamphlets as well. Freedom of the press was generally thought of in terms of the lone pamphleteer, not the freedom of *The Times,* the *Washington Post,* or *Le Monde.* Contemporary usage, however, is different. We do not ordinarily think of most books or many magazines as 'the press'. We still would include virtually all newspapers and many topical or political periodicals. We include radio and television, but usually not the theatre or the cinema. In the past 'press' often *included* what we now refer to as 'the news'. Now 'the press' is almost *defined* by whether the medium does or does not include 'the news', or at least some political reporting, analysis, or commentary. The meaning is not entirely settled in ordinary usage, but there has been a decided shift in emphasis.

These distinctions are important, because it is primarily in terms of the modern conception of 'the press' that arguments have been made for the recognition of a distinct principle of freedom of the press. In the main these arguments are derived from the perceived importance of the *political* content of the press, and to this extent the arguments for freedom of the press are inextricably linked to the argument from democracy. Although most of the editorial material that normally appears in the press would be covered by the principle of freedom of speech, the nature of the material presented and the method of presentation may argue for *particular* protection, either broader in scope or of greater strength than that available under a general principle of freedom of speech.

Under the argument from democracy, and under some versions of the argument from truth, speech with political content is not just another form of communication. It has special value in a system that professes to adhere to broadly democratic principles. Political speech, including public deliberation of political issues and open criticism of governmental officials and policies, is an important and arguably necessary method of retaining public control over officials, preventing usurpation of power, and acting as a check on the intrinsic force of the governmental apparatus. The press differs from other forms of communication not only by treating political issues with particular emphasis, but also by presenting those issues to a mass audience, thereby promoting the widespread public deliberation that is the ideal of a democratic society. Moreover, if public opinion acts as a check on governmental power, then a medium that can inform or mobilize the public is notably important.[15] The institutional press – newspapers, magazines, radio and television – is particularly suited to perform this function. This is well known to those who hold political power. As much in modern times as in the past, strong central governments with doubtful popular support exercise rigorous controls over the organized press, more so than over other forms of communication. In order to counteract this strong tendency on the part of those who govern to control the most effective form of criticism of government, it may be necessary to provide some particular protection for the press.

Thus it is primarily the argument from democracy, or at least one form of it, that generates the argument for special protection for the institutional press. From this perspective, however, it appears that it is not the format ('the press') that is in need of special protection, but rather the mass communication of ideas and information related to political issues. The organized press is indeed the medium most commonly used for the mass communication of political argument, but there is by no means a one-to-one correspondence. Mass public meetings have always been and remain a common method of communicating political ideas, and posters and billboards are frequently used as well. Conversely, many components of what we commonly call the 'mass media' have no political content at all, such as *Chess World*, *The Mickey Mouse Club*, and *Crossroads*. [16] I am not suggesting that such publications or programmes are undeserving of protection. It is only that nothing in them relates to the political justification for providing special protection for the press.

One reason for protecting the institutional press is that, unlike for example the mass meeting, it has the particular ability to alert what may be an otherwise apathetic public. Moreover, the fact that most mass communication of political matter appears in the press could argue on pragmatic grounds for an overall protection for the press, even if such protection would be to some extent both over-inclusive and under-inclusive. Yet one can question whether it is the function of the press to *force* interest on the public. A choice of *Kojak* over political discussion may indicate general satisfaction with government, or it may indicate a conscious preference to leave political decisions to others. Furthermore, there are insuperable problems in defining 'press' in this context. *The New York Times* and *The Economist* are plainly included, but what of the writer of books on political subjects (or currently working on his first book) or the basement pamphleteer? The problems caused may be greater than the gains. It seems preferable to look not at the medium of communication, but at the content of the communication. This is especially true when we realize that a great deal of very important political discussion takes place in quite private settings. The argument from democracy seems of equal or perhaps even greater import in the context of a political discussion at high table or at the corner pub. These settings much more closely capture the ideal of *deliberation* about public issues than does the publication of facts and opinion in a newspaper.[17] We may wish to say that some forms of communication represent a constraint on governmental power even greater than that established by a general Free Speech Principle, but this powerful constraint would properly be keyed to political content, and not to the presence or absence of a printing press or transmitter.[18]

THE PROBLEM OF ARTISTIC EXPRESSION

People generally use the word 'censorship' to refer to two topics. One is political censorship, and the other is censorship of art. Although I have addressed political censorship, I have yet to look closely at artistic censorship, and that is a gap that needs filling.

The importance of censorship of art to a discussion of free speech lies largely in the fact that history has many times seen the suppression, in the name of sexual morality or protection against offence, of many works now acknowledged as great masterpieces or at least valuable contributions. Although I discuss control of obscenity in chapter 12, the necessary foundation must be laid here. The question is whether art – visual, musical, theatrical, literary and poetic – is within the coverage of the Free Speech Principle.

The extent to which this is a problem deserving independent treatment involves consideration of the full range of aesthetic theory, an enquiry plainly beyond the scope of this book. For example, if there is no difference of importance between art and any other form of communication, then art may fit easily within all that I have previously discussed. But I am ahead of myself, and shall return to this shortly. The starting point should be the observation that there are works commonly referred to as 'art' whose content clearly places them within the range of the type of communication covered by the Free Speech Principle.

The easiest example of this is presented by those works of art that are intentionally, specifically, and perhaps explicitly political. Picasso's *Guernica* is the paradigmatic example. Also within this category would be some of the symphonies of Shostakovich, films such as *Z*, plays such as *Sizwe Bansi is Dead,* and the photographs of W. Eugene Smith. I use specific examples to make clear that I am not referring to those theories holding all art to be in some sense political. This is a much more limited argument. All I am saying is that those works of art that intend to make a political statement and are so taken by a substantial proportion of viewers or listeners (perhaps with the assistance of a helpful title or caption) lie at the centre of the Free Speech Principle. They lie within the principle not *because* they are art, but because they are political communications.[19] The artistic genre may be the medium of communication, but that is not important to the free speech issue.

Much the same can be said for those works that have a plain message that relates in some way to a matter of public interest, even if that message is not political in a narrow sense. Examples of works of this type would be the novels of Sinclair Lewis or Theodore Dreiser, the poetry of Henry Wadsworth Longfellow, Rudyard Kipling and Alfred Lord Tennyson, some French Romantic and Neo-Classical painting, and most religious art. Works like this carry a rather obvious message to the hearer or observer. They may contain elements not so easily characterized as communication, but there is sufficient communicative content that there is little difficulty in holding such works to be 'speech'.

For this reason, those who take art to be a form of communication need have no cause to question the inclusion of art within the Free Speech Principle, subject only to the same exceptions or limitations applicable to communication containing no artistic qualities. If, following Nelson Goodman, art and language are just two sides of the same coin, there would be no reason to treat art differently from purely linguistic utterances.

The problem arises if art is viewed as something other than mere communication. If, for example, art is so characterized because it is a mode of self-expression, or if there is taken to be a necessary gap between what is intended by the artist and what is perceived by the observer, then art does not fit so neatly into any of the accepted justifications for acknowledging the existence of the Free Speech Principle. To the extent that art is seen as something other than communication, it may not be within the scope of the principles of freedom of speech.

Of course there is nothing 'wrong' with saying that non-communicative art, no matter how beautiful or important, is not covered by the concept of freedom of speech. First of all, it is possible that artistic freedom might be included within some other principle of great strength. This could be a broad principle including artistic expression, or it could be a specific principle relating only to art. Such a principle might be based on the particular importance of protecting artistic self-expression, one that drew a distinction between this and other forms of self-expression. But the identification of such a principle is not my task here. Free speech is not the only liberty, but those who cannot or do not equate art with speech should not be disappointed when we say that free speech does not necessarily entail freedom of artistic expression.

Moreover, the fact that some form of conduct is not protected by a particular right or principle does not mean that the state cannot recognize that conduct as having important value. The list of rights against the state does not exhaust the list of rights the state may choose to create or recognize, or the list of values the state may deem important. If some art is not included within the Free Speech Principle, and is not included in any other principle of equivalent strength, the consequence is that art may be regulated when it is in the public interest to do so, the standard generally applied to exercises of governmental power. But in few cases could we find that suppression of art is in the public interest. Art is much less likely to cause harmful consequences than other forms of self-expression. The Free Speech Principle may be less applicable to art, but it also seems much less necessary.

From the perspective of freedom of speech, however, this whole problem of the proper characterization of artistic expression is most likely a false problem. We get into the type of difficulty I have just been discussing only if we focus on the objects of the regulation in determining the scope of the Free Speech Principle. But if, as with the problem of non-linguistic communication, we look to the purpose of the regulation, then the problem dissolves. Particularly under a justification for a Free Speech Principle that looks to the dangers inherent in governmental regulation of communication, what matters is not so much the effect of the regulation as the motive behind it. Thus the triggering factor is whether the government action is directed at the communicative impact of the conduct. If the regulation at issue is designed to limit the extent to which people will be *influenced* by a work of art, then free speech considerations are triggered, regardless of the format of the work, regardless of how some might characterize the work in philosophical terms, and regardless of the artist's own intent. Seen in this light, it is apparent that almost all instances of censorship of art are free speech cases, because the motivating factor behind the censorship is almost always the desire to prevent viewers or listeners from being influenced in a certain way. Thus artistic censorship is an act directed at the communicative impact of the work of art, and therefore is constrained by the Free Speech Principle. In the case of censorship of art, as with many other free speech cases, focus on the reasons for the regulation rather than the objects of the regulation solves what at first sight appear to be difficult puzzles. And under a justification for the Free Speech Principle that emphasizes the dangers of government control of communication, this focus on purpose and intent is the most logical course.

Bibliographical note to chapter 7

The discussion in the text of the distinction between coverage and protection is adapted from my 'Can rights be abused?', *Philosophical Quarterly* **31** (1981), 225–30. For similar distinctions, see Laurent Frantz, 'The First Amendment in the balance', *Yale Law Journal* **71** (1962), 1424. On the question of non-linguistic communication, additional sources are Louis Henkin, 'Foreword: on drawing lines', *Harvard Law Review* **82** (1968), 63; Melville Nimmer, 'The meaning of symbolic speech under the First Amendment', *UCLA Law Review* **21** (1973), 29. Also relevant to the subjects of this chapter are W. Crawford, 'Can disputes over censorship be resolved?', *Ethics* **78** (1968), 93; Robert Ladenson, 'Freedom of the press: a jurisprudential inquiry', *Social Theory and Practice* **6** (1980), 163; Stefan Morawski, 'Censorship versus art: typological reflections', *Praxis* **10** (1974), 154.

CHAPTER 8

What kind of freedom?

THE ANALYSIS OF 'FREEDOM'

In the previous chapter I examined some of the difficulties surrounding the word 'speech' as it is used in delineating the coverage of the principle of freedom of speech. I turn now to an attempt to clarify and illuminate the 'freedom' component of freedom of speech, a task whose difficulty is at least as great.

The word 'freedom' has spawned a voluminous literature. And for each different concept of freedom, there is a parallel conception of freedom of speech. To some people, such as Milton and Blackstone, freedom of speech consisted solely of an immunity from governmental licensing or other forms of pre-censorship. This view of freedom of speech still exists. It is the only way to explain, for example, such profoundly silly statements as that of Winston Churchill that 'In England there is absolute freedom of speech as long as the speech does not violate the law.'[1] To Mill, freedom of speech meant not only freedom from any form of governmental control, but also freedom from private social pressures that could also inhibit thought and opinion. Some take freedom of speech to include freedom from specific non-governmental sanctions, such as the exclusion of articles from newspapers, the exclusion of books from libraries, and the exclusion of certain programmes from radio and television. Others say that there is no 'real' freedom of speech unless people in fact have the *ability* to communicate their views to large numbers of other people. Those who hold this view advocate positive rights of access to newspapers, magazines, and broadcasting stations.

Accompanying each version of what freedom of speech can mean (and which its proponents claim free speech *really* means) is a particular but usually unarticulated philosophical notion of the concept of freedom, or liberty. Indeed one of the problems is whether we are talking about freedom or whether we are talking about liberty. Some thinkers, most notably Isaiah Berlin, have drawn a distinction between positive and negative liberty, while others, such as Joel Feinberg and Gerald MacCallum, have argued that positive and negative liberty are closely interrelated. In the context of a discussion of freedom of speech, it is often useful to concentrate on the distinction between positive and negative liberty, bearing in mind that this in no way denies that the two are related. If we look at freedom as ability and freedom as immunity as distinct issues, if we look separately at 'freedom to *do* what?' and 'freedom *from* what?', we can clarify some sticky problems in free speech theory. Rather than rehearse the entire philosophical question of the meaning and dimensions of 'liberty' and 'freedom', I think it best to look at this question as it applies directly to the problem of free speech.

An example may serve best to illustrate the complexity of the problem. Take that paradigmatic forum for free speech, Speakers' Corner in Hyde Park in London. Suppose I object to the taxation policies of Her Majesty's Government, and wish to offer those objections for consideration by the public. I go the station in Cambridge and purchase for £5.35 a day return ticket to London. Arriving in London, I make my way to Speakers' Corner, where I climb upon a podium and announce in a loud voice that I wish to speak about taxation. Immediately two hundred people, representing all strata of society, gather around to listen to my words. And fine words they are, presenting my arguments in a rational, articulate and persuasive manner. The audience listens attentively, and when I have completed my speech they ask questions, think about the issues, and discuss among themselves the ideas I have presented. Some are persuaded, some are not persuaded, but all have at least listened. I return to Cambridge on the evening train, happy that I have contributed to public debate, democracy and the search for political truth.

Now if this is in some sense an ideal free speech situation, let us look at the ways in which my freedom of speech could have been curtailed, making the free speech situation less happy. At the extreme I could have been unequivocally prevented by the government from speaking. For example, I might have been shot as I mounted the podium, or carried off by several large members of the army or the constabulary. This type of interference would make it totally impossible for me to speak, and equally impossible for the audience to hear what I had to say. Another possibility is that it might have been specifically unlawful for me to deliver this *particular* speech. This could happen if there had been a court injunction directing me not to give this speech, or if I had failed to secure a required license. In these cases I am in a sense free to deliver the speech, but I know to a virtual certainty that I will thereafter be cited for contempt of court or punished for not acquiring the licence. If I am willing to suffer these consequences, I am in this one sense free to speak. But I am not free in the sense that I will undoubtedly be punished for speaking, and as a result I will in fact be much less likely to speak.

There are other possibilities as well. Instead of there being a particular prohibition against this speech, there might be a *general* law making speeches of this type criminal. The penalty may be death, some period of imprisonment, or a fine of greater or lesser amount. In each case there is a possibility that I will not be prosecuted, or a possibility that I will be prosecuted but not convicted. I must take this into account, along with the expected penalty, in calculating the expected punishment. Having made this calculation, it is my choice whether to speak and risk the expected penalty, or refrain from speaking. I am free in the sense that no one is actually *preventing* me from speaking. But I am not free in the sense that the higher the expected punishment, the less likely I am to feel that the benefits are worth the risk. Similarly, there may be no law prohibiting my speech, but there may be a tax I am forced to pay if I wish to make a speech. The higher the tax, the more it is likely to have the effect of deterring me from delivering the speech.[2] Yet another possibility is that instead of being fined or taxed I could be forced to forgo a benefit. If I am told that I will be given £100, or a position with the civil service, if I do not speak, and given nothing if I do speak, then I am as prevented from speaking as I would be if it were a direct tax out of my own pocket.

These are not the only ways, however, in which the speech could be prevented, or the speech situation be less than ideal. If Speakers' Corner or its equivalent did not exist, then I would be prevented from speaking by the absence of a forum. If I could not afford £5.35, I would be prevented by poverty from speaking. If I had a soft voice, or no voice at all, I would be prevented by physical disability from speaking. If the audience were not there, or chose not to listen, or preferred to listen to another speaker who was talking about sex, I would again not be free to communicate my ideas to the public. If I were physically assaulted by a member of the audience, I would be prevented from speaking, just as I would effectively be prevented from speaking if a member of the audience played *Rule, Britannia!* on an amplified tenor saxophone during the whole of my oration.

In every permutation just described, there are elements both of freedom *to* and freedom *from*. In each there is something I am prevented from doing. In each there is an agent preventing me from doing it. In that sense it is true that positive and negative freedom are two sides of the same coin. Yet some of the constraints I have described, for example being shot by the army while speaking, are commonly thought of as restrictions on freedom of speech, but others, for example a soft voice or inability to afford train fare to London, are not usually taken to be limitations on freedom of speech. Some of the examples, like that of the interfering saxophone player, are more problematic. The example illustrates the many possible dimensions of freedom of speech, and at the same time shows the necessity of attempting to clarify just what the 'freedom' component of the principle means.

THE DIMENSIONS OF COERCION

There exists widespread agreement that freedom of speech includes at the very least some degree of immunity from direct governmental coercion or punishment. This much has been implicit up to now in this book, and in most of the writings on freedom of speech. Most of the balance of this chapter is devoted to the question of whether freedom of speech is *more* than just freedom from governmental sanction or control – whether freedom of speech is a concept that incorporates in some instances more of a notion of freedom *to*. But before turning to these fringes, we need further clarification at the core. What is it to be free from governmental coercion?

Formulating the Free Speech Principle in terms of a higher standard of justification for government action makes it possible to avoid the largely artificial distinction between punishment and other forms of control. Giving a cash bounty to those who refrain from criticizing the state and nothing to those who do criticize might not be a punishment in the very narrow sense. And we might say that it is not punishment in the strict sense if taxes are imposed on communicative activities, or if critics of government are made ineligible for public employment, or social welfare benefits. Yet in each of these cases a person does not get something he would have received but for the act of speech, and in each case the effect will be to influence behaviour, albeit by methods not identical to those of the criminal law.

There is a strand of analysis, now largely discredited, that would distinguish cases of this sort on the basis of a distinction between rights and privileges. Imprisonment for speech would be a free speech violation because there is a deprivation of the right to be free from confinement. But denial of social welfare benefits on account of speech would under the distinction be permissible, because social welfare benefits are not a right, but merely a privilege. We can argue about what counts as a right and what counts as a privilege, but the objection to the right–privilege analysis transcends any dispute about what are rights and what are privileges. If rewards are withheld on account of speech, clearly the effect will be to inhibit speech. If the effect is to inhibit that which is taken to be especially valuable, the principles of free speech are implicated regardless of whether the inhibition is by way of reward or punishment. And from the perspective of a negative justification for a Free Speech Principle, we can see that a selective system of rewards involves the state's questionable ability to distinguish on the basis of content every bit as much as a system of punishments.

It is of course true that in some sense *everything* the state does can have the effect of controlling speech. When those in positions of authority take a stand on any issue, they influence what people think and thereby influence what people say. But any system of rights and liberties presupposes some freedom of the will, and thus a distinction between punishment or reward for external activity, on the one hand, and argument or persuasion, on the other, remains a distinction of significance. The issue of government speech, propaganda and the like, is in its own way important, but it has little to do with any notion of rights.

Even if we take an aversion to content regulation by government as being at the core of the Free Speech Principle, there are instances in which content-based choice among communications is inevitable. Take the example of a journal published by a university controlled by the government.[3] The process of selecting and rejecting articles for that journal is a selection among communications by government on the basis of the content of the communications. Similarly, when civil servants or other government employees are selected, the selection is often based in large part on what the various applicants for the position have said or written. Yet the selection of a foreign policy adviser, for example, on the basis of the quality of or position expressed in writings about foreign relations is hardly thought to be a free speech problem. The same holds true for selection of university faculty, or selection of books by a public library. In these latter cases we think more often of free speech issues, but no one can deny that universities and libraries must of necessity often decide that some speech is valuable and that some other speech is not.

In order to get clear about this type of situation, it is important to recognize two crucial distinctions. The first is the distinction between *necessary choice situations* and *unnecessary choice situations*. A necessary choice situation occurs when there are scarce resources requiring allocation as a matter of necessity, whether it be money, shelf space in a library, pages in a journal or positions with the government. In these situations the existence of a scarce resource means that choices must be made. But where the resources are not scarce, then there is no necessity of making choices, and we have what I call an unnecessary choice situation. Examples would be social welfare benefits available to all who meet basic eligibility requirements, or tax deductions available to all taxpayers. The question to be asked in deciding whether there is a necessary choice situation or unnecessary choice situation is whether choice is inherent in the nature of the enterprise.

Drawing this distinction makes it possible to separate those cases that implicate free speech considerations from those that do not. Initially we can say that the injection of a choice based on speech into an unnecessary choice situation plainly involves free speech problems. Suppose there is an author who has written a book advocating that immigration be restricted to whites. If *on that basis* the author is deprived of a tax benefit generally available to all, or is excluded from social security benefits, a choice based on speech has been imposed on an unnecessary choice situation and we would properly say that these are free speech cases. But suppose that, again on the basis of the contents of the book in question, the author is denied a place on a government commission in favour of a candidate with more egalitarian views. Or suppose that the book itself is excluded from the shelves of a library, because the librarian chooses to allocate scarce shelf space and a scarce amount of budget money to better books. In these instances, where some selection must be made, we properly do not think of the issue in free speech terms.

The second important distinction, which is applicable to the necessary choice situation, is the distinction between relevant criteria for choice and irrelevant criteria for choice. If those who advocate Communist views are excluded from maintenance positions with the Department of Public Works, and if those who advocate Communist views are excluded from policy-making positions with the State Department of the United States, there is an important difference between the two cases. Only in the latter case is the criterion of political persuasion relevant to what is in both cases a necessary choice situation. The issue involves properly defining the purposes of the enterprise. If the purpose of a public library is taken to be the education of the public towards principles then currently in favour, then a selection of books that comport with those principles is relevant and therefore permissible. But if a public library is taken to be an institution devoted to the development of intellectual capacity in a neutral fashion, or the satisfaction of the public's intellectual curiosity, then the selection of books by intellectual quality is relevant; the selection by political content is not. If primary and secondary schools are seen as places for the indoctrination of the young, while universities are seen as centres of independent intellectual enquiry, then the political beliefs of primary and secondary school teachers are relevant although the political beliefs of university lecturers are not.

There are of course difficult and complex political, social and philosophical issues that are involved in determining just what the purposes are of these and other public institutions. I cannot explore those issues here. The point is only that it is meaningful to talk about coercion of speech and freedom of speech if we first examine the underlying purpose of the choice involved. Those who cry 'censorship!' in every case of choice are undoubtedly correct. All censorship is choice, and all choice is censorship. But these cries of censorship are usually pejorative, suggesting that the principles of freedom of speech have been violated. Those who make such claims should be required to explain the basis on which *they* would make the choice. I have the right to believe that the world is flat or that astrology tells us more about the universe than the theories of Newton and Einstein. I also have the right to express those views to anyone foolish enough to listen. But if I am Professor of Physics at a major university, it is silly to gainsay that such public utterances might validly cause my superiors to wonder if perhaps I am in the wrong line of employment, and to take action accordingly.

When we look at cases like this, we can see that the issue usually is not whether censorship exists, but that it is censorship based on criteria with which the speaker does not agree. This is an important distinction, and one that helps expose many claims of free speech as false problems.

PRIVATE CENSORSHIP

I closed the previous section with the observation that the word 'censorship', pejoratively suggesting a violation of the principles of freedom of speech, is often misused in the context of governmental action. In this section I wish to argue that that word is even more often misused in the context of private action, when the claim is that a person's freedom of speech has been restricted by the actions of some non-governmental agent.

Examples of such private 'censorship' are legion. *The Times* refuses to print my article or my letter to the editor, either because of the contents of the letter, or because of what they know about me personally from other sources. Or *The Times* does print the letter, but deletes a scurrilous reference to Mrs. Thatcher. Or the National Broadcasting Company refuses to schedule and broadcast a television show that I have produced, either because of the contents of the programme, or because of the private activities of the individuals involved. Or that same broadcasting company refuses to hire me as a commentator because I am a Communist. Or the broadcasting company broadcasts the programme I have produced but deletes all 'four-letter words' as well as a bedroom scene and a depiction of a gruesome murder. Or a privately-owned shopping centre excludes me and my picket sign from the premises because the management of the centre disagrees with the message on the sign.

In each of these cases I could claim that I have been the victim of censorship. In each instance I would have communicated some message to an audience but for the intervention of an external agent. Yet if we take the word 'censorship' to mean an improper interference with the principles of freedom of speech, then these may not be instances of censorship at all. They are all cases of choice, and they are all in some sense cases of interference, but they are not cases that call forth the application of the Free Speech Principle.

In order to comprehend the distinction between restraint by government and restraint by a private agent, it is important to take note of the crucial element of *choice* in any speech situation. When I hear something said, I make two kinds of choices, either immediately or after some reflection, with reference to what has been communicated to me. I decide if the statement is interesting or boring, important or trivial, useful or foolish, valuable or worthless. I also decide if the statement is true or false, valid or invalid, right or wrong. As a listener I engage explicitly or implicitly in the process of evaluating the content of the communication.

When we respond to speech in this manner, we do not ordinarily think of ourselves as censors, in large part because the evaluation does not seem to prevent anyone from speaking. But the issue is not this simple. When I have a dinner party, I am more likely to invite the wit than the bore, the person whose speech is interesting and full of insight rather than the person whose ideas I reject or whose statements add nothing to my knowledge. If I am the editor of a journal, I am more likely to solicit submissions from those whose past writings have indicated to me that they have something to say rather than from those who are unlikely to contribute anything of value. When the man who is known by me to talk much and say little starts talking, I am likely to go somewhere else, denying him part of his audience. In each of these instances I deny someone a forum for communication, and therefore have prevented some communication. Am I a censor?

The answer to this question parallels the discussion of governmental choice contained in the foregoing section of this chapter. In each of these instances I have to make a necessary choice and the previously spoken views of my 'victim' are relevant to that choice. I cannot invite everyone to my house, I cannot listen to everything, and as editor I cannot publish everything. Indeed as we go through our lives we are involved in a continuing series of choices. Evaluation of the content of communications is one type of choice in which we constantly engage.

When Mill talked about *social* censorship and *social* intolerance, however, he appears to have been referring to something else. He was concerned with condemnation of people because of their ideas, with censorship by *censure*. This form of disapproval is not wholly distinct from those I have previously discussed, but here there is less necessity of *choice*. We *could* listen, but we do not. We *could* tolerate, but we do not. At first sight it appears that there is something here very similar to the unnecessary choice situation I described earlier. But it would be a mistake to infer too much from this superficial similarity. The fact that there is an absence of governmental force behind private intolerance is a difference in kind and not a difference in degree. The absence of governmental interference leaves the choice with the participants in the communicative process. If social intolerance has a practical effect similar to that caused by governmental coercion, it is because people *choose* to respect the views of the majority, or because they choose to place their faith in particular arbiters of communicative value. That many people choose to allow others to make their choices for them is indeed unfortunate, and it is equally unfortunate that many people are willing to make decisions to reject ideas prior to gaining a full understanding of the idea they are rejecting. Social choice, however, is not the same as governmental punishment. If government is in a broad sense the servant of the people, government is

121

to that extent committed to a position of neutrality among competing ideas. Government derives its ideas from the population, it does not initiate them. To this extent private choice is inevitable and governmental choice often superfluous. The separation between the individual and government is central to the Free Speech Principle, and this feature is lost when, following Mill, we conflate social intolerance and governmental intolerance. Private intolerance was a worthy object of Mill's attention, but it is a wholly distinct problem from those questions of political philosophy that generate a political principle of freedom of speech.

I want to return to the examples that opened this section, because they illustrate an even more important dimension of the problem of private censorship. If *The Times* refuses to publish my article, I have in one sense been censored. But if the state *tells The Times* to publish that article, then *The Times* has been censored. *Its* freedom to decide what shall be on the pages of the newspaper is implicated, and *its* freedom to communicate *its* message is subject to governmental control. If the state forces a newspaper or magazine to be more tolerant, it is forcing that publication to include things it would not otherwise have included, and is therefore interfering with the freedom of speech of that publication. Part of the problem is that we tend to think of certain publications, especially the larger ones, as being ideally non-partisan. This may be because of the nature of the publication, or it may be because we think that publications of great size and power ought to have obligations of fairness and neutrality not dissimilar to those we impose on government. Thus, if ABC Television or the *Washington Post* restricts their editorial content to one political point of view, we may accuse them of being censors. But if the *Daily Worker* refuses to print articles by or favourable to Margaret Thatcher, Ronald Reagan, or General Zia, we would hardly be surprised and would probably not think in terms of 'censorship'.

There are of course important differences between the *Washington Post* and the *Daily Worker*, differences I seek to explore in the following section of this chapter. But the point I wish to make here is that the act of censoring by a private agent can in many instances be an act of speech by that agent, and that remedying this act of censorship by a private agent can be a governmental restriction on that act of speech. We cure the private censorship only by imposition of public censorship. What to some would be censorship is to the newspaper choice and press freedom. This additional dimension of private suppression as an act of speech, or at least a corollary to it, sharply distinguishes private from government censorship, and makes the notion of private censorship almost self-contradictory.

The problems are somewhat more difficult when the private censor occupies a monopoly position, as perhaps with a trade union, a church or some corporations. In the sense of censorship being a corollary to the monopoly's expression of its own views, the issues are the same. But it is possible that the balance between competing interests might be struck differently. The more a private censor occupies a monopoly position, the more likely it is that the effects on the amount of speech available will be greater. Moreover, we may be more inclined to equate monopolies with governments, both in terms of responsibilities and in terms of many of the flaws in real governments that generate the argument from democracy and the argument from negative implication. In this sense it would be plausible to recognize private censorship as a legal wrong, but such recognition would not detract from the fact that recognition of the legal wrong would impair the ability of the monopoly to express its own position most effectively. In some circumstances we might wish to pay this price, but it is a mistake to assume that there is no price at all.

This has relevance to the question whether free speech is a *claim* in the Hohfeldian sense. Is a deprivation of free speech the basis for a claim against another individual as well as a right against the state? Although it is sometimes asserted that this is the case,[4] that is neither an accurate statement of the law nor an unproblematic view of what the law should be. If, using Charles Fried's example,[5] I am prevented from speaking by a hostile mob, my cause of action against the mob members is based on interference not with speech, but with my person. If you destroy my books, or my printing press, my legal cause of action is based on loss of tangible property and loss of economic value, not on any non-economic value that might accrue from the use of books or a printing press. The presence of communication is immaterial. If the state prohibits me from putting up wall posters relating to Communism in a place otherwise reserved for posters, we would say that freedom of speech has been restricted. But if you put your poster *over* mine, I have no claim at all, even though my ability to communicate has been as effectively stifled.[6] A publisher's breach of a contract to publish my book is no different in the eyes of the law from any other breach of contract.

That something is not the law does not of course mean that it should not be. Perhaps the right to freedom of speech should include a claim against a private individual? Take the following example. I am delivering a speech in a small village to a group of willing listeners. Four people come by and circle the village green in their automobiles, sounding the horns constantly, and thus effectively drowning out my speech. Although this may be a public nuisance under the law, I have at the moment no claim against the four individuals. But maybe I should be permitted to recover against them for damages. There is precedent for the idea of parallel protection against government interference and private interference in the American law relating to the right of privacy. Some aspects of privacy are protected against state interference. In addition, most jurisdictions recognize a statutory or common law right that protects an individual against unauthorized use of his name or picture, and against unreasonable revelations about his past. One can imagine a similar multiplicity of free speech rights, including the creation of the tort of interference with freedom of speech. More precisely, it would be the tort of interference with communication, giving me in the above example a right of action for damages against the four horn-tooters who prevented me from speaking.

If the justifying principle for freedom of speech is the particular danger of governmental interference, and if free speech is based largely on the negative aspects of controlling speech rather than the particular benefits that come from speaking, then there is no special reason to protect against private interference. If, however, communication does have positive advantages, which can hardly be denied, then it is not unreasonable to desire some sort of protection against unreasonable interferences with this beneficial activity, regardless of the public or private character of the interferer. But when we are talking about the establishment of a mechanism for the enforcement of claims against individuals – the establishment of legal rights – we are talking about something very different from rights in the different and perhaps stronger sense of rights against state interference. For example, there is a legal right to contract (interference with a contract is a wrong), there is a legal right to reputation (interference with which gives rise to the tort of defamation), and there is a legal right to the use of property (giving rise to the tort of trespass). If communication is as valuable as it seems, then wrongful interference with communication could provide the basis for a private right of action.

There are, however, a number of problems that would militate against the creation of such a claim-right. One is that harms to communication, unlike harms to personal property, are difficult to measure in economic terms. But this is not an insurmountable problem. Despite similar difficulties, we have developed the law of libel and slander to protect the equally intangible value of reputation. A more serious objection is that a case of interference with speech alone is almost always trivial. Speakers and listeners can move to different locations, and most of the serious cases of interference will be connected with some more tangible wrong. Also, many cases of interference with speech are themselves acts of communication by the person who is interfering. This is the case with putting one poster over another, or with speaking loudly while someone else is trying to speak. It is not at all clear to me that a priority for one who speaks first is any more justified than a priority for one who speaks loudest. Finally, creation of a claim for damages might involve many of the same difficult distinctions that give rise to the Free Speech Principle. For example, will the value of the award vary with the truth or the utility of the words that the speaker wished to speak?

Free speech as a claim-right against other individuals is a subject that could be developed in more depth, and the arguments here are both superficial and tentative. But the deeper we get, the more we are involved in the technicalities of the law and the variation among different legal systems. The point I wish to stress here is that legal rights in the private law sense are very different from moral or political rights against state interference. A free speech claim against a private individual is different in kind from a free speech right against the state. When we make an appeal to the principles of freedom of speech we ordinarily refer either to rights against the state, or to a residual liberty recognizing freedom from state interference. One who claims a free speech right against a private person must realize that he is breaking new ground and that the arguments for such a legal right are not necessarily parasitic on the arguments for a Free Speech Principle. Recognition of such a claim might be valuable, but it would require argument developed along substantially different tracks.

THE ABILITY TO SPEAK

The distinction between freedom as immunity and freedom as ability is valuable in this context. Like positive and negative freedom, freedom as ability and freedom as immunity may be two sides of the same coin, but the distinction illuminates an important feature of free speech theory. If freedom of speech is solely an immunity from governmental (or even private) coercion, that does not mean that everyone will in fact have the ability to speak, or even have an equal ability to speak. This was the point of my examples about having a weak voice, or not having the fare for a journey to Speakers' Corner.

These problems may seem a trifle far-fetched, but there is a very practical application in reference to the instruments of mass communication. It is clear that those with access to radio, television, newspapers, magazines and book publishers have more ability to speak than those without that access, even though they all may be equally immune from governmental interference. Many have taken this economic and social phenomenon as a signal to argue that the open marketplace of ideas is a utopian fantasy, requiring that a *meaningful* freedom of speech rectify this imbalance.[7] They argue that the state should enforce some sort of right of access to these important channels of communication. If the marketplace of ideas is located in the airwaves and on news-stands, then my right to deliver a speech at Speakers' Corner, it is argued, is not the right to participate in the marketplace of ideas.

There are several objections to this argument. First, no one is prevented by direct governmental coercion from starting a newspaper or magazine, or from publishing his own book. They are of course prevented by economic considerations from so doing, but deprivation by a governmental or human agent is different from deprivation by economic circumstances. Certainly in many instances this deprivation is caused by the intentional acts of individuals or governments, and many of these deprivations could be cured by some particular re-design of society. But it does not follow that any remediable social condition is a free speech issue. Although they are interrelated, liberty and the conditions for its exercise are two different problems.[8] If the lack of economic resources with which to start a newspaper in some way implicates a *right* of free speech, then so too does almost any other remediable condition. Under such a view freedom of speech would support a right to an education, since education makes it possible to communicate more effectively. Freedom of speech might also support a general right to wealth or to a redistribution of income, since, even apart from the issue of access to the mass media, money can always be used to finance a wide range of communicative activities. It seems bizarre to hold that a right to free speech is the touchstone for a 'right' to virtually everything that might advance the condition of some people.

The fact that an argument may prove too much, or may be susceptible of a broad interpretation, or involve subtle gradations rather than clear distinctions, does not serve to strip the argument of all validity. It can still be argued that even if we recognize that rights and the conditions for their exercise are different, the instruments of mass communication are so distinctly important in modern society that it is necessary that everyone, or at least all different views, have a right of access. But this ignores the reasons why the mass media have become so important. There is certainly no compulsion to buy the *New York Times* or *Newsweek*. Moreover, many less traditional publications are sold at the same outlets as the major national publications, and many others are freely available through street vendors or subscriptions. If unorthodox views expressed in unfashionable publications do not have the impact of major newspapers, it is in large part because the consumers of information have chosen that result. If many people choose *The Times* over the *Socialist Worker*, or choose the cinema over Speakers' Corner, that in itself is not a free speech problem, although it may tell us much about society. It is one thing to say that the state must allow a forum. It is quite another to say that the state must provide the audience.

I wish deliberately to gloss over problems related to the electronic media – radio and television. The extent to which radio and television should be treated the same way as we treat newspapers depends in large part on technological arguments beyond the scope either of this book or my expertise. For example, if the number of broadcast bands were unlimited, then there might be few reasons for treating broadcast communication differently. But if there were a discrete number of bands that had to be limited in order to prevent chaos, there would be some reason for governmental intervention to secure equal access.[9] At the extreme this enforced access might take the form of state-owned monopolies of radio and television. In this area the relationship between technological fact and political theory is great, and I leave it to others to explore that relationship.

Still, there are problems inherent in any theory of access, whether it be an imposed obligation of fairness, a right of access to newspapers, or a state monopoly of radio and television. First, as I have previously suggested, state action to enhance speech is simultaneously state action to suppress speech. For example, when the government requires a newspaper to be fair, or to present different points of view, the government is in the first instance telling the newspaper what to say and, by necessary implication, telling it what not to say. Fairness, like neutrality, is itself a point of view. Imposed objectivity is a dilution of the ability strongly to take one side of the argument. This may not be obvious in all cases, but suppose that a government tells a newspaper that for every column inch of criticism of government that is printed, it must also print one column inch of support for governmental policies. When we require a newspaper to print a reply to an attack, we in many instances blunt the force of the attack. When the state co-opts the airwaves by monopoly of radio and television, it necessarily makes unlawful a powerful tool of private communication. I am not saying that any one of these policies is necessarily wrong. But we must recognize that in each instance the decision to enhance the actual ability of one individual or entity to communicate will at the same time create a legal restriction on the putative communication of others. At times the balance between the advantages and disadvantages or between the gains and the restrictions may make enforced access a worthwhile policy. But every such action must be evaluated with reference to the extent to which increasing some person's ability entails decreasing some other person's immunity.

Moreover, every enforced right of access involves the decision concerning to whom to grant the access, what ideas need additional exposure, and whether a presentation is fair or accurate. Even were it possible to attain such results with any degree of confidence, a legal right of access must involve the government in the process of selecting and distinguishing. If the aversion to such governmental involvement lies at the core of the Free Speech Principle, then governmental action to enforce fairness may do more harm than good. The issue is not whether newspapers should or should not be fair. Rather it is whether any governmental agency should be entrusted with the power to decide whether they are fair or not. It is not the concept of fairness that is troublesome, but the *institution* of enforcing fairness.[10] As soon as we say that something should be done about a particular instance of unfairness, we advocate a system to deal with all cases of fairness arising out of indistinguishable settings, and we must then concede the power of that system to make the distinctions. Such problems are inherent in taking freedom of speech to include a right to the actually occurrent ability to communicate, and the speculative benefits seem hardly worth the cost.

A LIBERTY IN THE NARROW SENSE

I have not been arguing that speech cannot be worthy of promotion, or that communication cannot be considered a 'good'. There are many instances in which communication can be promoted without involving an even greater restriction on speech. We might, for example, wish to provide funds to support aspiring authors or marginal but worthy periodicals. But a 'good' is one thing, and 'freedom' quite another. If speech were not a good thing, we would have little reason to spend public money on libraries, on art galleries and on public arenas. The point is not that speech ought not to be promoted, but that *free speech* is something different. Entangling the two serves only to confuse the argument.

The result is that the Free Speech Principle, or freedom of speech, is a 'liberty' in the narrow sense of that word. There are, I admit, almost as many senses of the word 'liberty' as there are of the words 'freedom' and 'right'. But there seems to be a developing consensus, at least in academic political philosophy, that a 'liberty' is the absence of 'interference, censorship, control, regulation, restriction, constraint etc.'.[11] It is closest to what Isaiah Berlin calls a 'negative liberty' and what Joel Feinberg calls the absence of 'external positive constraint'. Since I have already dealt with the exclusion of private censorship, freedom of speech is best characterized as the absence of governmental interference. It is liberty to communicate, unencumbered by governmental control but not necessarily unencumbered by other forms of control and not necessarily entailing the *de facto* ability to communicate.

It is important to recall the original discussion of the Free Speech Principle, which is in no way inconsistent with the conception of freedom of speech as a liberty in the manner just described. A liberty is not a total or absolute liberty. It is, in this context, only the creation of a higher burden of justification for interference or regulation. If a government may tell me what to do whenever it is in the public interest so to do, and if that power includes the power to tell me what to say and what not to say, then there is no liberty of speech. If a government may tell me what to do when it is in the public interest to do so, but may control my speech not at all or only when there is a compelling interest in so doing, then I have a strong liberty of speech. If a government may normally tell me what to do when it is in the public interest to do so, but may control my speech only when it has a substantial (or significant, or weighty) interest in so doing, then I have a weak liberty of speech, but a liberty nevertheless. Free speech is a guarantee of resistance to the normal principles of governmental action. The weight may vary. Liberties may be strong or weak. But it is the distinction from normal principles that constitutes a liberty in the political sense.

N.B. Some (such as Ronald Dworkin) have argued that a right against the government, or a liberty in the sense that I am using

here, is inseparable from some control on the majority or its designates, generally by a court exercising the power of judicial review.
This appears to be wrong. If a sovereign parliament, even though
unchecked by any other political body, thought that it had to have
a better reason to restrict speech than it had to have to impose
sanctions on other activities causing equivalent consequences, then
there would be liberty of speech, or a right to free speech, even
though it might be a fragile or ephemeral liberty. Whether that
parliament can be trusted to limit itself by respecting the right that
it acknowledges is a different issue. Dworkin's argument is valuable in demonstrating the relationship between the existence of a
right and the identity of the body that is protecting it. But it is one
thing to show a relationship and another to conflate two things
that are separate. That there is a close relationship between a right
and its enforcement does not mean that the two are one and the
same.

Bibliographical note to chapter 8

The problem of access to the forums of communication and to the sources
of information has generated a voluminous literature in the United States.
Important additional references are Lee Bollinger, 'Freedom of the press
and public access: toward a theory of partial regulation of the mass media',
Michigan Law Review **75** (1976), 1; Ronald Cass, 'First Amendment access
to government facilities', *Virginia Law Review* **65** (1979), 1287. The distinction between various forms of freedoms, rights, and liberties is a well
rehearsed subject in the legal and philosophical literature. Prominent
examples include Elspeth Attwooll, 'Liberties, rights and powers', in *Perspectives in jurisprudence,* E. Attwooll, ed. (Glasgow: University of Glasgow Press, 1977), 79; Gail Belaief, 'Freedom and liberty', *Journal of Value
Inquiry* **13** (1979), 127; Lon Fuller, 'Freedom – a suggested analysis', *Harvard Law Review* **68** (1955), 1305; John Garvey, 'Freedom and choice in
constitutional law', *Harvard Law Review* **94** (1981), 1756; Stephen Hudson
and Douglas Husak, 'Legal rights: how useful is Hohfeldian analysis',
Philosophical Studies **37** (1980), 45; David Lyons, 'Rights, claimants, and
beneficiaries', *American Philosophical Quarterly* **6** (1969), 173; Gerald
MacCallum, 'Negative and positive freedom', *Philosophical Review* **76**
(1967), 312; Thomas Perry, 'Reply in defense of Hohfeld', *Philosophical
Studies* **37** (1980), 203; Glanville Williams, 'The concept of legal liberty',
in *Essays in legal philosophy,* R. S. Summers, ed. (Oxford: Basil Blackwell,
1970), 121; David Lyons, 'The correlativity of rights and duties', *Noûs* **4**
(1970), 45.

CHAPTER 9

The strength of the liberty

FREE SPEECH AND OTHER VALUES

The two preceding chapters both have been devoted to problems of delineating the scope of the doctrine of freedom of speech. In each the issue was, broadly, whether the principle of freedom of speech applies. In chapter 7 the question was whether the principle of free speech applies to certain forms of conduct; in chapter 8 the question was whether that principle applies to certain forms of restraint. To neither of these questions can there be a clear answer. The boundaries of the Free Speech Principle are fuzzy. Freedom of speech, like any other principle, has its core of clear cases and a fringe or penumbra where the application is less certain and the issues more complex. Furthermore, the process of defining the boundaries of a principle involves a balancing of interests. The derivation of a political right from broader principles involves choosing and balancing among those broader principles, and a definition of the boundaries of the right is parasitic on the original balance. Still, the goal of this process is to determine whether the principle of free speech applies; whether an appeal to free speech is relevant to the enquiry.

An affirmative answer to this question, however, does not dispose of a free speech problem. It only tells us that one exists. Having determined the applicability of a principle of free speech, we must then determine its *strength*. A principle does not prevail just because it applies, and in this chapter I look to the strength of the Free Speech Principle within its area of coverage. In chapter 1 I described the Free Speech Principle as a greater burden of justification for government action, a higher hurdle. It is necessary now to look at the height of that hurdle and the types of justifications that will clear it. What interests prevail in the face of the Free Speech Principle, and under what circumstances? What does it take to overcome the Free Speech Principle, or, conversely, how strong *is* that Principle?

By highlighting the other-regarding nature of speech, and by incorporating that fact in the definition of the Free Speech Principle, I have made this a more difficult problem than many perceive it to be. If freedom of speech is premised on speech being self-regarding, then a simple demonstration that in a particular case speech causes harm is sufficient to justify restricting the speech.[1] But this capacity for harm exists in almost all speech. Recognition of the Free Speech Principle entails protecting some speech despite its harmful effect. Therefore a showing that certain utterances or certain categories of utterance cause harm does not *eo ipso* compel the result that the utterance should be restricted. The Free Speech Principle has already taken this into account. The mere observation that some speech causes unpleasant consequences is an insufficient solution to a free speech problem. A Free Speech Principle requires to justify restriction consequences more serious than those that would normally be required to justify governmental action. There is no way around the difficult task of evaluating the strength of the free speech interest, the strength of the opposing interests, and the balance between the two. To suggest that this task is not present in all cases is to ignore the full dimensions of the problem. I have made the task here more difficult, but I have no wish to define away important problems.

I am not suggesting that any simple formula will enable us to deal with all free speech problems. The ideals within a society vary, and so therefore will the weights of the opposing interests vary. The balancing of such complex variables cannot be reduced to precise verbal or mathematical formulas. It is still useful, however, to look for a method of evaluating opposing interests.

THE PROBLEM OF PRIORITY

At bottom the question is one of establishing some principles of priority between freedom of speech on the one hand and various inconsistent interests on the other. The notion of inconsistency is important. Were it possible in any given instance completely to accomodate unlimited speech as well as the unimpeded advance of another interest, there would be no need to consider the free speech issue. Difficulty arises only when speech will impair some other interest, or when protecting some other interest necessitates restricting speech. Freedom of speech is not necessarily inconsistent with recognition of other interests, but only when there is inconsistency is there a problem that calls for balancing and establishing priorities.

Where this inconsistency does exist, the problems of priority are of two types. I hope to show shortly that the distinction is only one of degree, but initially it is useful to draw the distinction. One type of priority problem occurs when we must balance freedom of speech against the general public interest. Take the example of a person who distributes pamphlets advising young men to resist conscription into the army to serve in a war currently being waged. Suppose that the war is being waged because it is in the public interest to do so (preservation of security, sanctity of national boundaries and so on), and suppose further that as a consequence of the distribution of the pamphlets some people will not serve who otherwise would have served. In this case we can say that the speech (distribution of pamphlets) is harmful to the public interest. A putative restriction on distribution of the pamphlets would involve balancing the interests supporting the principle of freedom of speech against the potential harm to the public interest. But it is insufficient merely to say that we are balancing. If there is force to the Free Speech Principle, then the presumption must be against the restriction – not necessarily an irrebuttable presumption, but still a presumption. The burden of proof is on the public interest. It is for those who support the restriction to show why it is needed, and to show why the public interest is in special jeopardy in this instance. To show merely that the restriction would advance the public interest would be insufficient, because that would ignore the higher burden of justification imposed by the Free Speech Principle. In all cases of balancing freedom of speech against the general public interest, where no particular individual rights are involved other than the right to free speech,[2] we do balance the interests, but with our thumbs on the free speech side of the scales.

Compare the foregoing example with a case involving specific individual rights on both sides of the balance. A good example is the case of newspaper publicity prior to a pending criminal trial. Assuming that some prospective jurors will read about the facts of the case if there are no restrictions, and assuming that some aspects of the newspaper account will not parallel the forthcoming courtroom evidence, it is likely that this publicity will impair the defendant's chances of obtaining a fair trial.[3] On the other hand, a restriction on newspaper publicity is plainly within the Free Speech Principle. Publicity relating to the judicial process, including the prosecution of crimes, is one of the more important justifications for the principle. Now although there is a public interest in granting fair trials as a matter of course, there is also a strong individual right of *this* defendant to obtain a fair trial. The right to a fair trial supports different procedural devices in different systems, but it is a right of great power in almost all modern societies. Thus in this case, unlike the previous example of national security, we must balance one special right against another special right. Just as a restriction on freedom of speech requires a particularly strong justification, so too does a restriction on the right to a fair trial. There is a Fair Trial Principle just as there is a Free Speech Principle. When these two principles collide, as in the example just given, we must determine the priority between the two principles, the strengths of the interests involved in this *type* of application of the principles, and the strengths of the interests involved in the *particular* application in this case. Where freedom of speech is set against the public interest we do not know the answer in every case, but we do know that the analysis must provide for special deference to the free speech interest. In this case, however, where one distinct limitation on state power is set against another, we do not know from the existence of the free speech interest that the presumption should be in its favour. In some cases the Fair Trial Principle may be more important than the Free Speech Principle. The Free Speech Principle is important in all cases within its scope, but it is only necessarily more important in cases where no identifiable individual right is present on the other side of the balance.

It would seem therefore relatively uncontroversial to assert that freedom of speech is not and cannot be an absolute right. This broad statement, however, must be tempered by two highly pertinent qualifications. First, it is important to recognize not only the distinction but also the relationship between the strength of a right and the scope of a right. This terminology is but another way of expressing the distinction between coverage and protection that I discussed earlier, but the terms 'strength' and 'scope' are particularly illuminating here. The scope of a right is its range, the activities it reaches. Rights may be narrow or broad in scope. Defining the scope of free speech as freedom of self-expression is very broad, defining it as freedom of communication substantially narrower, and defining it as freedom of political communication narrower still. The strength of a right is its ability to overcome opposing interests (or values, or other rights) *within* its scope. This distinction is nothing new, although it is often ignored in popular dialogue about freedom of speech. The point I wish to make here is that although the scope of a right and the strength of that right are not joined by a strict logical relationship, they most often occur in inverse proportion to each other. The broader the scope of the right, the more likely it is to be weaker, largely because widening the scope increases the likelihood of conflict with other interests, some of which may be equally or more important. Conversely, rights that are narrower in scope are more easily taken to be very strong within that narrow scope. It is much easier, for example, to say that there is a very strong, almost absolute, right to purely verbal political speech than it would be to say that a right to self-expression can be as strong. Any examination of rights must first recognize this interrelationship and then try to preserve some equilibrium between scope and strength. This is easiest but not necessarily best at the extremes. Meiklejohn, for example, defined freedom of speech as freedom of political speech by those without profit motives. Within this narrow scope it was easier for him to define the right as absolute (which he did) than it would have been had he broadened the scope to include other forms of communication. Yet the more narrowly we define a right, the more likely we are to exclude from coverage those acts that may fall within the justification for recognizing the right. Freedom of speech as freedom of political deliberation gains simple absolutism at the cost of excluding much that a deep theory of the Free Speech Principle would argue for including.

Second, there is an important distinction between the absoluteness of a political right and the absoluteness of a legal right. A strong but not absolute political right may still at the level of application be converted into an absolute legal right. The question concerns the level at which the weighing process will take place, and which people or institutions will be entrusted with the weighing process. In this respect the issues parallel the considerations involved in act-utilitarianism and rule-utilitarianism. We may balance the issues at the rule-making level, concluding that it is best to have an absolute right in order to preclude judges, juries, or (in the case of constitutional rules) legislatures from possibly giving insufficient weight to the Free Speech Principle in a particularized balancing process. Or we may instead allow the balancing to take place at the level of application, thus permitting judges, for example, to determine in the individual case whether countervailing interests outweigh the strength of the Free Speech Principle. It is commonly supposed that this type of *ad hoc* or particularized weighing results in an insufficiently strong principle of freedom of speech, that there is danger of freedom of speech being 'balanced away'.[4] This is probably true as an empirical observation, but it is hardly a necessary truth. It is possible to create principles of insufficient strength at the rule-making level, and it is equally possible for a judge at the level of application to apply a principle in a way that gives it great power. A full analysis of any political principle must deal with the degree to which any institution can protect that principle, and hence the problem of the strength of a principle is intertwined with the problem of designing institutions for the protection of political principles in general.

For these reasons it is difficult to discuss the question of priority as a wholly distinct problem. Questions of priority are intertwined with the definition of the interest whose priority is at issue and with the identification of the institution that is to make the determination of priority. But having issued this disclaimer, I still think it useful to discuss separately some important problems in evaluating the priority between freedom of speech and other important interests.

In looking at the question of relative priority, it is helpful to look to the analytical methods of the statistician. The indifference curve analysis so often used in dealing with questions of distributive justice is most illuminating when there is in fact some scarce resource to distribute. We can learn a great deal from indifference curves when the two axes represent commodities that, but for scarcity, would not be inconsistent. There is nothing inherently inconsistent about guns and butter except that we do not have the resources to buy all we want of both. Freedom of speech, on the other hand, involves a balance between interests that are necessarily inconsistent. Distribution of literature advocating immorality is inconsistent with full promotion of a certain public morality; criticism of government opposes establishment of strong central authority; extensive pre-trial publicity conflicts with the interests in a fair trial. Moreover, many of the reasons underlying the Free Speech Principle are derived from notions of uncertainty, whether in the search for knowledge, in confidence in government, or in the process of regulating speech. Here the application of the techniques for decision-making under uncertainty seem especially appropriate. Although in these cases I find the error analysis of the statistician more illuminating than the indifference curve analysis of the economist, I do not claim that what I have to say might not also be expressed in other terms.

A useful starting point is Blackstone's maxim that it is better that ten guilty men go free than that one innocent man be punished. Several important points are embedded in this example. First, the example would be meaningless in a perfect (error-free) system. If we could with complete assurance of accuracy identify those who are guilty and those who are innocent, then this ratio would tell us nothing, since in no event would we ever have occasion to punish the innocent or free the guilty. But once we acknowledge that we make mistakes in the process of determining the facts relating to any alleged crime and that we also make mistakes in applying the law to the facts, then we must also recognize the possibility that we will come to the wrong conclusion in some cases. The errors produced can be errors of under-inclusion or errors of over-inclusion. Because we do not have certain knowledge of the true state of affairs, we cannot be absolutely certain that a verdict of innocent is not a decision to free one who is in fact guilty (an error of under-inclusion), or that a verdict of guilty is not a decision to punish one who is in fact innocent (an error of over-inclusion).

Free speech problems present analogous issues. If a person is tried for the crime of seditious libel, for example, he is being tried for uttering words constituting a threat to the national security. Again we are presented with the possibility of errors of under-inclusion or over-inclusion. Someone may be found innocent whose words did injure the national security, or someone may be found guilty whose words did not have the relevant effect. Similarly, in an action for defamation, a court may impose liability in a case where the allegations were true, or where there was no injury to reputation, or a court may fail to impose liability where the words were both false and injurious to reputation. Or in an obscenity trial, works not in fact obscene may be found obscene, and works that are obscene may be found not obscene.[5] Because the enforcement of any control on speech is through a court or other decision-making body, the possibility of the two different types of error is as present in the process of regulating speech as it is in the application of the criminal law.

Blackstone recognized these two different types of error. He also recognized that in the criminal law we do not take the two errors to be of equivalent seriousness. Implied in the ten-to-one ratio is the belief that the erroneous deprivation of individual liberty is far more serious than the erroneous release of one who is in fact guilty. It is not that the erroneous release of the guilty causes no harm. Failing to impose punishment upon the guilty detracts from the retributive goals of the criminal law by allowing the guilty to escape sanction. It also harms the goal of deterrence by lessening the certainty of punishment, and it harms the goal of security by releasing someone more likely than the innocent person to commit future crimes. The release of the guilty thus harms the public interest in a variety of ways. But the opposite error, the punishment of the innocent, causes harm to the *individual* interest in personal liberty, an individual interest held to be especially important, and also harms the social interests in justice, fairness and the efficient use of the criminal process. For these reasons, among others, we deem the latter error more serious and we design the system of criminal procedure and punishment in a way such that errors of one type are preferred to errors of the other type. By the use of procedural devices such as the burden of proof, the presumption of innocence, the requirement of unanimity of jurors to convict, and the privilege against self-incrimination, we make it especially hard to convict anyone of a crime. By so doing, we make it more difficult to convict the innocent, but at the price of simultaneously making it also more difficult to convict the guilty. Because of the different weights we assign to the harms of the two types of errors, it is a price we are willing to pay.

This approach is a method for balancing interests. If personal liberty for the innocent were taken to be an inviolable right, then we would want to ensure at any cost that no innocent man was ever convicted. We could accomplish this goal by convicting no one. And if punishing all guilty people were taken to be the overriding public interest, we could so treat it by punishing everyone, thus ensuring that all guilty people were punished. By electing a middle ground between these extremes we balance the interests. But by skewing the process in favour of the defendant, we recognize that one interest is more important than the other.

It is important to recognize that any skewing of the decision-making process involves a cost in terms of optimal accuracy. Whenever we distort the impartial fact-finding process to take account of interests other than the accurate determination of the truth, we pay a price in terms of an increased frequency of erroneous results. In terms of the burden of proof, we would achieve maximum accuracy by establishing as a decision-rule that we punish whenever it appears that the defendant was more likely guilty than not (50.1%). Whenever the defendant was more likely innocent than not we would not punish. This decision-rule would make the fewest errors at any level of uncertainty. But when, recognizing the superior value of personal liberty, we hold that there must be proof beyond a reasonable doubt, we say that we will convict and punish only when there is, roughly, 95% assurance of guilt. In so doing we commit ourselves to acquitting in many cases (50.1% to 94.9%) where the defendant is *probably* guilty. We thus pay a price, in accuracy, for our preferences. We make more mistakes in all, but we make fewer of the kind of mistake that we find most harmful.

I wish now to return from criminal procedure to freedom of speech.[6] If we acknowledge the existence of a Free Speech Principle, of a right to free speech in a strong sense, then freedom of speech occupies the same place in the equation as does personal liberty in the criminal process. When weighed against the general public interest, freedom of speech is taken to be the superior value. To take account of this, the system must treat a wrongful infringement of freedom of speech as a harm more serious than a wrongful damage to the public interest. The ratio of errors of course need not be the same as that we employ in criminal procedure. But if the design of rules does not reflect at least some imbalance in order to minimize free speech errors, even at the cost of increasing other errors, then we are not incorporating the Free Speech Principle into our institutions.

Examination of this statistical relationship illuminates the extent to which we sacrifice accuracy in order to respect weightier values. We are willing to increase errors of one type in order to decrease errors of another, more serious, type. An important point now becomes apparent. The identification of a particular instance in which freedom of speech is erroneously recognized is not the basis for a valid argument against a free speech rule. The argument is invalid because acceptance of any doctrine of freedom of speech entails, in a world of uncertainty, instances in which a free speech claim is erroneously recognized, just as the principle of personal liberty entails instances in which the guilty are acquitted. Because such errors are built into the system, the identification of a particular error in no way shows that the system has been improperly designed. A perfect rule is unattainable. We are faced with only two alternatives – under-protection or over-protection. When we recognize a strong principle, we are selecting under-protection as a greater harm than over-protection.[7] We over-protect speech not because we want to, but because it is the only alternative to under-protection. Since errors of over-protection are incorporated into this choice, the identification of one such error tells us nothing we did not already know when we made the initial choice to recognize a Free Speech Principle.

This is not to say that the balance cannot be struck too far on the side of freedom of speech. It is entirely possible that a rule will be unsatisfactory because it allows *too many* of the errors of the less harmful kind, just as a rule of criminal procedure will be held to be unacceptable if it releases too many guilty people. But this argument must be made on the basis of multiple instances, forcing us to reevaluate the balance between the aggregate of errors. One error tells us nothing. What is relevant is the ratio between all or a statistically significant large number of errors.

All of this merely reflects the fact that recognition of a Free Speech Principle entails a cost to society. For example, when we recognize a right to criticize the government we accept a diminution in efficiency and authority. Only if we are willing to accept the cost should we recognize a Free Speech Principle. Unless we are trying to get something for nothing, we have no cause to complain about the costs.

Balancing of interests is difficult because the process is empirical and statistical. The benefits are rarely clear, and we only know the costs after a number of trials have been run. There is unfortunately no escape from a trial and error approach. We recognize the potential conflict between freedom of speech and another interest, we estimate the extent of priority of the free speech interest, and we establish a rule incorporating as best we can that relative priority. After some time has passed we attempt to estimate whether freedom of speech is flourishing to the extent we desire, and whether the costs are bearable. If we are displeased with the result, we adjust the rule, and keep doing so until we are satisfied with the result. It is a continuing process of fine tuning, proceeding from coarse adjustments to finer ones. I do not intend this description as a manual of arms for society's rule-makers, but merely as a description of an existing but rarely stated process.

Where the conflict is between free speech and another strong principle, a rule that accommodates the two may not give priority to speech. In dealing with pre-trial publicity, for example, we may take a fair trial to be more important than an uninhibited press, and this would be incorporated into the rule.[8] But here the complexity is compounded. If the individual interest underlying the imbalance in the criminal process is the interest in protecting against erroneous deprivations of liberty, this interest can be accommodated merely by releasing any defendant injured by pretrial publicity. But this would pay insufficient heed to the public interest in enforcing the criminal law. We are thus balancing on three axes: the strong interest in a free press; the weaker but still important public interest in punishing the guilty; and the strong interest of the defendant in a fair trial. Additional interests can be imagined, making the calculus still more complex. There is no escape from the subjective evaluation of the competing interests, but the process is more rational once we recognize the multiplicity of interests and the questions of priority and error that surround any attempt to formulate a specific rule.

As I have repeatedly emphasized, recognizing a Free Speech Principle entails establishing a burden of governmental justification greater for those governmental actions directed at communication than for governmental actions directed at other forms of conduct. The particular words adopted to characterize this burden will reflect the balance struck between freedom of speech and other interests. Take the rule, adapted from American free speech doctrine, that speech may be restricted only when there is a clear and present danger that the speech will cause a significant harm to the public interest.[9] By comparison, we can hypothesize a rule that might exist in the absence of a Free Speech Principle: speech may be restricted when that speech is likely to cause harm.[10] The comparison between the two rules is illuminating. The strong rule requires that the danger be clear, but the weak rule allows regulation when the danger is less certain. The strong rule requires that the danger be immediate, but the weak rule allows regulation of a danger more remote in time. The strong rule requires a significant harm, but any harm is sufficient to meet the standard set by the weak rule. If we imagine a scale of dangerousness, incorporating all of these elements, then we might say that that the clear and present danger standard requires a reading of 90 on the danger scale, and the weaker test requires a reading of only 55. Thus, under the clear and present danger standard, all dangers falling between 55 and 89 inclusive are immune from state control, *despite the fact that they are dangers*. The allowed dangers are the price we pay for accepting a Free Speech Principle. The hard question is to determine the point at which the number or effect of the allowed dangers becomes so intolerable that their total strength outweighs the admittedly stronger unit-weight of freedom of speech. We cannot even begin to address this question, however, until we realize that there *are* allowed dangers.

The question of national security is a useful example because it emphasizes the predictive aspects of free speech decisions, the estimates of cause and effect inherent in making a decision under conditions of uncertainty about the future. The following over-simplified example, which substitutes bright lines for gradation, helps to make this point clear. Suppose that a group of people are advocating armed revolution against the state. Two outcomes of their activities are possible. One outcome is that people will listen to this advocacy and reject the ideas that are advocated. The other is that a substantial minority will be persuaded of the necessity of armed revolution, and as a consequence will take up arms and topple a democratic government supported freely by a majority of the population. We must now make a decision whether to suppress this advocacy of armed revolution, although we can only guess which of the two possible outcomes will occur. Once we incorporate the decision whether to suppress, there are four possible outcomes: 1) we can suppress speech that would, if allowed, have caused a revolution; 2) we can suppress speech that would, if allowed, have been harmless; 3) we can allow speech that, having been allowed, will cause a revolution; 4) we can allow speech that, having been allowed, will be harmless. Outcome 1 is a correct decision, as is outcome 4. The errors lie in outcomes 2 and 3. But because we cannot know with certainty at the time of the decision what will happen, the decision to suppress entails a risk of erroneous outcome 2, and the decision to permit the speech entails the risk of erroneous outcome 3. Under a Free Speech Principle, outcome 2 must be considered a more serious error than outcome 3, *ceteris paribus*. When we incorporate this by use of a standard such as 'clear and present danger', we accept a risk of actually occurrent revolution higher than it would be under a standard of less force. From this perspective it is not surprising that highly volatile political systems have no room for a Free Speech Principle, and that stable political systems are more able to take the risk.

The balance inherent in something like the 'clear and present danger' standard shows that balancing of interests may take place on different levels and may be entrusted to different institutions. Compare the following two rules: a) police officers shall seize and destroy all publications whose danger to the national security outweighs the intellectual value of their contents; b) police officers shall seize and destroy all copies of the May 1979 number of *The Radical Revolutionary*. The differences between these two rules point up the difference between balancing to come up with a rule and balancing in the individual case, and also the difference between entrusting the task of balancing to those who make the rules as contrasted with those who enforce the rules. Balancing to create a rule sacrifices the ability to weigh the interests in a particular case to the advantages of predictability, and at the same time entrusts the balancing process to the legislative body. Balancing in the individual case attempts to gain fairness and accuracy in every case, but at the expense of predictability, and in some cases at the expense of entrusting the balancing process to people not sufficiently sensitive to free speech concerns.

A balance may also be struck either in a substantive or a procedural rule. To the extent that we protect all speech that would not cause a clear and present danger, for example, we have incorporated the priority of speech into a substantive rule. To hold, on the other hand, that speech may be restricted only if a unanimous jury so decides, or if the government bears the burden of proving by clear and convincing evidence that there must be a restriction, is to incorporate the same priority into a procedural rule.

Thus, every problem of balancing freedom of speech against other interests presents four questions. First, what is the relative priority between freedom of speech and the other interest? Second, should that relative priority be established in a rigid rule or determined on a case-by-case basis? Third, who should decide what the balance is to be – constitution, legislature, court, administrative tribunal, jury, or enforcement officer? Fourth, in what types of rules should the balance be incorporated? All four of these questions are interrelated, but failure to consider them all often leads to a rule that varies from the intended result.

It is equally important to recognize that the way in which we characterize the interests to be balanced can predetermine the results. For example, take a libel case based on the allegation by John Smith that the highest ranking admiral in the navy is psychologically unfit to command large numbers of people. If we characterize this problem as one involving the competing interests of national security and military authority against the interest of John Smith in making psychological conjectures, the result seems pre-ordained. But if we characterize the problem as one involving the competing interests of Admiral X in avoiding criticism against the interest of the public in evaluating their leaders and participating in political decisions, then the result is as pre-ordained, but with the opposite conclusion. The characterizations of the interests are parasitic on the underlying justifications for the Free Speech Principle. Under the argument from democracy, the balance in the case of Admiral X would be described as the interest of Admiral X in his reputation compared to the interest of the public in evaluating the qualifications of its leaders. If freedom of speech is premised on the perceived inability of government effectively or fairly to regulate speech, then the characterization would look more to the future. Under this argument the question of seditious libel, for example, would be characterized not only in terms of whether the particular words were seditious, but also in terms of whether any governmental body should have the authority to decide what is seditious and what is not. It is always easy to argue against a free speech claim by noting the danger of the particular words at issue, but the problem is properly addressed by noting as well the danger of entrusting a category of decisions to a particular body.

Always present is the question of whether different *categories* of speech are entitled to different weights on the balance. Is political commentary more valuable than the commercial cinema? Is textual literature more valuable than pictorial magazines? Is academic discourse more valuable than pulp novels? Are economic theories more valuable than commercial advertising? In large part different weights for different categories are generated by a particular deep theory for a principle of freedom of speech. Under the argument from democracy, political speech is more deserving of protection than, say, literature or art. Under the argument from individuality, speech published for commercial motives deserves less weight. It is bizarrely over-simplified to hold that all types of speech deserve the same weight, at least if we look at categories of speech rather than whether particular utterances are on one side or another of a given issue. To say that there shall be no political marches is very different from saying that there shall be no marches by fascists, or socialists, or whatever.

Although distinctions among categories appear inevitable, there are still problems. For one thing, much speech spans different categories. Obscene pictures may be used to make a political argument; commercial advertising may be artistically creative; literature may carry an economic message. The activity of categorizing is substantially more difficult than the abstract establishment of categories. Moreover, establishing categories entails entrusting to some institution the responsibility of distinguishing among those categories. Distinguishing among categories involves many of the same problems involved in distinguishing within a category. This is not to say that categorization by classes of speech is never possible, but only that deciding if words are an X or a Y carries many of the same problems as are involved in deciding if words are true or false, right or wrong, or valuable or worthless.

The reader expecting a master-plan for the balancing of interests will be disappointed to learn that none is to be offered. Balancing interests cannot be reduced to simple formulae, much as we might wish that this could be so. I have tried to suggest considerations that make intelligent balancing possible, and to point out pitfalls to avoid. This will, I hope, improve and refine the dialogue of balancing in those cases where freedom of speech is one of the interests to be weighed.

CAN RIGHTS BE ABUSED?

Quite often in the context of discussions of freedom of speech one hears things such as 'the right to free speech does not include the right to abuse that freedom', or 'that is not free speech, that is an abuse of freedom', or 'people who abuse their freedom have no right to it', or 'there is a right to free speech, but people are responsible for abuses of that right'. But *can* freedom of speech be abused? 'Abuse of rights', 'abuse of freedom', and 'abuse of liberty' are locutions that invite closer analysis than is seen in popular discourse. Analysis of these locutions reveal them to be importantly ambiguous. The speaker who uses one of these expressions often leaves unclear whether the conduct referred to is inside or outside the right in question.

Suppose I tell my son he may use the car tonight. He takes the car, picks up several friends, and embarks on an evening of drinking and carousing, resulting in complaints to the police and damage to the car. In this case it would seem quite natural for me to say to him that he abused the right (or privilege) to drive the car.

Suppose instead I tell my son he may take the car tonight, but only for the purpose of going to a concert in Oxford. He drives to London. When I learn of this, I do *not* say he abused the right. Rather, I simply say he disobeyed me.

In the first example I say the right has been abused because his conduct (taking the car) was *within* the right granted by me. I did not say what could or could not be done with the car. I merely said he could use it. My son has abused the right *by exercising it,* but in a wrongful or irresponsible manner. The logic of 'abuse' presupposes that the right is in fact exercised. In the second example I do not say that he has abused the right, because he did not have the right to drive to London, nor did he have an unrestricted right to use of the car. By driving to London he has not abused a right; he has gone outside it.

Recall the saying, 'Your right to swing your arm ends where the other fellow's nose begins.' Is punching me in the nose an *abuse* of the right to swing your arm? No. It is beyond the right.

This demonstrates that an abuse of a right must be at the same time an exercise of that right. When a speaker says that *A* has abused his right to free speech by speaking in a particular way, the logic of 'abuse' means that the speaker necessarily presupposes that A's right to say these particular words was within the right to freedom of speech. And if this is so, then A had the right to say those words. To punish A for saying those words would mean that there is no right to utter them, and thus A did not abuse his right to free speech at all, but merely went outside it.

Thus, it is internally inconsistent to say, 'You have a right to free speech, but you are responsible for abuses of that right.' This means that an abuse would be punished. But if an 'abuse' is punishable it is outside the right. On such an interpretation there is no such thing as an impermissible or punishable abuse of a right. A speaker who uses 'abuse of rights' to refer to conduct that is outside the scope of the right is simply talking nonsense. 'Abuse' cannot be used to define or limit a right. If the speaker intends to say that some form of speech is outside the right to freedom of speech, and therefore subject to punishment, 'abuse' is the wrong word because it means just the opposite. If the speaker means that the right to free speech is not in fact a right to engage in all forms of speech, but only to engage in certain forms of speech, the locution 'abuse' is again misguided and misleading. The speaker is arguing that the right to free speech is not unlimited, that some forms of speech are not within the right. In this instance 'abuse' is unfortunate, because the proper use of 'abuse' implies that the conduct referred to is within the scope of the right, and that is inconsistent with the speaker's arguing that that conduct is outside that scope.

A use of 'abuse of the right to free speech' that *is* internally consistent is derived from the distinction between criticism and punishment.[11] To say that A abused the right to free speech by distributing, say, Nazi literature, can mean that A is subject to criticism for distributing Nazi literature, but is not subject to punishment for that act. To say that one is not permitted to abuse a right is not the same as saying that one *should not* abuse a right. Although there is no such thing as an impermissible or punishable abuse of a right, there can be an unwise or morally offensive exercise of a right, which is for that reason considered an abuse. If 'abuse' is a call for criticism but not a call for punishment, then A can at the same time have a right to distribute Nazi literature and still abuse his right to free speech by so doing.

Frequently one who criticizes an unpunishable act wishes that that act were subject to punishment. A speaker who uses 'abuse of the right to free speech' possibly is arguing that the right to free speech ought to be redefined or narrowed in order to exclude a particular form of speech, in the future making that form of speech not an abuse of the right to free speech, but rather a punishable act outside the scope of the right to free speech.[12]

In the *Philosophical Investigations* Wittgenstein says: 'Someone says to me: "Shew the children a game." I teach them gaming with dice, and the other says "I didn't mean that sort of game." ' Wittgenstein's intended meaning is not germane here. But the passage itself suggests that unexpected applications of language may lead us to be more precise in future uses of the same word or phrase. This is particularly applicable to 'freedom of speech', because that right is both more complex and more qualified than is suggested by the general word 'speech'. To say that someone has abused the right to free speech may be to say that the right ought to be clarified to ensure that it is clear that this particular form of speech is not within the right to free speech even though it is 'speech' in the ordinary language sense.

Finally, it is possible to justify and explain locutions like 'abuses of rights are not permitted' in terms of the distinction I have drawn between coverage and protection. From this perspective conduct can be at the same time both within a right yet not protected by it. By being within the right the conduct is presumptively, but not absolutely, protected. The presumption in favour of protection is rebuttable, and 'abuse' may be the generic term for those strong reasons (such as 'clear and present danger') with sufficient power to penetrate the presumptive protection of a right.

Arguments about the abuse of freedom of speech often appear in the context of words that are alleged to be crude, vulgar or offensive. The argument is made that moderate, reasoned, intellectual argument is protected, not speech that is inflammatory or offensive. Thus Archibald Cox has argued that although reasoned objection to conscription ought to be protected, the wearing of a jacket bearing the words 'Fuck the Draft' should not be, since it lowers the standard of public debate.[13] It has been argued also that although religious disagreement ought to be allowed, blasphemous publications should be prohibited because they only cause offence without contributing to serious debate about religious matters. In all of these cases the argument is essentially that people should not be permitted 'to go too far'.

It is certainly true that lessening the quality of public debate is one of the costs of a strong protection of freedom of speech. It is a particularly paradoxical cost since public debate itself is one of the primary advantages of a system of freedom of speech. Thus this cost not only opposes the justification but also detracts from it. Yet it is nevertheless difficult to accept such a limitation. Under the argument from truth it is extreme ideas that are in the greatest need of protection because it is here that failure to recognize our own fallibility is most likely. And under the argument from democracy the right to appeal to and mobilize public opinion is important. Dirty words and shocking speech are often more likely to do this than sober reasoned argument. This is unfortunate, but acceptance of democracy and the arguments derived from it involves accepting the standard of debate that in fact exists. It may be salutary for some to impose their ideas of proper debate on the population, but this approach is more opposed to a concept of democracy than based on it. The same considerations apply under the individualistic arguments for freedom of speech, for again the style of speech chosen by a speaker is as much a part of individualism as is the strictly propositional content of the message. But perhaps the strongest argument against such limitations comes from the argument from distrust of government. The more that words are caustic and angry, the more the regulatory authorities may see them as outside the range of permitted liberty. The power to impose rules of debate is all too often the power to decide which views shall be expressed and which shall not.

I do not mean to be taken as intimating that offence to individuals is not a harm that could in some circumstances outweigh freedom of speech, or that offence may not be a valid justification to respect in setting the boundaries of the Free Speech Principle. But if we do so it should be because we have identified offensiveness as a significant countervailing interest, not because the concept of free speech itself incorporates a set of rules for the 'proper' exercise of that freedom.

THE CONCEPT OF PRIOR RESTRAINT

Although I have considered the possibility that the weight of the Free Speech Principle may vary with the objects of the restriction, I have yet to deal with differing standards depending on the *form* of the restriction. I turn now to this important topic, important because the history of free speech doctrine has been pervaded by a distinction based solely on form – the concept of previous restraint, or prior restraint.

Prior restraints, as contrasted with subsequent punishments, constituted the primary evil towards which many of the earlier writings on freedom of the press were directed. Milton's *Areopagitica* is addressed solely to the problem of *prior* restraint represented by licensing of books and newspapers. It is the only form of restriction that Milton thought wrong. As long as no censor prevented the first publication of printed matter, Milton saw no objection to subsequent punishment based on the contents of the book. Similarly Blackstone, in volume IV of the *Commentaries*, defined freedom of the press as consisting solely of immunity from previous restraints. Any form of punishment for matter already printed was outside of his principle. Considerable evidence also exists that the First Amendment to the United States Constitution was intended merely to restrict prior restraints, although such an interpretation is not embodied in current American constitutional doctrine.

This dichotomy between previous restraint and subsequent punishment is reflected in contemporary legal doctrine. For example, a defamatory publication will not be restrained under English law if the publisher merely asserts that he will raise truth as a defence. In cases of subsequent punishment by civil damage remedies or criminal penalty, on the other hand, the publisher has the burden of proving truth in order to avoid the penalty. In the United States, prior restraints must meet an especially heavy, almost insurmountable, burden. It is a burden that is substantially greater than that which must be met to justify other forms of restriction on speech. Thus the United States Supreme Court refused to permit an injunction prohibiting the publication of the Pentagon Papers, although a majority of the justices thought it likely that the newspapers could thereafter be criminally prosecuted for endangering national security.[14] The question presented is whether we can justify this special aversion to previous restraint. Is there a principled distinction between prior restraint and subsequent punishment?

Prior restraint, or 'censorship' in the strict sense,[15] can take various forms. Under a licensing system, whether for books, films, newspapers or speeches in the park, *all* putative communications must be offered in advance to the censor or licensing body, which then approves or disapproves. Where such a system prevails, publication without securing advance approval is an independent offence without regard to the content of the publication. Such systems are still quite common for films, for example in England and the Republic of Ireland, but in the West are virtually non-existent for books or newspapers. A somewhat milder form of prior restraint occurs where there is no requirement that all publications be submitted in advance, but a publication found to be outside the protected range will be banned, either from further distribution of

149

that particular issue, or possibly any further distribution of that newspaper or magazine at all. I prefer to reserve the use of the word 'ban' for this type of prior restraint, where a named publication is prohibited although future issues so affected have yet to be printed or written. The third significant form of previous restraint is the judicial injunction, prohibiting a specific individual from publishing particular matter, punishable by sanctions for contempt of court. This may occur where the court has already seen, *in camera,* the entire publication at issue, as in the Pentagon Papers case in the United States and the thalidomide case in Great Britain, or where the injunction applies to a category of publication or category of subject matter, as in the normal pre-trial 'gag order' designed to prevent publicity prejudicial to a fair trial.

Despite the fact that these forms of control are in many ways more different than they are similar, they are all grouped together under current legal doctrine because they all seek to prevent rather than to punish, a distinction based on the temporal aspects of the official action. Under the doctrine of prior restraint, the timing of the governmental action commands a different result, or erects a higher barrier for justification. This distinction, however, appears on closer analysis to be without justification.

Several characteristics of systems of prior restraint are thought to justify the special apprehension of such restrictions. Standards are often broad and vague, inviting suppression of materials that ought to be protected, suppression based on personal prejudices and animosities, and an especially high risk of the error of over-suppression. Second, censorship boards are rarely in the hands of lawyers and almost never in the hands of judges. This leads to a lack of appreciation of applicable legal standards, to decisions more political than legal, and to application of the popular views of the moment without sufficient regard for minority rights or the long-range public interest. Third, censorship boards can be said to have a vested interest in prohibiting some speech. Censors are in business to censor. The compulsion to justify and exercise authority may lead to an aggressive and over-repressive exercise of the power to deny licences. Fourth, unlike formal judicial proceedings, licensing proceedings are rarely public. The public does not have the opportunity to scrutinize the actions of the licensing authority and thereby require strict adherence to the governing standards. Fifth, a prior restraint does not allow matter to be said or printed even once, thus keeping the information totally from the public, a feature not present with subsequent punishment. Sixth, violation of an injunction or suppression order involves an almost certain probability of punishment, because the order is directed at a particular act and at a particular individual, whereas subsequent punishment is in practice far less restrictive.

Although many of these reasons appear superficially persuasive, the justification for a distinct prior restraint doctrine collapses once we look at the issue in terms of what any free speech rule is designed to accomplish. In any area relating to freedom of speech, there will be a rule separating the protected from the unprotected. The existence of a sanction, prior or subsequent, means that some words have been found to be outside the protection of the Free Speech Principle. Whether the particular rule is correct is always open to question, but that substantive issue has little to do with the mechanics of the restriction. Given a rule, any rule, the primary aim, assuming the existence of any strong Free Speech Principle, is to accomplish the restriction while minimizing the suppression of that speech not covered by the rule.

In these terms we can see that subsequent punishment can have the effect of effectively suppressing protected speech even more than prior restraint. If, for example, the penalty for distributing an obscene motion picture is five years imprisonment, and if sentences of that magnitude are imposed with some regularity, then the effect is to impose on a putative film producer or distributor a certain amount of caution. Legal proceedings are of course not always 'correct' in their outcomes. Recall the previous discussion of uncertainty in the legal process. It is not unlikely that some films that are not in fact obscene will be found obscene by a court, and the possibility of such an outcome increases with the imprecision, as here, of the governing legal standard. A rational producer, therefore, will refrain from producing anything even close to the borderline, even if the film is not in fact obscene. The effect of the possibility of punishment, therefore, will be to prevent some publications from being made or distributed even though they would not or should not actually be punished. This risk is not, however, present in a system of prior restraint. Where subsequent punishment is the rule, borderline materials never see the light of day. But where some form of advance determination is possible, there is no risk in submitting even the close cases to the censor. Thus, those materials that are protected, although not plainly so, are more likely to emerge in a prior restraint system. Of course this works the same way for materials just on the unprotected side of the line. Something that is unprotected but only slightly so will not survive the censorship process. But given the uncertainty of criminal actions, such materials have a fair chance of remaining untouched. But if the regulating rule is correctly drawn, there is no reason to consider it a value that some unprotected materials can in fact be published. If the regulatory rule is incorrectly drawn, then subsequent punishment counteracts the error, but it is the error in the rule and not the method of enforcement that is at the nub of the problem.

The same can be said of the arguments based on the assumption that under a subsequent punishment system something can be said at least once, or that injunctions and some other prior restraints involve an absolute certainty of punishment. The short answer to this is that it is just not true that all material will surface at least once where subsequent punishment is the rule. An appreciation of the deterrent effects of a system of criminal or civil liability shows at once that a scheme of subsequent punishment prevents publication just as does a licensing scheme. But even if some material that would be prohibited by a licensing scheme will emerge under a punishment system, it is hard to see the value in this. Assuming that the rules and procedures applied by, say, a licensing board sufficiently satisfy the requirements of the Free Speech Principle, there appears little social utility in permitting the publication of that which has been properly determined to be without the protection of the principles of freedom of speech. In many cases objections to prior restraints are really objections to the underlying substantive rule, but that has nothing to do with the timing or method of restraint. And if someone feels that the importance of what they have to say is worth breaking the law to say it, they can as easily ignore a prior restraint as a criminal statute. To be sure the probability of punishment is higher in the former case, but it is hard to see how a *legal* principle can be based on the value of protecting civil disobedience.

Many of the objections based on the discretion, motives and qualifications of the censors are quite valid. But these flaws, although most often associated with prior restraints, are not necessarily part of them. Unchecked administrative discretion with frequent over-suppression can exist with subsequent punishment. The doctrine of prior restraint focuses on the largely irrelevant *timing* of the restraint, to the detriment of attention to those flaws that are the actual source of the objection. It is the identity and discretion of the restrainers and not the timing of the restraint that is important. Unfortunately, this factor remains obscured by continuing obeisance to the doctrine of prior restraint.

Bibliographical note to chapter 9

A parallel discussion of uncertainty and the risk of error, but in the context of specific American cases, is my 'Fear, risk, and the First Amendment: unraveling the "chilling effect" ', *Boston University Law Review* **58** (1978), 685. Important references on prior restraint include Vincent Blasi, 'Prior restraints on demonstrations', *Michigan Law Review* **68** (1970), 1482; Thomas Emerson, 'The doctrine of prior restraint', *Law and Contemporary Problems* **20** (1955), 648; Paul Freund, 'The Supreme Court and civil liberties', *Vanderbilt Law Review* **4** (1951), 533.

CHAPTER 10

Freedom for whom?

In *On Liberty* Mill excepted from the principles he advocated those societies still in a primitive or backward state, and those individuals who because of immaturity or mental disease could not be trusted to make decisions for themselves. In these classes of humanity the value of individualism was weakened, and independence of mind would lead more easily to folly and error than to wisdom and knowledge. Open discussion was only to be for those who could profit from it.

James Fitzjames Stephen seized on this exception to make an easy debater's point against Mill's entire argument. If there are individuals and societies not yet mature enough for liberty, Stephen argued, then it must be that the strong can and should guide the weak. And if this is so, Stephen went on, then consistency requires that on all levels of maturity and wisdom the strong should guide the weak. If the average should guide the dim, then why should not the bright guide the average? Although Stephen deployed this argument more against Mill's objections to paternalism than against Mill's position on the liberty of thought and discussion, the issue is directly relevant to a study of freedom of speech.

Most of the justifications for freedom of speech rest on some notion of popular competence. This is seen most starkly in those versions of the argument from truth that presume that the public has the ability consistently to separate truth from falsity. Even the weaker fallibility formulation of the argument from truth presupposes some considerable broad-based competence, since that argument presumes that as a rule errors will be identified to our benefit more often than errors will prevail to our detriment.

Similarly, the argument from democracy is premised on the ideal of equal and universal participation in the governmental process. The assumption is that the population is, if not perfect, at least competent to decide the general policies with which they will govern their lives. To do so they must deliberate about these policies. By respecting the argument from democracy we assume that this deliberation will have on balance beneficial results.

The arguments from individuality require if anything an even greater presumption of competence. When we say that everyone knows best how to run his life, or to make the choices that affect him, or that everyone's opinion is important, we assume that in some respects the similarities among people are more important than the differences, at least in terms of how government treats those people.

Finally, we should look at the arguments based on the perceived disadvantages of governmental control, whether by reason of incompetence or bias. By distrusting government, these arguments show at least a comparative faith in the public, holding that on average the population as a whole is more to be trusted than those it might select as its governors.

One difficulty with all of these arguments is the empirical basis on which the assumption of comparative popular competence rests. It seems clear that all people are not equally able to separate foolish ideas from wise ones, and that all people are not equally capable of making informed and rational judgments. If this is the case, then would it not be preferable to recognize these differences, and substitute the judgment of a wise and informed minority for the open deliberation of a possibly mediocre majority that produces unpredictable and often undesirable consequences? Should not government have an important educative function?

Casting government in the role of educator and enlightener is to a large extent inconsistent with recognition of a strong Free Speech Principle, because the educative function, when taken to its greatest extremes, requires the educator to promote good ideas and inhibit bad ones. This point was well recognized by Stephen in the last century, and by many others in this century. Nor is it a position that follows standard ideological categories. This view is seen in much of Marxist thought, and is seen as well in recent works such as Tussman's *Government and the Mind*, which those with a penchant for over-simplified characterizations would probably call 'conservative'.

Although there is a conflict between an educative government and a government constrained by a strong Free Speech Principle, a government that performs educative functions need not reject an independent principle of freedom of speech. Recognizing freedom of speech as a liberty in the narrow sense does not preclude a government from expressing its own views. Nor does the exis-

155

tence of liberty of speech deny to government the power to establish institutions that are educative or indoctrinating, such as public schools, state universities, public libraries, state-financed journals and government information agencies. Some of these institutions are more indoctrinating than others, but all represent some degree of governmental influence on the process of public deliberation. In large part the existence of these institutions does not create free speech problems. As long as we accept the notion of freedom of the will in the design of our institutions, we can maintain the distinction between governmental action to influence the mind and governmental action to foreclose from consideration certain ideas and information that others are willing to put forth. The latter presents free speech problems, but the former in most cases does not.

The difficulty with any strong limitation on freedom of speech supported by the belief that some people are more competent than others is that we have yet to devise a satisfactory system for reliably separating the more competent from the less competent. Although it is necessary that we select some to make decisions for us (and that may be a majority), and although ideally those so selected have considerable competence in general, this does not mean that those individuals are infallible or even more competent as to every issue that may come before them. A system of freedom of speech in one sense embodies the belief that the teachers may be wrong, and that the teachers frequently have much to learn from the students. There is a distinction between recognizing the educative role of government and designing a government on an educative model. When we design a government on the educative model we assume that education is a one-way process from the educator to those who are to be educated. When we recognize that this is not always the case, especially where government is the educator, then education and openness become not inconsistent but rather mutually supportive.

In extrapolating a general principle from Mill's exception, Stephen made the mistake of failing to recognize that Mill's exception for the immature was based on a balance of utility. Mill's exceptions were implicitly premised on the belief that those of insufficient maturity could not contribute enough to the search for knowledge to counterbalance the possibility that they might come to believe erroneous ideas. The presumed mediocre majority is not in the same position. The majority may too be misled. But not only is the danger less, the likelihood of the majority making a valuable contribution is also more. We must evaluate and balance both of these factors before we say that a group's argued lesser competence excludes it from participation in the process of public debate and deliberation.

Mill has been accused, by Maurice Cowling among others, of being an elitist. That is, Mill is said to have desired liberty of thought and discussion in order that a superior few might be free from the constraints imposed by a mediocre majority. I do not dispute this interpretation, for it points up an important distinction between for example Mill and Holmes, on the one hand, and critics such as Stephen and Tussman on the other. They all believe that some people are more gifted than others, and they might even all agree that in an ideal system the few should guide the many. But the latter group believes that we have the ability to identify those who are gifted and entrust them with the educative responsibility. The so-called elitists, however, are wary of this process of identification of the gifted, and are fearful that the selectors[1] may choose not those who are best but rather something short of that standard. Particularly in a majoritarian democracy there seems little possibility that the electorate will have the foresight and the perception to identify accurately those who are most gifted. This has certainly not been the experience in most existing democracies. Recognizing the danger that any system for selecting philosopher-kings is more likely to select kings than philosophers, we grant freedom of speech to the many as the only practicable way to insure freedom of speech for the best. Freedom of speech, as a means of facilitating communication, serves therefore as a means of lessening the gap between the rulers and the ruled, between those who decide and those who are bound by those decisions.

In lessening the gap between the rulers and the ruled, we of course lessen the power of the rulers. This is at times salutary and at times harmful. Those who wish to emphasize the teacher and student model for government implicitly adopt the belief that the gap between rulers and ruled ought not to be lessened, because the benefits are not worth the cost. This is an extraordinarily optimistic political philosophy, premised on the assumption that we are able to identify and entrust with power those who in practice are more likely to make the best decisions. Stephen was a great admirer of Hobbes, and Hobbes' views on the validity and efficacy of strong central authority are embodied in Stephen's views on freedom generally and freedom of speech in particular. For those who are more sceptical of strong central power and more sceptical of the ability of a population to select those who should wield it, freedom of speech is a palliative to the concentration of power and

157

is also a corollary to the view that the leaders may not have much less clay in their feet than those whom they lead. A Free Speech Principle need not acknowledge that all people are of equal competence; it only supports the belief that there is a fundamental distinction between knowing that some people are more competent and knowing who those people are; between recognizing that an elite exists in theory and having the ability to identify it in practice.

IS MOTIVE RELEVANT?

People speak for a countless number of reasons. Not only are there many different kinds of speech acts, but there are also for every possible speech act a large number of different motives that may have caused the speaker to engage in that speech act. The precise nature of those motives, although important for many purposes, is not central to a discussion of freedom of speech. One motive in particular, however, does appear especially relevant to a full analysis of the coverage of the principles of freedom of speech – the profit motive. In the prototypical free market economy, one who communicates solely in order to make a profit would be just as happy selling soap or iron bars. Under these circumstances can we justify holding that communication for profit is entitled to less free speech protection (or perhaps none at all) than those who communicate for 'higher' motives?

This is by no means a silly question. Some people who have thought very seriously about freedom of speech have found it inapplicable to profit-making activities. Alexander Meiklejohn, for example, believed that radio was not entitled to the protection of the First Amendment because 'it is not engaged in the task of enlarging and enriching communication. It is engaged in making money.'[2] This is a rather startling statement. Meiklejohn speaks as if the task of enlarging and enriching communication and the task of making money were mutually exclusive. There is no reason why this must be so. One can enlarge and enrich communication for the purpose of making money.

Still, we do perceive freedom of speech as in some sense a personal or individual right. If that is the case, then on what basis do we grant a right to free speech to corporations whose sole motive is profit? There are many people who are in the *business* of communication. Newspapers have a profit motive, *The Times* and *The Washington Post* as well as the sensationalist tabloids. Book publishers have a profit motive – they too are in the 'speech trade' just as other companies may be in the 'rag trade' or the 'shoe trade'. Even corporations whose main business is not communication may still communicate for money. I am not referring to advertising a product for sale, but rather to corporate communication that resembles the kind of speech traditionally covered by the Free Speech Principle. Thus, when an oil company publishes an advertisement arguing against restrictive environmental controls or in favour of import quotas, that company is speaking out on a matter of current political concern, but it does so in the service of a long-range profit motive. So too with a consortium of banks that speaks out in opposition to a proposal to nationalize large banks, or even a company that more abstractly extols the philosophical advantages of the free enterprise system. Is this kind of speech protected? Are corporate speakers as free from governmental interference as are individuals speaking solely from personal emotional or intellectual motives?

If freedom of speech is based on the interests of the speaker, and if the speaker's dignity or self-respect is the determinative factor, there seems little reason to extend that freedom to those whose only motive is profit. From this perspective a restriction on speech is a restriction on a product, no different to the corporation than requiring anti-pollutant devices on automobiles, prohibiting the sale of misbranded pharmaceuticals, or forbidding use of crocodile skins in the manufacture of belts and handbags. Of course not all profit-making enterprises are concerned solely with maximizing profit without regard to the product involved. I have no doubt that those who control *The Economist, The New York Times* and the like, have personal commitments to the process of communication that transcend the profit motives of an artificial creature of law. But a putative restriction on *corporate* communication would leave intact the ability of those *individuals* to communicate for whatever reasons and in whatever manner they chose.

If this conclusion sounds uncomfortable, and it does to me, I submit that it is because we do not think of free speech primarily as an interest of the speaker. True, it is speakers that we are protecting, and it is speakers who 'create' or 'produce' the ideas and information that under a Free Speech Principle we take to be so important. But under most versions of the argument from truth and the argument from democracy it is society's interest in knowledge and information that is important. The interest of the speaker is recognized not primarily as an end but only instrumentally to the public interest in the ideas presented. As a result the motives or corporate status of the speaker are almost wholly irrelevant.

Indeed, Meiklejohn's exclusion of radio because of its profit motive is particularly anomalous since it was Meiklejohn who first stressed that freedom of speech is primarily an interest of the listener. If that is so, then the motives of the speaker are beside the point.

Similarly, if the foundation of the Free Speech Principle is the notion of individual choice, as it is in the argument of Thomas Scanlon, then again it is the hearer's interest that is our primary concern. Freedom of speech makes possible, under such a theory, a wider range of choice, and a choice not artificially cramped by governmental intervention. But the choice is made not in the act of speaking, but in acting upon what is spoken. Speech informs us of the alternatives from which we can choose. So again if we are concerned with the range of arguments brought to bear on the individual's decision, we should care not about the source of the alternatives or the motives of those who suggest them.

The mistake made by those who talk of motives, or of 'deserving' a right to free speech, is that they fail to consider fully the nature of the interests being protected. To 'deserve' or 'earn' a right assumes that the right is granted for the sole benefit of the actor. As the example of profit-making speech shows, this view is too simple. Many great works have been produced for quite pedestrian reasons. *The Prince* was written not to provide the world with an important and controversial work, but to curry favour in the crassest sense. Much beneficial technology was developed for the original purpose of killing human beings during time of war. And for every worthless occupant of the pages of an academic journal that is written solely to gain promotion or tenure, there is an important contribution to knowledge published for precisely the same reason.[3] In dealing with free speech problems it is especially important that we look to the value of the product more than we look to the motives of the producer.

THE PARADOX OF TOLERANCE

The question of the deserving speaker is presented in stark relief in the context of what Karl Popper has called the 'Paradox of Tolerance'.[4] According to Popper, it may be paradoxical to allow freedom of speech to those who would use it to eliminate the very principle upon which they rely. There exist individuals or groups who believe that freedom of speech should be eliminated or greatly curtailed. Allowing freedom of speech to such people, it is argued, is allowing freedom of speech to be used for its own destruction. By permitting such individuals or groups to speak, we increase the probability of their gaining power (or so the paradox presumes), thereby undermining the process that generates the Free Speech Principle. Popper presented the paradox in reference to his version of the argument from truth, but it is present with reference to other arguments as well. The question is whether freedom of speech should be available to those who would, were they in power, eliminate or significantly restrict the liberty of speech under which they claim the right to speak.

The problem presented by the paradox is more than hypothetical. The argument from the paradox has been employed in England by those who seek statutes, regulations, judicial decisions, or enforcement practices restricting the activities of the National Front. In the United States the same argument was relied upon by those who sought (unsuccessfully) to ban the march of the American Nazi Party in Skokie, Illinois. It is an argument that has been and is to some extent still employed in opposing freedom of speech for Communists and others of the political left. It is also a principle that has been specifically embodied in the Universal Declaration of Human Rights and the European Convention on Human Rights, the latter providing that 'Nothing in this Convention may be interpreted as implying for any State, group, or person any right to engage in any activity or perform any act aimed at the destruction of any of the rights and freedoms set forth herein or at their limitation to a greater extent than is provided for in the Convention.' This article has been interpreted to permit the outlawing of the German Communist Party, and an analogous provision in the German Constitution was relied on to support the banning of neo-Nazi parties.

I concede that I may not have presented the argument in its most favourable light. The argument becomes stronger when it is related to a particular justification for freedom of speech, especially a justification based on the premises of fallibilism. If, with Popper and Mill, we say that any belief may be wrong, that knowledge advances by the continual process of identifying error, then the end of such challenges to accepted doctrine would mark the end of the progress of knowledge. Because this would be such a serious consequence, the progress of knowledge in general can be taken as more important than the gaining of any particular piece of knowledge. Thus the end of open enquiry is a harm greater than that caused by any particular error, because open enquiry is the foundation of the identification of all errors. With this as the assumed premise, it is not surprising that Popper argues that the goals of tolerance may demand that we not tolerate the intolerant.

161

Those who would destroy the continuing process of open enquiry threaten the basis of all knowledge and therefore ought to be suppressed, at least if the danger to the system of freedom of speech is real and not purely imaginary.[5] Popper did not relate his discussion of the paradox of tolerance to specific groups, but it appears that he would support the current argument that freedom of speech ought not to be allowed to those whose goal is the destruction of open enquiry.

This position is consistent with the fact that the argument from truth in any strong form establishes the advance of knowledge in a position of lexical priority over all other values, a question I discussed in chapter 2. Because the advance of knowledge stands above all other values, attacks on this advance, whether by speech or otherwise, must, according to the proponents of this theory, be opposed.

Popper, the seeming opponent of ideology, has been criticized for himself supporting what is also an ideology, an ideology of the advantages of openness.[6] This of course parallels the objection that has been made to other forms or applications of scepticism. A sceptic is one who doubts all statements except this one. But this is not the place to discuss scepticism as a general epistemological problem. The point here is that whether Popper is right or wrong about the underlying theory, he *is* consistent. One who takes a version of the argument from truth as the sole basis for freedom of speech must fight against attacks on that foundation, even if those attacks are in the form of speech. If we allow people to question the assumption that more speech leads to more knowledge, then we risk having the whole system toppled.

This resolution of the problem, however, assumes that some governmental body will have the ability to identify those individuals or groups that constitute a threat to the continuing existence of a system of freedom of speech. But if we see freedom of speech as based on a perceived inability to perform this type of function, then the resolution of the paradox differs from that which might be reached under other theories of free speech. For here the regulation of the speech is the very evil at which the Free Speech Principle is addressed. The issue is not whether totalitarian groups should be allowed to speak, but whether anyone should have the power to decide which groups are totalitarian and which are not – whether we can with confidence entrust to a licensing authority, to a county council, or to a court the power to withhold privileges from groups because they are *perceived* as being totalitarian, anti-democratic, or fascist. The problem is not whether the Nazis should be allowed to speak, but whether we can establish an institution to decide which groups threaten freedom and which do not. As I tried to emphasize in Part I, the very inability to perform this type of categorizing provides one of the strongest arguments for a principle of freedom of speech, and therefore the denial of free speech rights to those who are 'fascists', 'racists', or 'totalitarians' is as much at the core of the Free Speech Principle as would be the denial of the same rights to Democrats, Republicans, Liberals, Conservatives, or Catholics.

Bibliographical note to chapter 10

Also of interest in reference to this chapter are Marvin Glass, 'Anti-racism and unlimited freedom of speech', *Canadian Journal of Philosophy* 8 (1978), 559; Glenn Schram, 'The First Amendment and the educative function of law', *American Journal of Jurisprudence* 20 (1975), 38.

PART III

APPLICATIONS

CHAPTER 11

Defamation

THE VALUE OF REPUTATION

The theoretical validity of some form of remedy for defamation (libel and slander) has been in the past so much of a problem for free speech theory that it was not treated as a problem at all. Faced with the incontrovertible fact that defamatory statements can and do cause serious harm to individuals, traditional arguments for freedom of speech chose to avoid the problem by holding defamation simply to be an exception to the principles of free speech. But defamatory speech does in many instances share the characteristics of the speech that is covered by the principles of free speech, and merely stating that it is outside the Free Speech Principle is analytically unsound. If defamation is not encompassed by the principles of freedom of speech there must be a reason why, a reason drawn from the deep theory underlying the Free Speech Principle.

Harm to reputation is in many cases an immediate and visible harm. If I am accused of being dishonest or untrustworthy, or if a reviewer of this book charges me with professional incompetence, I am injured in any way imaginable except physical pain and bodily damage. Communication of defamatory statements, especially if the objects of the communication are those whose esteem I value, causes me clear harm, perhaps more if the statements are false but not much less so, as far as *I* am concerned, if the statements are true. This direct and highly visible harm has led many people to treat defamation as an exception to the Free Speech Principle, but this follows only if we erroneously view the protection of speech as based on its harmlessness. If speech is protected because it is taken to be a self-regarding act, then the plainly other-regarding nature of defamatory utterances takes those utterances out of a Free Speech Principle based on grounds of harmlessness. And if speech is protected because it does not cause particular and immediate harm to the interests of others, then again libel and slander fall wholly without the scope of the principles of free speech. But once we realize, as we must, that virtually all speech acts are other-regarding, and that a great variety of communication can cause particular and immediate harm to the interests of others, then an exception for defamation is less comprehensible. If the mere existence of harm excludes utterances from the scope of the Free Speech Principle, then the Free Speech Principle becomes co-extensive with a Harm Principle, and the former is no longer a distinct doctrine of political philosophy. But when we perceive the Free Speech Principle as recognizing the other-regarding quality of speech but still establishing a higher standard of justification for its restriction, then the notion of an 'exception' for defamatory words seems odd, at least where the defamatory harm provides the basis for the alleged exception.

It is or should be clear that reputation is itself a valuable personal interest. Iago's observation that 'he that filches from me my good name . . . makes me poor indeed' strikes a responsive chord for most people. It may be that a harm to reputation is so serious that it is sufficient to meet the higher burden of justification established by the Free Speech Principle. The value of reputation may be so great that its protection outbalances even the added weight of the interest in freedom of speech. But these are problems that must be addressed, and uncritical acceptance of an 'exception' is of little assistance.

THE PROBLEM OF SELF-CENSORSHIP

The intricacies of the law of defamation have occupied numerous books, law journal articles and court cases. It is not my intention here to delve into the legal niceties of defamation law. For purposes of initiating this discussion, it is sufficient to note that defamation includes libel (written) and slander (oral), and is defined as the publication (communication) to a third person of words (and sometimes other forms of communication) containing an untrue imputation against the reputation of another.[1] Although criminal libel is nominally recognized in most common law countries, libel and slander are most commonly treated as torts, giving the person whose reputation is damaged a right of action for money damages (and occasionally a retraction) against the person who uttered the defamatory words. Civil law countries recognize an analogous but not identical wrong, but the remedy is more often through the criminal law rather than a basis for a private suit for damages. For the purpose of this book it will be satisfactory to work with the basic common law definition, which is accepted in virtually all countries whose law is derived from the English common law.

The conflict between the law of defamation and freedom of speech is not always fully appreciated, in large part because it is *false* factual propositions that are penalized by the remedy for libel and slander. If I charge a person with having committed an act he did not commit, or owing money he does not owe, or having characteristics he does not possess, it is difficult at first to see that there is any problem. After all, falsehood does not normally contribute to public debate, but rather detracts from it.[2] To the extent that we punish harmful falsity, it can be said, we punish that which has no value to the exchange of ideas and thereby raise the standard of public discussion.

Standing alongside the presumed lack of value in misstatements of fact are two other goals, both of which are closely aligned with some of the goals of a principle of freedom of speech, especially those goals derived from the argument from truth and the argument from democracy. First, there is the goal of actively encouraging the dissemination of accurate information. Although one solution to the problem of erroneous information would be to inhibit the flow of all information, such a solution would unduly sacrifice the value of the advance of knowledge and also the value of information to public and private decision-making. So although falsity is bad, its suppression must accommodate the affirmative advantages of fostering truth. Second, there is, especially under the argument from democracy, great value in the uninhibited flow of evaluative commentary. Opinion and comment are less susceptible of characterization as true or false. Nevertheless, opinion and comment contribute greatly to public discussion, and the goal of eliminating misstatements of fact should, where freedom of speech is an acknowledged principle, not cause an excess sacrifice of comment, criticism, opinion and evaluation.

The traditional view has been that all of these goals are compatible. Thus there is in the common law the defence of fair comment, under which a statement on a matter of public concern is not actionable if it is solely a comment, however critical or harmful, founded on accurate statements of the underlying facts. By requiring that the statements of fact be accurate, it is supposed, we foster truth in public dialogue while still giving free rein to the expression of opinion on matters in which the public has a legitimate interest. On the level of abstract theory the common law has aimed to protect commentary while at the same time recognizing the lack of social value in the publication of errors of fact.

This approach, however, assumes a congruence between the legal rule and its practical effect. It is more realistic, however, to look at the imprecision in any system of enforcing legal penalties, and the effect of that imprecision on human conduct. The recognition of that imprecision was one of the leading contributions of the school of jurisprudence known as American Realism, and the law of defamation provides one of the clearest areas for application of the theory of the American Realists, in particular the fact-scepticism of Judge Jerome Frank.

As Frank often pointed out, courts are frequently wrong. Some error is inherent in any process of fact-finding, and the legal process is no different. Thus, in applying the law of defamation, it is necessary to recognize that judicial determination of truth or falsity may occasionally be in error. That which is true may be found by a court to be false. To the extent that this happens, a rule penalizing factual falsity may penalize truth. Thus a publisher of defamatory matter he knows to be true must still consider the possibility that a court will hold otherwise and impose liability. To the extent that the burden of proving truth is on the publisher, the risk is increased, since there is added to the possibility of judicial error the possibility that the burden of proof as to truth will not be met, even if the published statements are true. Thus a rule that punishes falsity may at times punish truth, and a putative publisher may refrain from publishing truth for fear that it will erroneously be found to be false and therefore be penalized.

Even more importantly, a publisher may at times be mistaken in his belief in the factual truth of what is published. Because it is often either not feasible or not possible to verify every statement made to a demonstrable certainty, a publisher must either publish the facts knowing that liability may be incurred, or refrain from publishing owing to a desire to avoid that risk. To the extent that the latter course of action is chosen, some degree of *self-censorship* exists. Self-censorship is of course salutary when the unpublished statements are not true. But the important point is that the uncertainty and risk inherent in the legal process means that some impelled self-censorship exists as to statements that are true. The desire to avoid liability will produce caution, and some of that caution will extend to statements that are indeed accurate, although it will not always be possible to prove them to be so.

Finally, the expense and inconvenience of litigation serves to magnify the deterrent effect, because a publisher may effectively be penalized even if he ultimately prevails in the legal system. And if he does not prevail, the litigation costs, when added to the damages to be paid, serve to increase the penalty and therefore magnify the risk.

Because of these uncertainties and risks in the process of ascertaining truth, a rule penalizing falsity has the actual effect of inducing some self-censorship as to statements *that are in fact true.* Just as a rule that seeks to maximize the extent of punishment of guilty persons will also punish some innocent persons, so too does a rule that maximizes the deterrence or punishment of falsity deter and punish some truth as well. The problem is inevitably one of balancing interests, because we penalize falsity at the expense of inhibiting the presumably valuable dissemination of truth, but we grant the greatest freedom for the spread of truth only by adopting rules that will permit the circulation of an increased amount of defamatory falsehood. Given the value of the circulation of accurate information, and given the harm of defamatory falsehood, no solution at either extreme seems tenable.

Recalling the discussion of error analysis from chapter 9, it is easy to see two possible errors. One error is an erroneous prohibition of valuable speech, as when true statements are either penalized or deterred. If there is value in the search for knowledge and in public deliberation, then truth that remains unspoken is as much if not more of an error than statements of truth that are punished. The other error occurs when we wrongly permit unprotected speech to be circulated, as when we fail to punish that which is both harmful and false. Now harm to reputation is often a very serious harm, and reputation is an important value worthy of strong protection. But if we recognize a strong principle of freedom of speech, then the balance must be struck in a way that recognizes that an erroneous penalty on speech is a harm of special magnitude.

This method of looking at the problem is exemplified by the recent and extreme divergence from the common law of the American law of defamation. Because the First Amendment to the Constitution of the United States specifically protects freedom of speech and freedom of the press, and because there is no *constitutional* protection of reputation, what results is a *stipulated* strong priority for freedom of speech. Given this priority, it follows that an error of over-suppression or over-deterrence is treated more seriously than an error of under-protection of reputation. An unpublished truth is a more serious error than a wrongful injury to reputation. As a result, the American law of defamation has been drastically modified in several respects.

First, a public official or a public figure may recover damages for defamation only if he can show not only that the allegations against him were untrue, but also that they were published with actual knowledge of their falsity, or at least a suspicion of falsity and subsequent disregard of whether the statements were true or false. It should be clear, as in fact has been the result, that this is a burden virtually impossible for any defamed person to meet. As a result, many false allegations against public officials and public figures remain unpunished. However, awareness of the degree of protection on the part of publishers results in a great deal more being published, most of it true, about public officials and public figures than would have been the case in the absence of such strong protection. In many instances reputations are indeed sacrificed to the goals of a strong and free press, but this is thought to be a price worth paying when the alternative is the protection of reputation at the sacrifice of the loss of some publication of important truth.

Similarly, in the United States the burden of proving falsity in all cases is now on the defamed plaintiff, although at common law it is up to the publisher to prove truth as an affirmative defence. This is more than a procedural technicality. The burden of proof is one way in which the balance between protection of reputation and protection of freedom of speech is determined. There may be many cases in which the published statements are in fact true, but where a publisher will not be able so to demonstrate to the satisfaction of a jury. In such cases publication of truth is penalized, and in other cases the existence of this burden deters the publication of truth. The remedy, shifting the burden of proof to the defamed individual, also has its cost, for then there will be cases in which the published statements are false but the injured party will be unable to prove them so in court, resulting in the error of permitted defamatory falsehood. But where freedom of speech has a priority over the interest in a good reputation, it is the former error that is more serious than the latter, and recognition of the priority relationship leads to a shift in the burden of proof.

Only those who ignore reality would suppose that the defence of fair comment in English law, which requires factual accuracy, does not deter some truthful commentary as well. But where speech is not by stipulation pre-eminent such deterrence of publication of truth may be an acceptable price to pay for an effective system of protecting individual reputations. But if freedom of speech is assumed to be more important than virtually everything else, as it is under the American Constitution, then the inevitable balancing process must be heavily weighted in favour of protecting speech, and therefore heavily weighted against the protection of other interests.

PUBLIC FIGURES AND PRIVATE LIVES

Recognition of uncertainty in the legal process and the consequent recognition of the possibility of self-censorship means that under a strong Free Speech Principle reputations must at times be sacrificed to the goals of freedom of speech. But this result is compelled only if the statements at issue come within the coverage of the Free Speech Principle. If some categories of speech are not covered at all, then the weighted process just discussed may be inapplicable. It is therefore useful to look more closely at the various types of defamatory utterances, because it is possible that some are totally outside the coverage of the Principle.

Let us look at two examples. First, suppose a newspaper reports that a cabinet minister owns shares in a company that is subject to the control of that cabinet minister in his official capacity. Second, imagine a conversation in a pub between two men, in which the first tells the second that a third man, not present, is a thief.

In looking at these examples we tend to think instantly of free speech issues for the first example, but not for the second example. Although the public discussion of official conduct plainly involves free speech considerations, private gossip appears far-removed from the goals of the principles of freedom of speech. Cases lying between these extremes are more problematic. The differences are explained by looking at the types of discourse that relate to the aims of the Free Speech Principle.

The argument from democracy provides a justification for special treatment of discussion of public issues and the conduct and qualifications of public servants. The qualifications and performance of our leaders is of such vital concern to the public that the loss of some of that information further detaches governmental officials and policies from responsibility to and control by the populace. Here the loss of truth is most serious, and this can be avoided only by sacrificing some number of individual reputations. In some ways this is a lesser harm than it would be in the case of the reputation of a private individual. One entering public life offers his qualifications and performance for evaluation by the public and invites public scrutiny of his actions. He has in effect assumed the risk. In these cases the principles of freedom of speech compel a strong weighting in favour of public discussion, including the occasional falsity that comes with vigorous discussion of issues, and away from a strong interest in reputation. A rule either denying any remedy or making the remedy very difficult most effectively serves the goals of the Free Speech Principle.

There is a fine line between individual qualifications and public performance, and there is also a fine line between what is perceived as an attack on one's reputation and what is criticism of one's policies. As a result, libel actions brought by public officials can in many cases seem remarkably similar to actions for seditious libel. If the argument from democracy and the arguments from separation of citizen and government have validity, then the danger of allowing public officials to bring actions based on attacks on their official conduct is so great that it outweighs any interest in the reputations of public officials.

The case of the public figure not involved in the governmental process is more difficult. In many instances individuals not in government have as much if not more effect on political policy than those with official positions. There is legitimate concern with the performance and qualifications of the president of General Motors, the leader of the Trades Union Council, or the administrator of a major private hospital. But on the other hand the private lives of pop stars and professional footballers, for example, while clearly of interest to the public, are of less legitimate concern. Information that interests the public is not necessarily information whose dissemination is in the public interest. It is true that public figures, like public officials, assume the risk of unfavourable publicity. But assumption of the risk is a circular concept. The risk of publication of false information exists for the very reason that there may be insufficient legal protection. If falsity were more stringently penalized, presumably there would be less publication of falsity and therefore less of a risk to assume. Moreover, public interest in the lives and qualifications of many public figures is of a different order of legitimate importance than it is for governmental officials. Obviously there are gradations here, and this is not the place to suggest the exact legal rules that might properly take account of these gradations. But the point is that the legal rule enacted must take account of a great number of variables: the degree to which an individual assumes the risk of unfavourable and erroneous publicity; the degree to which the individual benefits from and perhaps solicits or encourages publicity; the degree to which the private activities of an individual are relevant to that person's public performance; and the degree to which the public interest is furthered by the dissemination of additional information about that individual or others in a similar position.

Where purely private individuals are concerned, however, there is substantial doubt as to whether the principles of freedom of speech apply at all. Where the communication as well as the subject matter is private, as in back-fence gossip, there appears no reason to hold such communication to be covered by the Free Speech Principle. A review of the various justifications underlying recognition of the principle reveals none that justify any special protection for conduct of this type. Because the communication does not bear on any issue as to which public truth is important or public error harmful, none of the more positive justifications is helpful. And because the issue arises in the context of a private legal action, with no governmental body making the determination of truth or falsity, freedom of speech as a protection against governmental determinations of doctrine is inapplicable. This is not to say that legal rules dealing with private defamation necessarily need to be strict. It only means that the balance of policy considerations that yields the ultimate legal rule need not be warped by an inapt application of the principles of freedom of speech.

A more difficult problem arises in the context of the treatment of private individuals in the public forum, for example in books, newspapers, magazines, broadcasting or public speeches. If a private person is involved in a matter that has some public importance, should the rules of defamation be the same as those applied to communication not involving a public issue? Although there might be more concern for free speech here, the important point seems to be that in discussions about private individuals the concern about the freedom to name the particular person involved (as opposed to describing the event) is so slight that again the rules ought not to be influenced by free speech considerations. It is not unreasonable to say that he who makes a private person into a public figure assumes the risk of falsity, and thus acts at his peril. The interest in avoiding falsity where private individuals are concerned seems greater than the interest in acquiring and disseminating knowledge.[3] Unless we place very little value on privacy, we ought not to encourage its unwarranted elimination.

PRIVACY AND TRUTH

If we acknowledge a category of communication in which the public interest in avoiding falsity is greater than the public interest in acquiring knowledge, then we have accepted the view that the interest in the acquisition of knowledge may at times fall before the weight of stronger interests. This also entails the proposition that some knowledge is more valuable than other knowledge. In many cases the acquisition of knowledge or the identification of error constitutes a benefit either to a particular individual or to society at large. But in other cases it is difficult to see how the acquisition of knowledge advances any worthy interest.

Thus, in terms of publishing information about other people, there are instances in which truth is not necessarily desirable. If I reveal someone's long-past criminal record, for example, I may very well damage his reputation with accurate information. Moreover, I can through revelations of truth cause damage other than injury to reputation. For example, if I were to publish in a newspaper an explicit photograph of a husband and wife engaging in 'normal' sexual relations, I can imagine no way in which their reputations would be damaged, assuming that there was no question but that the photograph was taken without their knowledge or consent. Nevertheless the obvious embarrassment and humiliation they would suffer is undoubtedly a very real injury. One can imagine a similar consequence from the disclosure of a physical deformity, even though again there has been no damage to reputation.

In the United States but not in England the tort of invasion of privacy would cover many instances of this type. In this respect invasion of privacy and the validity of truth as an absolute defence to defamation actions present an almost identical issue. Does the disclosure of the truth always create free speech problems? Is the public interest in private information sufficient to outweigh the harm caused? I find it difficult to justify an affirmative answer to this question. It is superficial to say that all knowledge is necessarily valuable. Knowledge as to the affairs and past of purely private persons serves little if any public purpose. Moreover, disclosure of private facts, in addition to causing embarrassment and humiliation, infringes on the individual's interest in controlling certain aspects of his life. When facts about me that I prefer to keep secret are disclosed by another, I have been denied control over my life, my choices and my personality.

It may be that in many instances there is something to be gained from such disclosures. Certainly that is the case where the person is standing for or holding public office and is thus placing his personality before the electorate for scrutiny. The same may hold true where by entering the public arena some persons desire to benefit from publicity about their lives. Perhaps in these instances the control over private facts has been relinquished. But in the absence of such relinquishment of control, and in the absence of some public interest in the particular truth asserted, it is hard to see why truth *per se* entails an unrestricted right to speak.

It is not an easy matter to decide whether a particular truth is or is not in the public interest. Nor is it any easier to decide in all cases which individuals have relinquished their privacy and which have not. But when an action for compensation is brought by an individual not holding any governmental position, and when the decision is made by a jury not beholden to any governmental authority, the dangers inherent in governmental selection among forms of speech are not present. A private lawsuit is not always the answer to any free speech problem. To take it as a remedy, for example, for the abuses that may occur when criticism of government is concerned is in some sense to extend to the majority the determination of what is a right against the majority. But purely private speech involves no such problems, and developing legal principles and rules to separate the public from the private is central to both enforcing the Free Speech Principle and keeping it within its proper scope.

Bibliographical note to chapter 11

A more specifically legal discussion is my 'Social foundations of the law of defamation: a comparative analysis', *Journal of Media Law and Practice* **1** (1980), 3. Useful additional references are Stanley Ingber, 'Defamation: a conflict between reason and decency', *Virginia Law Review* **65** (1979), 785; Melville Nimmer, 'The right to speak From *Times* to *Time:* First Amendment theory applied to libel and misapplied to privacy', *California Law Review* **56** (1968), 935.

CHAPTER 12

Obscenity

THE CONCEPT OF THE OBSCENE

The legal and philosophical issues surrounding the regulation of obscene publications have traditionally been a fertile field for the application of free speech theory. In large part this interest has been occasioned by the excesses of the past. When works such as Theodore Dreiser's *An American Tragedy*, Radclyffe Hall's *The Well of Loneliness*, and James Joyce's *Ulysses* have been found to be obscene and therefore suppressed, we are properly wary of granting to government the authority to ban publications on the grounds of obscenity. But most powers are susceptible of excess or erroneous application, and we should not let the existence of abuses be a substitute for close analysis of the issues involved in the problem of obscenity.

The regulation of obscenity is thought to serve a number of different goals. First, it is argued that obscene publications are immoral, and that the community's interest in maintaining its standards of morality allow or even compel the restriction of publications that are inconsistent with the prevailing moral norms. This was the argument first employed to support the regulation of obscenity in the eighteenth century, and it is an argument frequently made today. Second, many people have argued and have sought to demonstrate that obscene publications cause certain antisocial acts. In the weaker form of the argument, it is claimed that obscene publications cause people to engage in activities that are themselves quite controversially the subject of legal control. Examples would be adultery, homosexuality and various forms of sexual 'perversion'. The controversy about the harm of the effects is not present in the stronger form of the argument, which seeks to demonstrate that obscene publications lead to acts whose illegality is beyond moral question, such as rape and child molestation. The strength of this argument depends on the strength of the underlying empirical evidence. This evidence is quite inconclusive, with some studies finding that there is no causal link between obscenity and crime, others holding that the causal link is quite strong, and still others falling somewhere in between. Third, it is argued that regulating obscenity is justified on environmental grounds. One form of this argument appeals to the notion of a moral environment, but in this form the argument duplicates the arguments based on morality *per se*. More recently, however, some have argued that the proliferation of sexually explicit materials makes a community uglier and leads to urban decay. Under this argument obscenity should be regulated for the same reason that we regulate architecture, urban development, location of factories and the use of green spaces in city planning. Finally, there is the argument from offensiveness. One version of the argument holds that people are offended by being forced to see obscene materials, and therefore it is justifiable to restrict public displays of obscenity. The stronger version of the argument holds that people are offended by the knowledge that such materials are available, and that the offence is not eliminated by removing the materials from public display. Under either version the argument is that offensiveness, as much as harm in the strict sense, is a legitimate justification for governmental control.

Although legal usage has often caused us to associate obscenity with sex, the etymology of the word 'obscene' compels no such conclusion. 'Obscene' refers to that which is repugnant or disgusting to the senses, or offensive, filthy, foul, repulsive, or loathsome. 'Pornography', however, from the Greek for 'harlot' and 'writing', refers only to erotic sexual depictions. Thus obscenity may or may not be pornographic, and pornography may or may not be obscene. It is not incorrect to say that war or gory violence is obscene, nor is it incorrect to describe a pornographic work as beautiful or important. Yet despite this divergence in dictionary definition, there is considerable overlap in current usage.[1] Most of what the laws of most countries include within the term 'obscenity' is in fact pornographic, and much of what is pornographic is widely held to be obscene. Recognizing, therefore, that non-sexual material such as depictions of violence may be within the concept of obscenity, and intending to return to that theme later in this chapter, I still wish to stay close to current usage and therefore commence with a discussion of sexually oriented obscenity.

The continuing debate over the propriety of regulating obscene publications has produced an avalanche of literature – political, legal, sociological, psychological and historical. There is no indication that the speed of this avalanche is decreasing. Unfortunately, what most of this literature shares is a juxtaposition of two related but still separate issues. One is the general issue relating to the proper extent of governmental power over the lives and activities of individuals. The other is the free speech issue, which is frequently mentioned because obscene materials most often occur in verbal or pictorial form.[2]

The arguments relating to governmental power in general appear in several different versions. It is often argued, for example, that obscene publications should not be controlled because their use is either private or causes no harm to others, and that activities causing no identifiable harm to others are no proper concern of the state. Another form of the argument is that morality in general, or certain types of moral judgments, should not be enforced through the legal system – that the immorality of obscene publications, however plain, is insufficient to justify legal proscription. Finally, some people have contended that obscene materials in particular, or open sexuality in general, are positively good, either by providing an outlet for sexual frustration, or by encouraging a healthier view of sexuality, or by breaking down irrational sexual taboos, or by encouraging sexual experimentation.

This debate is a long tunnel with no apparent end. But I want to emphasize here that this debate is largely irrelevant to a discussion of free speech. The arguments about obscenity parallel the arguments about homosexuality, adultery, and 'unnatural' sexual practices. There is also a close connexion with the arguments about regulating gambling, alcohol, and marijuana, and requiring the wearing of motorcycle helmets and automobile seat belts. I wish to stay well clear of this well-rehearsed topic. In the context of an analysis of freedom of speech, the question is whether the verbal or pictorial character of obscene materials demands, in deference to the principles of free speech, a different mode of analysis. Does a Free Speech Principle provide a distinct argument against regulation of obscene publications, independent of arguments relating to enforcement of morals, paternalism or self-regarding conduct? Does a heightened free speech interest diminish the force of the arguments in favour of regulating obscene publications in a way that it does not with respect to arguments in favour of regulating other forms of sexual conduct? This separation of free speech considerations from other principles is one of the central themes of this book, and it is particularly important in the context of a discussion of obscenity.

IS OBSCENITY SPEECH?

Because obscene publications are by definition verbal or pictorial, it is natural to assume that they are a form of speech and that their regulation is consequently a free speech problem. But if we bear in mind that the word 'speech' in the concept of freedom of speech is a term of art bearing a close relationship to the justifications undergirding the concept of free speech, then it is less clear that all forms of pornography are necessarily speech in this technical sense.

Let us suppose a hypothetical extreme example of what is commonly referred to as 'hard core pornography'. Imagine a motion picture of ten minutes' duration whose entire content consists of a close-up colour depiction of the sexual organs of a male and a female who are engaged in sexual intercourse. The film contains no variety, no dialogue, no music, no attempt at artistic depiction, and not even any view of the faces of the participants. The film is shown to paying customers who, observing the film, either reach orgasm instantly or are led to masturbate while the film is being shown.

I wish to argue that any definition of 'speech' (or any definition of the coverage of the concept of freedom of speech) that included this film in this setting is being bizarrely literal or formalistic.[3] Here the vendor is selling a product for the purpose of inducing immediate sexual stimulation. There are virtually no differences in intent and effect from the sale of a plastic or vibrating sex aid, the sale of a body through prostitution, or the sex act itself. At its most extreme, hard core pornography is a sex aid, no more and no less, and the fact that there is no physical contact is only fortuitous.

Thus a refusal to treat hard core pornography as speech in the technical sense at issue is grounded in the belief that the prototypical pornographic item shares more of the characteristics of sexual activity than of communication. The pornographic item is a sexual surrogate. It takes pictorial or linguistic form only because some individuals achieve sexual gratification in that way. Imagine a person going to a house of prostitution and, in accord with his particular sexual preferences, requesting that two prostitutes engage in sexual activity with each other while he becomes aroused. Having achieved sexual satisfaction in this manner, he pays his money and leaves, never having touched either of the prostitutes. Or imagine a person who asks that a leather-clad prostitute crack a whip within an inch of his ear. These are hardly free speech cases. Despite the fact that eyes and ears are used, these incidents are no more communicative than any other experience with a prostitute. This is physical activity, the lack of physical contact notwithstanding.

If the above examples are not free speech cases, there seems no difference between the same activity when presented on film rather than in the flesh. Consider further rubber, plastic or leather sex aids. It is hard to find any free speech issues in their sale or use. If hard core pornography is viewed merely as a type of aid to sexual satisfaction, any distinction between pornography and so-called 'rubber products' collapses. The mere fact that in pornography the stimulating experience is initiated by visual rather than tactile means is irrelevant if every other aspect of the experience is the same. Neither involves communication in the way that language or pictures do.

My point is that much pornography is more accurately treated as a physical rather than a mental experience. This is of course an over-simplification. Physical sensations, including sexual arousal, have mental elements. Pain, for example, is both physical and mental. But the presence of a mental element in what is primarily a physical act does not create a communicative act. That I adore escargots, while others find them disgusting, is not caused by any physiological differences in taste buds. It is primarily a mental distinction. But that does not make the sale or ingestion of escargots an activity covered by the principles of freedom of speech.

It has been argued, however, that serious literature as well as hard core pornography may evoke this same type of physical or quasi-physical arousal. No doubt many people have been aroused by *Lady Chatterley's Lover*, and there are probably people somewhere who are aroused sexually by the plays of Shakespeare, by the *Kinsey Report*, or even by *Bambi*. People may become sexually excited by art or music; it is said that Hitler's speeches had the effect of arousing some of his listeners. I do not dispute any of this, but it misconceives the issue. It is not the presence of a physical effect that triggers the exclusion from coverage of that which would otherwise be covered by the principle of free speech. Rather, it is that some pornographic items contain *none* of the elements that would cause them to be covered in the first instance. The basis of the exclusion of hard core pornography from the coverage of the Free Speech Principle is not that it has a physical effect, *but that it has nothing else.*

It is important here to recognize the distinction between advocacy of conduct and the conduct itself. I may on the one hand advocate the assassination of the President of the United States, and on the other hand actually attempt such a deed. It is not inconceivable that my attempt will encourage others to do the same, but we properly would not say that the attempted assassination is a communicative act covered by the principles of freedom of speech. I may argue that adultery is a desirable activity, and I may quite separately commit adultery. Although frequent adultery, if known, may cause others to do the same thing, the act itself is not communicative.

So too with pornography. It is one thing to suggest or argue that pornography is good, or that the laws prohibiting it should be repealed. But the pornography itself is not such advocacy, it is the act. To confuse the act with its advocacy is a substantial mistake in free speech analysis. It is possible to argue that the purpose of pornography is to present the activities depicted as desirable, or to present a vision of sexual openness. But if that is the purpose then we are no longer dealing with hard core pornography. What defines pornography is its lack of intended intellectual appeal. Freedom of speech would be boundless if we were not able to draw a distinction, however fuzzy, between communication and the communicative potential of physical acts. Implicit in recognition of freedom of speech as a distinct principle is the notion that we can separate advocacy of an act from the act itself, even though the act may contain some elements of advocacy. Thus although arguments for sex are covered by the Free Speech Principle, sex is not. Sex in and of itself is not a free speech problem. And if sex is not covered, then two-dimensional sex is not covered any more than three-dimensional sex, visual sex no more than tactile sex. And it is this conception of pornography as sex and no more that explains its exclusion from the coverage of the Free Speech Principle.

I am not suggesting that clear lines can always or ever be drawn. More likely they cannot. But it is possible to imagine that the tools of communication can be used for purposes not significantly communicative. Whatever may be the problems of line-drawing, to which I shall return presently, it is apparent that at one extreme there exists material with neither propositional, emotive, nor artistic content. It thus contains none of the properties that are defined by the technical sense of the word 'speech', and is thus outside the scope of the Free Speech Principle.

I have argued that there is a category of material that is not speech in the free speech sense, just as many other uses of language, such as making a contract, are not speech in the free speech sense.[4] Thus the Free Speech Principle is not relevant to determining whether hard core pornography should be regulated. But it does not follow from this that hard core pornography should necessarily be regulated. There remain serious issues of privacy, choice, and the relation of law to morality that may argue against regulation of pornography. There may even be a Free Sex Principle. The point is only that the issue of controlling hard core pornography is not a free speech issue, and we cloud the enquiry when we talk of free speech rather than the relevant questions of privacy, choice, autonomy and the role of government.

FREE SPEECH AND OBSCENITY CONTROL

I have argued that there is a category of usually pictorial but possibly linguistic activity that is not significantly communicative. This category is, however, but a small subset of the universe of pictorial and linguistic acts, and also only a small subset of the universe of all printed material dealing with sex.

Under almost any justification for a Free Speech Principle the advocacy of a different sexual morality is covered by the Principle. Advocacy of adultery, homosexuality, sado-masochism, pederasty, foot-fetishism, bestiality or whatever is plainly communicative and well within the coverage of any moderately broad Free Speech Principle.

Similarly, conveying sexual information for the purpose of informing is also covered. The informational content of a sexual instructional manual, or anthropological, sociological, medical or historical accounts of sex is sufficient to bring the material within most Free Speech Principles. In some non-ideological face-to-face settings we might say that providing information has no free speech implications (such as providing the plans of a bank vault to a potential bank robber), but these are the aberrational exceptions to the general principle that providing information to the public is in most cases covered by the Free Speech Principle.

For similar reasons, depicting or describing sex in art is covered by any Free Speech Principle that includes art, no matter how explicit the sexual depiction might be. If art is covered, then sexual art is covered as much as any other subject of artistic expression.

The Free Speech Principle also covers the use of offensive words, even if those words have sexual connotations. The use of such words in political argument is now common, and they are equally prevalent in serious literature. People do not use the word 'Fuck' in order to provide sexual stimulation, and thus the arguments in the previous section of this chapter are wholly inapplicable.

Finally, my argument for the exclusion of hard core pornography does not in any way apply to what is often referred to as 'violent pornography'. This term is ambiguous. In the sense that pornography, intended to produce sexual stimulation, can feature violence for those so attracted, then violent pornography is no different in free speech terms from pornography that features other sexual stimuli. But in the sense that violence alone is offensive, or harmful, or repulsive, then violence would not make something pornographic. It might make it dangerous, or even obscene, but neither characterization would suggest that the publication is not covered by the Free Speech Principle. There may be reason to suppose that some violent depictions are so dangerous that the interest in their control would meet even the heightened standard of the Free Speech Principle, but the arguments that relate to the exclusion of pornography from the coverage of the Free Speech Principle are inapplicable to violence as such. The sex-aid approach to hard core pornography that shows such pornography to be scarcely communicative at all does not appear relevant to the depiction of violence. Although it is possible that a refined categorization approach to freedom of speech might grant publications featuring violence for its own sake (such as a martial arts movie) less protection than would be granted to, say, political speech, this would create problems because of the frequent use of violence to emphasize a moral or political argument, as, for example, with the use of vivid depictions of violent death in a motion picture intended to point out the horrors of war.

The fact that most sexually oriented publications other than hard core pornography are covered by the Free Speech Principle does not of course mean that those publications are necessarily protected by the principle. It may be that some or all of the arguments put forth in favour of regulation of sexually explicit materials are sufficient, at least as to some classes of publications, to overcome the presumption against regulation established by the Free Speech Principle. I do not propose to attempt to answer that question here. Such an effort would entail a full analysis of the empirical evidence and philosophical foundations of each argument advanced in support of the regulation of sexual materials. As to the empirical evidence, this would require analysis of literally hundreds of volumes of studies that have been performed by people in a wide range of academic disciplines. And as to the philosophical foundations of some of the proffered justifications, full treatment would take me further into the relationship between law and the enforcement of morals than I wish to go in a book dealing with freedom of speech. All I want to say here, admittedly by way of conclusion rather than argument, is that, given the high burden of justification established by the Free Speech Principle, the verdict for me as to both the empirical evidence and the philosophical justifications must be 'not proven'.[5] This does not mean that the justifications are not good ones. It means only that they are not good enough to outweigh the heavy presumption in favour of freedom of speech.

If hard core pornography (or for that matter other forms of sexually explicit material) is to be regulated, the legal rules established for the identification of such material must incorporate the notions of uncertainty I discussed in chapter 9 and applied to the question of defamation in chapter 11. Indeed, the history of imprecision in the regulation of obscene publications mandates that we pay more attention to uncertainty and the possibility of erroneous results here than we would in most other areas of application of the Free Speech Principle.

Thus, if we were to construct the legal rule in a way that duplicates as best we can that abstract distinction between what should be regulated and what should not be regulated, mistakes would still occur. Some of these mistakes would be mistakes of under-regulation, publications that are hard core pornography would not be found so to be and thus would escape the sanction. Other mistakes would be mistakes of over-regulation, publications that are not hard core pornography would be found to be so and would therefore be punished. But, as I have said before, recognition and adoption of a Free Speech Principle entails the conclusion that the mistake of over-regulation must be treated as a more serious mistake than the mistake of under-regulation. Failing to impose sanctions on regulable pornography weakens the assumed public interest in regulating pornography but hurts no specific right. But imposing sanctions on publications that are indeed protected by the Free Speech Principle cuts into a right we take to be of special importance.

Because one type of mistake is more serious than another, setting the legal rule at the same point as we would set the 'ideal line' is an error, because it assumes that the two types of error caused by uncertainty are of equal danger. In order to avoid this error, we must move the legal rule away from the ideal line, and create a legal rule that in practice protects some hard core pornography. If this is done, then mistakes in application, which are inevitable, will, unless extraordinarily erroneous, only result in punishing that which ideally ought not to be protected. By moving the actual legal rule away from the ideal rule, and by moving it in the proper direction, we create a 'buffer zone' designed to reflect the special weight of the free speech interest, and therefore designed to minimize free speech errors even if the result is to increase the number of errors of the opposite kind. I do not want here to get into the precise formulation of legal rules, but I do wish to stress the importance of skewing those rules to reflect the principles of uncertainty and the comparative harm of error.

The foregoing discussion, concentrating as it does on identification of pornography in specific works, is most applicable to obscenity control through use of the criminal law. Other forms of control are also possible, and one that has received considerable attention recently is that of restriction without prohibition.[6] Thus, establishments dealing with sexually explicit materials, such as 'adult' bookstores and theatres, might be permitted to operate, but with restrictions on where they could be located, or on the type of advertising permitted on the exterior of the establishment, thus avoiding offence to the sensibilities of passers-by. This type of approach has considerable appeal, because it deals with some of the justifications for control of such materials, while at the same time permitting those who desire them access with relative ease. In so far as such restrictions cover only that which could be called hard core pornography, these restrictions create no free speech problems, for reasons I have just detailed. If material is totally outside the coverage of the Free Speech Principle, and therefore subject even to criminal sanctions as far as the question of free speech is concerned, then *a fortiori* a form of restriction less onerous than a criminal penalty would be permissible as well.

The problem comes when the definitions employed in the restrictive mechanism go beyond hard core pornography. It is tempting to hold that since no one is subject to criminal prosecution, and since no material is absolutely prohibited, then broader restrictions would cause little harm to free speech interests. But in many cases restrictions on the location or manner of distribution could have serious effects on the communicative impact of a publication. If a serious newspaper or magazine that contains some sexually oriented matter is to be restricted as to the locations in which it can be sold, then that message will reach far fewer people, or at least a different class of the population. The same holds true for motion pictures that might be restricted to certain areas because they contain nudity, violence or coarse language. The result is likely to be either that some serious messages will not reach as wide an audience than might otherwise be the case, or that publishers will change their publications to remove legitimate uses of nudity, sexual references or coarse language. Either of these consequences entails serious free speech problems, especially under those justifications for freedom of speech that stress the interests of the recipient or the interests of society at large, rather than merely the interests of the speaker. This is not to say that no restrictions are ever appropriate, but only that schemes for geographic or similar restriction must take account of the extent to which publications of undoubted free speech value will lose much of their effect by being drawn into a large net designed primarily to restrict materials with little or no free speech value. [7]

Bibliographical note to chapter 12

The literature dealing with obscenity and pornography is enormous. Works of philosophical interest not yet cited include Fred Berger, 'Pornography, sex, and censorship', *Social Theory and Practice* 4 (1977), 183; Rajeev Dhavan and Christie Davies, eds, *Censorship and obscenity* (London: Martin Robertson, 1978); Joel Feinberg, 'Pornography and the criminal law', *University of Pittsburgh Law Review* 40 (1979), 567; John Finnis, ' "Reason and passion": the constitutional dialectic of free speech and obscenity', *University of Pennsylvania Law Review* **116** (1967), 222; Louis Henkin, 'Morals and the Constitution: the sin of obscenity', *Columbia Law Review* **63** (1963), 391; David Holbrook, ed., *The case against pornography* (London: Tom Stacey Ltd., 1972); Douglas A. Hughes, ed., *Perspectives on pornography* (New York: Macmillan, 1970); Harry Kalven, 'The metaphysics of the law of obscenity', *The Supreme Court Review* (1960), 1.

CHAPTER 13

Free speech and the rights of the state

DOES A STATE HAVE RIGHTS?

It is commonly supposed that freedom of speech is subject to restriction in the name of national security. If free speech conflicts with a nation's right of self-preservation, then, it is argued, the freedom to speak must yield to the superior interests in defending the state. In some cases the threat to the state is thought to be external, and in some cases it is thought to be internal, but in both situations the state includes within its arsenal a range of verbal crimes, such as sedition, incitement, conspiracy to overthrow the government and lists of illegal organizations. There is also a range of offences not necessarily verbal, but which can be committed by verbal acts, such as treason and espionage.

Offences of this sort appear to presuppose a model in which the state and the perpetrator have opposing and mutually exclusive interests. Although that presupposition is largely accurate in a monarchy or similar monolithic state, the issues become substantially more complex where democracy of some sort is the appropriate model. On the assumptions of democracy, it is not quite so easy to understand how some of the people can be guilty of a crime for attempting to change the government. In order to have some understanding of free speech and national security issues in a democracy, we must first determine what national security means in a system of government where the state and the people are taken to have an identity of interest.

Although I suggested in chapter 3 that popular sovereignty cannot plausibly be taken as a sufficient condition for the existence of what is generally taken to be democracy, some degree of popular control in the making of laws is certainly a necessary condition. In theory the laws and official policies of a democracy are made *and changed* by the people or their responsive representatives. The element of change is crucial, for a society in which all laws were immutable would hardly comport with our understanding of democracy, no matter how democratic were the processes that led to the enactment of those laws. Yet for this power to change the laws to be effective, the population must retain the power not only to propose new laws and comment on the advisability of the laws so proposed, but also the power to comment upon and to criticize existing law, with the aim, express or implied, of urging repeal or modification.

Where a society acknowledges democratic government formulated broadly along these lines, the state *qua* state cannot be said to have a legitimate interest in the preservation of particular laws. Because the laws that do exist owe their legitimacy to popular support, it would be anomalous to hold that those laws are or should be immune from popular rejection or change. And if popular rejection or change is implicit in the concept of democracy, then speech advocating such action must be protected as well, for without it the raw power to change the laws would be ineffective.

None of this is controversial. No state can consistently suppress criticism of existing law and at the same time claim to respect even a relatively weak principle of freedom of speech. But all of this presupposes peaceful change, obedience to law, change within a constitutional structure or of that constitutional structure by means 'within the law'. What then of illegal change, or of violence, or of breach of peace? What of arguments to break the law rather than to change it? It is here that we encounter many of the most difficult issues in free speech theory.

Superficially, we might say that advocacy of legal change should be permitted, but that advocacy of violent or unlawful means of change should not be protected by the Free Speech Principle. After all, people should not be able to rely on freedom of speech derived, here, primarily from the argument from democracy, for the purpose of going outside the process of democracy. It is not that fairness or consistency requires that those who claim rights under a principle must themselves subscribe to that principle, although such an argument is quite plausible.[1] Rather, speech that produces extra-legal change undermines the process of rational deliberation that is the *a priori* value of a democratic system.

Assuming that speech directed towards producing unlawful activity is a legitimate concern of the state, it is necessary to look beyond the specific verbal formula employed by a speaker. Specific advocacy of illegal acts may indeed increase the probability of occurrence of those illegal acts, but so too may illegal acts flow as a consequence from statements not containing specific references to breaking the law. Regardless of intent, public denunciation of a law will increase the likelihood that someone somewhere will disobey that law.[2] And in many cases a speaker who intends for members of his audience to break the law will not have to use the specific formula of disobedience in order to produce the desired result. A series of lectures on university campuses dealing with the lack of harm and positive benefits of smoking marijuana is likely to increase the incidence of violation of the marijuana laws, and this result would probably be independent of whether the speaker was a serious proponent of drug law reform or the city's largest distributor of illegal drugs.

Because few utterances *invariably* lead to illegal activity,[3] the question is one of probabilities. Statements that explicitly encourage unlawful acts will in most instances have a higher probability of causing those illegal acts to occur than statements lacking explicit encouragement, but the correllation is by no means perfect. And in terms of probabilities, virtually any criticism can be meant or taken as encouragement to disobedience. Holmes may have been guilty of overstatement in observing that 'every idea is an incitement', but the point is valuable. It is not the ritualistic utterance of 'you ought to break the law' that produces disobedience to law, but rather a complex mixture of behavioural factors including but not limited to the particular words chosen by the speaker.

Identifying the probabilistic nature of the relationship between the speech and the consequent action makes it possible to identify an illuminating mistake. I have argued that implicit in the Free Speech Principle is the view that speech is less subject to regulation than non-speech conduct causing commensurate harm. Someone might suggest, therefore, that if speech advocating the murder of a specific individual (or even advocating some lesser crime) caused a murder, recognition of the Free Speech Principle would make it less possible to punish the speech than the murder. This might be so, but the appropriate comparison is not between speech causing murder and murder. It is between speech potentially causing murder (or other crimes) and other activity potentially causing murder. Legislation can be separated into that dealing with primary harms and that dealing with secondary harms. Primary harms are the evils that society wishes to prevent. Secondary harms are those harms or acts that are likely to lead to primary harms. For example, curfews are rarely based on the primary undesirability of people being out at night, but rather on the belief that under some circumstances certain primary evils (burglary, assault, looting, etc.) are more likely to occur when people are out at night. And prohibition laws are less often based on the primary evils of drink than they are on the assumption that drinking increases the probability of other evils occurring, such as fighting and reckless driving.

Under this distinction we can see that in almost all cases speech would be a secondary evil rather than a primary one. The desire to regulate would stem from the belief that the speech would be likely to cause a primary harm. Recognition of a Free Speech Principle means that the correlation between speech and the primary evil must be higher (the probability greater) than would be necessary to regulate other secondary evils. If there is a probability that speech advocating looting will cause some looting, and if there is a probability that people being out at night will cause some looting, the probability must be higher to justify a restriction on speech than it would to justify a curfew. Recognition of the Free Speech Principle does not disable the state from regulating those speech acts likely to cause crime, but it does require a higher showing of likelihood than for those other acts also likely to cause crime.

Nor is there anything in the Free Speech Principle that prevents the state from estimating questions of intent and effect, as long as the standards are appropriately stringent. In defending the concept of implied causation in this area, Holmes noted that 'guessing at motive, tendency and possible effect' was 'pretty much the whole body of the law, which for thirty years I have made my brethren smile by insisting to be everywhere a matter of degree'.[4] Yet although speech not mentioning illegal acts can still cause those illegal acts, there is no doubt that requiring expressed incitement provides some measure of certainty. Perhaps, therefore, it is best to look at criticism of law or government policy as a spectrum. At one end is pure non-inflammatory criticism. At the other is speech specifically, directly and exclusively devoted to inciting disobedience. Two further categories fall between these extremes. One, closest to the criticism only end of the spectrum, contains no words of incitement, but the tone and context of the criticism may encourage disobedience to law. Marc Antony's oration over the body of Caesar is an oft-cited example of this type, and so is Mill's example of the corn-dealer. The other intermediate category, closer to pure incitement, involves general criticism coupled with specific admonition to violate the criticized laws.

Looking at these four categories, we can see that government regulation in the first category would most resemble the most oppressive uses of the crime of seditious libel and would seem fundamentally inconsistent with the premises of any of the arguments for a Free Speech Principle. Disobedience may in some or many cases be the consequence of non-inflammatory criticism, but there is no way to prevent this while recognizing even a rather weak Free Speech Principle.

Similar arguments compel the exclusion of most speech in the second category from the range of permissible regulation. If criticism may incite, then it is incumbent upon us to balance the value of the criticism against the risk of actual law-breaking and the consequent harm should that danger be realized. Recall the discussion of the weighing process from chapter 9. In a case like this we are balancing the Free Speech Principle against the general public interest in obedience to law. Recognition of the import of the Free Speech Principle entails the conclusion that limiting criticism of government is a more serious harm than is the risk of some violation of law. After all, laws are broken every day. But the fact that suppression of criticism is in general the greater harm does not entail the conclusion that disobedience to law in a given instance can never outweigh the interest in permitting criticism of government. If the disobedience to law is virtually certain to follow from the words spoken, and if the disobedience to law is especially serious, then suppression of criticism of government may be justified. We might say that no harm can be imagined that would justify the suppression of criticism unaccompanied by express advocacy of disobedience. Such a position is quite inviting, in that any other position involves the risk that prosecutions will be based on a desire of those in power to suppress criticism rather than to prevent the violation of law. If the Free Speech Principle is founded on a distrust of this very type of power, then this position is especially compelling. This approach is a fairly accurate representation of current American constitutional doctrine, under which no criticism of law not containing direct words of incitement may be prosecuted, regardless of the possibility that some criticisms may as well cause a 'clear and present danger' of serious disobedience to law. Results less protective of speech are also possible. We might for example say that serious risks of dangerous disobedience should be sanctioned, even though no explicit words of incitement were employed by the speaker. But this involves not only the actual suppression of some criticism, but also suppression by self-censorship, or 'chilling', that emerges from any method of enforcement that is imprecise in application. Recognition of the Free Speech Principle thus leads to the conclusion that, in this second category of potential implicit incitement, restrictions on speech are either totally impermissible or must be restricted to those statements having a virtually inevitable tendency to produce some serious unlawful act.

In the third category, that containing speech with both words of criticism and words specifically advocating disobedience to law, the analytic difficulties are fewer. This is because these two elements are severable in almost all instances. There is little reason why a rule could not at the same time allow all criticism but prohibit advocacy of unlawful action. There would be close cases, but this could be taken into account by again setting the line of demarcation at such a point that it would incorporate a 'buffer zone' minimizing the instances of restrictions on criticism. Only those utterances that were plainly directed towards advocating illegal conduct would be proscribed, and both the rule and its application would resolve all doubts in favour of permitting the speech in question. As long as such a division between criticism and specific words of incitement is theoretically possible, then this third category dissolves, partially into the second category and partially into the fourth.

The fourth category, that of words specifically directed towards violation of law, is the most troublesome. The central question is whether anything contained in the Free Speech Principle compels, or even suggests, that advocacy of illegal activity, in isolation, should be protected. The answer to this question depends in turn on whether the Free Speech Principle is derived from legal or prelegal values. That is, if freedom of speech is justified by its relationship to the legal system, and especially if it is justified by its ability to ensure the functioning of a system of laws, then speech directed at weakening or destroying that legal system would appear to have little claim to protection. But if on the other hand freedom of speech is pre-legal, if it is derived from precepts not contingent on any particular legal system, then there is nothing so special about advocacy of unlawful acts that should occasion special treatment.

Speech advocating illegal action appears most inconsistent with the argument from democracy. If the processes of democratic government generate the Free Speech Principle, then speech that would circumvent those processes, that would impose a form of government other than rule by the people,[5] cannot fall within the coverage of the Principle. Perhaps paradoxically, the argument from democracy can justify protecting speech advocating violation of law when and only when democracy does not exist. Underlying the argument from democracy is faith in the value of popular sovereignty. The use of communication to mobilize, to persuade, and perhaps to unite the population provides the justification for this particular view of the Free Speech Principle. When a government is so constituted that the people are not in control, and when there is no lawful mechanism by which the people can take control, then it would appear that the advocacy of unlawful acts of revolution (and perhaps only this type of unlawful act) should be available in order that unrepresentative governments can be removed. There is, however, a difference between the moral permissibility of such advocacy and the likelihood or feasibility of any government recognizing such a right. Yet there is nothing contradictory about establishing a procedure whereby government may be checked. Permitting some advocacy of 'illegal' revolution is merely an extreme example of such a procedure. Thus, the current American constitutional doctrine allowing advocacy of revolution or other illegal conduct may be viewed as a wholly logical recognition of the fact that unlawful revolution may at times be the only way to remove a government that has removed itself from popular control. It is hardly surprising that a nation founded on this very basis would at the least recognize in its laws the possibility that such a need would again arise.

The analysis under the argument from truth is not dissimilar. The argument presupposes a system of rational discourse. Advocacy of illegal action, especially advocacy of violence, is fundamentally inconsistent with the assumptions upon which the argument from truth is founded. One who seeks to impose his views by force, or seeks to have others do it for him, can reasonably be said to have forfeited his claim to protection under a system premised on the supremacy of reason. But just as democracy does not always exist, even where it represents the ideal, so too does reason not always prevail. It is not totally irrational to suppose that some laws may directly or indirectly have the effect of limiting a system of rational discourse. Although it is possible that advocacy of illegal action need not be protected if all laws are the product of and changeable by rational discourse, the degree to which we may wish to protect advocacy of unlawful conduct may vary directly with the extent to which the system falls short of the ideal.

Moreover, it can be argued that advocacy of illegal conduct ought to be protected under the 'catharsis' theory described in chapter 6. Allowing people to say 'We ought to blow up Tower Bridge' may not in the abstract be as subject to protection as 'We ought to get Parliament to allow us to blow up Tower Bridge', but it may be that allowing people to advocate destruction is the safest course.

If we do not allow people to talk about blowing up Tower Bridge, they may react by actually blowing up the bridge. If we accept the psychological assumptions upon which the catharsis theory is premised, advocacy of illegal conduct may be less likely to lead to illegal conduct than would prohibition of that advocacy, paradoxical as this may at first appear.

Still, these arguments seem strained. And well they should, where freedom of speech is conceived as a principle instrumental to some overall good of society. An argument based on the public interest, even the long-range public interest, accommodates only with considerable difficulty the view that advocacy of disobedience to the law is itself in the public interest. But if public interest does not provide the starting point for freedom of speech, then speech that is not in the public interest need not for that reason alone remain unprotected.[6] The argument from truth, the argument from democracy, and the various arguments from distrust of government are all consequentialist arguments, deriving their force from some conception of the long-range general welfare. By contrast, the arguments from autonomy and individuality are non-consequentialist. Their force is undiminished by a particular instance in which speech would be deleterious to the general welfare, or even that suppression of a category of speech would be advantageous to the general welfare. The fact that some speech may encourage me or others to break the law may under non-consequentialist theories provide strong arguments for overriding the Free Speech Principle. But in determining whether 'pure' advocacy of illegal acts is covered by the Principle, the fact that the conduct advocated violates the law is largely irrelevant. Indeed, under Thomas Scanlon's argument from autonomy, speech directed at encouraging (although not facilitating) the violation of law lies at the core of the Free Speech Principle, because it goes directly to the priority of individual autonomy over state power.

Where speech is merely critical of existing law, or where speech advocating disobedience is inseparably combined with such criticism, protection is mandated by any strong theory of freedom of speech. It is only in the pure case of unalloyed and specific advocacy of illegal action that the result varies depending on the underlying justification for the Free Speech Principle. Such utterances are indeed quite rare. More common are those where words of incitement are combined with words of criticism, or where words of criticism may have the likely and perhaps intended effect of inducing disobedience to law. We have determined that such speech is *covered* by the Free Speech Principle. But that does not necessarily entail protection. It may be that the state interest in preserving the rule of law is sufficient in some cases to outweigh even a heightened free speech interest. This issue is present in all cases in which speech may cause disobedience to law, but it is drawn in starkest relief in those cases where the violation of law may jeopardize the 'national security', and it is to this that I now turn.

NATIONAL SECURITY

The interest in the security of the nation is often thought to be a trump card in free speech disputes. Whatever the strength of the Free Speech Principle, a threat to national security is commonly held to be a danger of sufficient magnitude that the interest in freedom of speech must be subordinated. But 'national security' is a rather loose term. Before we can evaluate the strength of an appeal to the interest in national security, we should attempt to clarify just what it is that is thought to demand such extreme deference.

One important distinction is the distinction between national security and personal security. The latter as well as the former may be jeopardized by various acts of speech. This indeed is the very point of Mill's famous example of 'an opinion that corn-dealers are starvers of the poor . . . delivered orally to an excited mob assembled before the house of a corn-dealer, or when handed about among the same mob in the form of a placard'. Mill and some contemporary scholars have attempted to explain the lack of protection in such instances by noting that such utterances are substantially or wholly *action*, rather than speech. But this begs the question. All speech is a form of action. And most speech is intended to produce some response in the form of other action, so we cannot define out of the coverage of freedom of speech all speech that attempts to produce some physical action, at least not without reducing the coverage to only that speech that would be ineffective.

In saying that some speech is 'really' action, the claim appears to be that some speech causes harmful action without the opportunity for reflection or deliberation. Holmes' example of falsely shouting 'Fire!' in a crowded theatre is the paradigm example, and Mill's corn-dealer example also seems to fit this description. Most of the justifications for a Free Speech Principle relate in some way to the process of deliberation. To the extent that some speech acts operate with such immediate effect that the opportunity for deliberation is absent, then the applicability of the Free Speech Principle is substantially less. And to the extent that the consequences of such speech are incontrovertibly dangerous, then the arguments against protection are even stronger. Hence the lack of protection in Mill's example, and maybe even the lack of coverage in Holmes', which combines immediate effect without deliberation with a complete lack of political, normative or informational content.

Looking at examples like this helps us to get clear about national security. In some cases an existing state of national emergency may prevent deliberation on a large scale just as it does on a smaller scale in the theatre or in front of the corn-dealer's house. During time of war, for example, rumours are frequently taken as truth, and the passions of war often interfere with rational deliberation. Moreover, war or other national emergency often require action more immediate than in calmer times. Again there may not be time to trust the deliberative process for separating truth from error, even if we assume that such separation normally occurs. Therefore the appeal to national security as overriding freedom of speech is often a claim that the underlying presuppositions of a system of freedom of speech are inoperative in certain circumstances of national emergency. In this form the claim is strong, but there remains the difficult issue of determining just what is to count as a national emergency. It is hard to lay down hard and fast rules for this determination, but acceptance of this 'exception' requires that we be wary of the possibility that those who wish to restrict speech can all too easily claim that an 'emergency' exists. The implementing rules for such an exception must ensure that a claim of emergency is only availing when the conditions for deliberation do not exist. This is the point of the 'clear and present danger' doctrine in American free speech theory, and it is equally useful in other contexts as well.

Thus, one basis of the claim of national security is that certain threats to national security prevent the operation of the deliberative process. In this form the claim is not dissimilar to the claim made when national security is not at issue, as for example in the corn-dealer example. Another basis of the appeal to national security, however, relates not to the conditions for the exercise of freedom of speech, but rather to the strength of the countervailing interest. Thus, it can be argued that the destruction or enslavement of the nation is of such great danger that it always outweighs the free speech interest.

Danger, however, is a function not only of the magnitude of the harm, but also of its imminence. If I were to stand in front of the Capitol in Washington and suggest that the government of the United States ought to be overthrown so that we could institute a monarchy, the danger should such an event occur would be great, but the likelihood of it happening would be so small that few would consider my speech to be dangerous. Yet on the other hand there are occasions when a possible harm might be so great that we would consider it a real danger even if its occurrence were less than certain and less than immediate.[7] A good example of this is the recent American case permitting a restriction on plans for construction of a hydrogen bomb.[8] The court that decided the case was not certain that the plans to be published would make it possible for such a bomb to be constructed by another nation not currently having the capability of building a hydrogen bomb. Nor was it certain that the bomb, if it could be built at all, could be built immediately. But implicit in the decision was the determination that the building of such a bomb was of such potential harm that somewhat less certainty and immediacy were necessary in this case than would be necessary in other cases where the possible outcome was less devastating.

Thus, evaluation of the interest in national security requires a determination of the extent of the harm should the argued effect actually occur, the probability of that effect occurring, and the immediacy of the effect. The more serious the effect, the less certain and less immediate that effect need be. But this relationship operates only within a limited range. There are great dangers to free speech interests if improbable and distant dangers can be used to justify limitations on speech. Thus there must be a minimum threshhold level of both probability and immediacy in order to provide sufficient deference to the weight of the Free Speech Principle. But if the dangers to national security are highly probable, likely to be immediate, and of great magnitude, then a restriction of freedom of speech in the name of national security is consistent with recognition of the Free Speech Principle.

Bibliographical note to chapter 13

For more detailed analysis of 'clear and present danger' in American constitutional doctrine, see Alan Fuchs, 'Further steps toward a general theory of freedom of expression', *William and Mary Law Review* 18 (1976), 347; Gerald Gunther, 'Learned Hand and the origins of modern First Amendment doctrine: some fragments of history', *Stanford Law Review* 27

(1975), 719; Hans Linde, ' "Clear and present danger" reexamined: dissonance in the Brandenburg Concerto', *Stanford Law Review* **22** (1970), 1163; Alexander Meiklejohn, 'The balancing of self-preservation against political freedom', *California Law Review* **49** (1961), 4.

CHAPTER 14

Speech in the streets

SPEECH IN THE CONTEMPORARY STYLE

Much speech takes place in settings in which the only issues as to regulation are those that relate to the content of the communication. Whether we should regulate matter appearing in books, newspapers, and Hyde Park Corner orations, for example, is determined by what is said, and our estimation of the dangers that might flow from the particular communicative content of the speech.

Traditionally, these concerns with content have constituted the only important free speech questions. But as speech has moved into new settings, new considerations not related to content have appeared. When people communicate by picketing, through the use of demonstrations or in parades, interests not related to the content of the communication are implicated. Parades interfere with the flow of traffic, demonstrations may prevent people from going where they wish to go, and picketing may interfere with the operation of a business or office. All of these are legitimate concerns. Yet these settings for communication are becoming increasingly prevalent in contemporary society. Reconciling the free speech interests with the acknowledged importance of traffic- and crowd-control has as a result become an increasingly important problem for free speech theory.

It is tempting to say that this type of communication is less important. Communication by parades, demonstrations and picketing is more emotional than intellectual, and more fully argued statements of the positions involved are available in books, newspapers, magazines and other less obstructive communicative formats. If we cut off 'speech in the streets', there remain readily available alternative forums, and there is little danger that some ideas will remain unsaid. Indeed, restricting speech of this type may well support some of the values protected by a system of freedom of speech, by forcing communication into channels more conducive to rational argument and deliberation, thereby increasing the overall level of civility in public discourse.

Acceptance of such a position, however, requires that we ignore an important phenomenon in contemporary communication. When people first started talking and writing about freedom of speech and freedom of the press, there existed only a few forums for communication. There was no radio or television or cinema, few newspapers, few periodicals, and comparatively few political tracts published for private distribution. It was not at all unreasonable to assume that a mildly expressed and closely reasoned political or social or theological argument would in fact be read or heard by most people having any interest in such matters. But now, with radio, television and film, with almost innumerable newspapers, magazines, books and pamphlets, and with so many people speaking out on so many different subjects, there is perhaps 'too much' speech, in the sense that it is impossible to read or hear even a minute percentage of what is being expressed. There is a din of speech, and our limited capacity to read or to hear has resulted in effective censorship by the proliferation of opinion rather than by the restriction of opinion.[1] We learn no more from a thousand people all speaking at the same time than we learn from total silence.[2]

Under such circumstances it is frequently necessary, literally or figuratively, to shout to be heard. One method of gaining a listener's attention is by the use of offensive words or pictures. Another, more relevant here, is through the use of placards, large groups of people, loud noises and all the other attention-getting devices that are part of parades, picketing and demonstrations. To restrict these methods of communication is to restrict the effectiveness of speech, and also to restrict the extent to which new or controversial ideas may be brought to the attention of potential listeners.

Moreover, important free speech values are served by emotive utterances. This is most apparent under the catharsis argument discussed in chapter 6. But it is equally important under the argument from democracy. As a voter I am interested not only in what others feel about a certain issue, but also in how many people share that view, and in how strongly that opinion is held. As a public official I am equally concerned (or should be) with gauging the extent and the strength of public opinion. In addition, freedom of speech serves a legitimizing function, in holding that people should be bound by official policy if they have had, through speech, the opportunity to participate (even if unsuccessfully) in the process of formulating official policy. In terms of this function, parades, picketing and demonstrations are a way of attempting to influence official policy and are thus a part of the total process.

I am not arguing that parades, demonstrations and picketing should always be protected. Nor am I arguing that there are not good reasons for restricting speech when it takes these forms. What I am arguing is that there are good reasons for recognizing this type of speech as being important, and that there seem to be no good reasons for relegating these forms of communication to some inferior status in the free speech hierarchy. The question is not one of balancing a less legitimate form of speech against legitimate governmental interests in peace and order, but rather is one of balancing an important and legitimate form of communication against important and legitimate governmental interests. When so formulated the problem is a difficult one, but one that is fortunately slightly more susceptible to rational resolution than some other free speech problems.

EXPLORING THE GOVERNMENTAL INTEREST

The regulation of parades, picketing, and demonstrations provides the perfect example for the application of some of the ideas dealt with in chapter 7. More particularly, the question is one that is best looked at not in terms of the object of the regulation, but instead in terms of the purpose or the intent of the regulation. Suppose that the Communist Party wishes to march down the High Street on May 1. If the governing authorities were to prohibit the march because they did not want Communists to march, we would properly think of this as a free speech problem. But if the governing authorities were to prohibit the march because the High Street had previously been scheduled for repair on that day we would be much less troubled. The effect of the governmental action is the same, prohibiting the march, but the different reasons behind the regulation produce different results.[3] Similarly, a law prohibiting marches by Communists would strike us as a free speech problem, while a law prohibiting obstruction of the High Street would not, even though the effect might be the same in many cases.

The difference between the free speech cases and those that are not free speech cases is that in the free speech cases the governmental action is directed intentionally at the communicative impact of the conduct. But when the governmental action is not directed at the communicative impact we do not think in free speech terms. If the governmental interest is unrelated to the speech itself, if it is unrelated to communicative impact, then the action is in most cases not even within the coverage of the Free Speech Principle. For example, governmental action designed to control traffic, prevent the obstruction of public ways, prevent noise or prevent the destruction of public property, would be outside the scope of the Free Speech Principle, although some *incidental* restriction of communication was the result.

The distinction between regulations directed at communicative impact and those not so directed is derived most naturally from those justifications for the Free Speech Principle that focus on the dangers of governmental regulation. For under these arguments it is government we most want to check. It therefore makes sense to look at what government is doing in the particular case. Where the regulation itself contains a distinction based on the content of the communication, the impermissible governmental motive will be most apparent. For example, an ordinance prohibiting marches by Communists but permitting marches by certain other political parties can obviously not be one that is designed to prevent obstruction of traffic, or prevent noise. Marches by Communists are not necessarily more obstructive or noisy than marches by other groups, so it becomes plain that an ordinance of this type is not truly directed towards those ends. Similarly, if an ordinance prevents the carrying of picket signs, but permits any other form of congregation in a public place, it would be hard to claim that the anti-picketing ordinance was designed to prevent obstructive congregations of individuals.

This approach runs into difficulty, however, under some of the more positive justifications for the Free Speech Principle. A regulation, for example, that prohibited any obstruction of the streets and walkways at any time for any reason would have the effect of prohibiting all demonstrations, picketing and parades. Under the analysis previously suggested, this regulation would create no free speech problems because the governmental action was not directed in any way at communicative impact. Yet if we look at the positive values of freedom of speech, such as those supported by the argument from truth and the argument from democracy, something still seems wrong here. The regulation, although 'pure' in its purpose, still has the effect of restricting a number of important modes of communication.

If we are to respect these positive justifications for freedom of speech, the Free Speech Principle must be considered relevant even in those cases where the regulation is not directed at the communicative impact of the conduct. But freedom of speech cannot be as high a trump card in these instances, both because of the legitimacy of the countervailing interests in order, traffic flow and the like, and also because the absence of an intent to interfere with communication weakens the free speech interest. Perhaps it is best to imagine a series of concentric circles, or a ring that surrounds the central core. The core application of the Free Speech Principle would be where the regulation has the purpose of interfering with communication. In this core the strength of the Free Speech Principle is greatest. Surrounding that core is a ring, in which fall cases where there is no intent to restrict communication, but where the effect is to accomplish that result. Within this ring the free speech interest must still be accommodated, but the absence of the governmental purpose to deal with communicative impact eliminates one justification for a Free Speech Principle and thus produces a weaker free speech interest. It thus seems quite plausible to say that here the conduct is still covered by the Free Speech Principle, but with a somewhat lesser amount of protection. The standard of justification is less here than it is in the core cases.

In order to accommodate the acknowledged but weaker free speech interest in this area, the process of balancing the interests need be less skewed than it is in the core cases. One way of recognizing the state's interests to a great extent while still accommodating some free speech interest is to respect the state's justifications concerning ends, but hold the state to a stringent standard with respect to means. Thus, if a free speech interest is present, then it ought not to be restricted for the sake of another legitimate interest unless there is no way to accommodate the two. Restrictions on speech should be permitted only when the restrictions cannot be avoided. If it is possible to protect the other interest with less of a restriction on freedom of speech, then a restriction of speech in the name of that interest is gratuitous. 'Surely the end cannot justify the means unless it at least requires them.'[4] Thus, if peace and order, or prevention of noise, or prevention of obstruction of traffic can be accomplished without a total prohibition of parades, picketing and demonstrations, then such means must be used. Only if all other alternatives have been exhausted can a restriction on an important method of communication be tolerated, even in this area outside the central core.

It is true that governments rarely engage in purely gratuitous regulation. Whether some form of regulation is 'necessary' to serve some legitimate governmental objective is usually a question of degree. Thus, adoption of the standard suggested in the previous paragraph means that governments would be held to a higher standard of necessity for their non-speech-related regulation when that regulation has an effect on covered communication than when no such effect is present. In this sense, the formulation is quite similar to that for the Free Speech Principle even in the core cases. The standard may be different, but the crucial element of comparison is still present. The speech interest heightens the scrutiny of the state's means as well as its ends, although nothing in the structure of the Free Speech Principle dictates how much higher the scrutiny must be.

The lesson of the 'least restrictive alternative' approach goes far beyond the specific issue of parades, picketing and demonstrations.[5] Throughout history many of the arguments for restricting freedom of speech, either generally or in specific instances, have been made under the umbrella of 'necessity'. But a *claim* of necessity does not make necessity a fact. If we examine more critically the claims of necessity, many of them will be seen to be false claims. Close scrutiny both of the ends that are argued to be sufficient to justify restrictions on freedom of speech, and of the means that are argued to be necessary to accomplish those ends, will in many cases show that it is possible to recognize free speech interests and other important interests without undue sacrifice of either. There will always remain hard cases, but many of them are not as hard as they at first sight appear.

Bibliographical note to chapter 14

The tension between the demands of effective communication and the efficiency of society are well treated in Geoffrey Stone, 'Restriction of speech because of its content: the peculiar case of subject-matter restrictions', *University of Chicago Law Review* **46** (1978), 81; Geoffrey Stone, 'Fora Americana: speech in public places', *The Supreme Court Review* (1974), 233.

Notes

Notes to chapter 1

1 The reference to independent principles suggests aspects of what Rawls calls 'intuitionism', but which is more descriptively characterized as 'pluralism'. See Brian Barry, *The liberal theory of justice*. Works in the pluralist tradition include Isaiah Berlin, *Four essays on liberty;* Isaiah Berlin, *Concepts and categories: philosophical essays,* ed. Henry Hardy; Isaiah Berlin, *Against the current: essays in the history of ideas,* ed. Henry Hardy; Joel Feinberg, 'Rawls and intuitionism'; Ruth Barcan Marcus, 'Moral dilemmas and consistency'; Bernard Williams, 'Ethical consistency'; Bernard Williams, 'Conflicts of values'.

In opposition to pluralism, and to the possibility of conflict inherent in it, are what might be called 'coherence' theories. These are of two types: those that recognize a plurality of principles, but incorporate secondary rules establishing priorities and relationships among the primary principles; and those that are based on a singular, all-encompassing principle. Among the most prominent of coherence theories are Alan Gewirth, *Reason and morality;* John Rawls, *A theory of justice;* pp. 34–40; David A. J. Richards, *A theory of reasons for action;* David A. J. Richards, *The moral criticism of law;* Ronald Dworkin, *Taking rights seriously;* Ronald Dworkin, 'Liberalism', in *Public and private morality,* pp. 113–43.

I do not want to rehearse the opposing arguments here, except to note that universal overriding principles are often formulated at such a level of abstraction as to be of negligible utility. Although my arguments in this book fit slightly less comfortably into coherence theories, the problems are minor at this book's level of particularity.

2 It therefore is included in the more general liberal theories of Dworkin, Rawls, and Richards. See also Richard Flathman, *The practice of rights,* pp. 44–5.

3 See Joel Feinberg, *Social philosophy,* p. 26. I have also learned much from some not yet published work by Alan Fuchs.

4 This follows Thomas Scanlon, 'A theory of freedom of expression'. See also Harry Wellington, 'On freedom of expression'. The argument in the text is consistent with Dworkin's view of rights as trumps, *Taking rights seriously,* pp. 190–2.

5 Side constraints appear most often in deontological theories, and are

often taken to be absolute. See Charles Fried, *Right and wrong*, p. 81; Robert Nozick, *Anarchy, state, and utopia*, pp. 28–33. Nozick concedes, as do most deontological theorists, a 'catastrophe' exception, but my point is that the notion of a side constraint is equally useful even though it only creates a higher threshold of justification short, even well short, of absolute prohibition. Moreover, consequentialist or goal-directed theories may also, if they are attentive to certain long-run consequences, generate side constraints. See D. W. Haslett, 'The general theory of rights'. David Lyons, 'Human rights and the general welfare'.

6 *Taking rights seriously*, p. 26.

7 In some respects the argument in the text resembles the notion of *prima facie* rights, but talk of *'prima facie* rights' is misleading. See A. I. Melden, *Rights and persons*, pp. 13–14; Rex Martin & James Nickel, 'Recent work on the concept of rights', pp. 165–80. When a right is of insufficient strength to withstand the force of other exigent interests, the right does not evaporate, even in that instance. If a right is taken to represent the right-holder's power to require an especially strong reason for restricting the conduct covered by the right, then the right persists even when in a given instance those especially strong reasons do not permit the exercise of a particular act. In this sense, having a right to speak does not mean that in every instance covered by the right a person must be permitted to speak. It means only that in every instance covered by the right a person can require a very good reason before being prohibited from speaking.

8 The importance of recognizing an independent Free Speech Principle is in inverse proportion to the size of the group of liberties that would also include freedom of speech. When free speech is a component of a small class of political liberties, more is said about free speech than if free speech is a component of, say, freedom of action, or freedom to engage in any form of self-expression.

9 Voltaire, in *Liberté d'imprimer*, argued that freedom of the press should be protected because of the impotence of speech and press. If that were true, then it is hard to see what motivated Voltaire to write.

10 I do not wish here to go deeply into the question of just what Mill claimed in *On liberty*. Even less do I wish to join the debate over whether *On liberty* represents what Mill 'really' believed. My point is only that freedom of speech and freedom to engage in self-regarding acts are importantly distinct.

11 In rejecting an ordinary usage approach to clarifying the concept of free speech, I follow Hart's similar treatment of 'law'. H. L. A. Hart, *The concept of law*, pp. 4–6.

12 Where freedom of speech is recognized in a written constitution, the problems are somewhat different. Independent principles of fidelity to written law *may* require that the words in a written constitution be interpreted with greater deference to ordinary language definitions. This problem is not present at the level of political theory. Still, con-

stitutional language is not ordinary language, and there is nothing inimical to the idea of a written constitution in developing and applying constitutional definitions of the words employed. Thus, 'freedom of speech' in a written constitution may refer only to the concept of free speech, and not to the ordinary language meanings of either 'free' or 'speech'. I have developed this point further in 'Speech and "speech" – obscenity and "obscenity" ', and in 'Categories and the First Amendment: a play in three acts'.

13 In this respect freedom of speech is like many other concepts of political theory, such as equality, democracy, and liberalism. See Richard Flathman, *The practice of rights*, p. 44.

Notes to chapter 2

1 Holmes' most prominent opinions on free speech theory are his dissents in *Abrams* v. *United States*, 250 U.S. 616 (1919), pp. 630–1, and *Gitlow* v. *New York*, 268 U.S. 652 (1925), p. 673. For the views of Brandeis, see his concurrence in *Whitney* v. *California*, 274 U.S. 357 (1927), pp. 375–8; for Frankfurter, the concurrence in *Dennis* v. *United States*, 341 U.S. 494 (1951), pp. 546–53; for Hand, the opinions in *United States* v. *Dennis*, 181 F.2d 201 (2d Cir. 1950), and *International Brotherhood of Electrical Workers* v. *NLRB*, 181 F.2d 34 (2d Cir. 1950).

2 See Zecheriah Chafee, pp. 36–7.

3 For example, see J. M. Finnis' imaginative 'Scepticism, self-refutation, and the good of truth', pp. 247–67.

4 Bryan Magee, *Popper*, p. 27.

5 I am concerned now to deal with that form of scepticism that concentrates on the lack of certainty. Other versions of scepticism are concerned more with objectivity than with certainty, admitting that some epistemic states are better than others, but denying the existence of objective criteria for making that determination. I will treat this variety of scepticism presently in the discussion of the 'consensus' theory of truth.

6 Holmes' theory of the marketplace of ideas has its epistemological roots in the American Pragmatists, by whom he was greatly influenced. The term 'survival theory of truth' comes from Carl Auerbach, 'The Communist Control Act of 1954: a proposed legal–political theory of free speech'. See also Max Lerner, *The mind and faith of Justice Holmes*, p. 290.

7 Holmes' scepticism is embedded not only in his views on free speech, but also in the American Realist school of jurisprudence of which he was a founding father. See 'The path of the law'.

8 *Constitutional theory*, p. 158.

9 For example, Milton asked rhetorically, 'who ever knew Truth put to the worst, in a free and open encounter?' *Areopagitica*, p. 126. In the Third Book of Esdras (4:41) it is said that 'truth is mighty and will prevail', and Walter Bagehot held that 'in discussion truth has an

advantage' and 'arguments always tell for truth'. 'The metaphysical basis of toleration', p. 425.

10 Here I am grateful to Hyman Gross for valuable comments.

11 'Being free to speak and speaking freely', in *Social ends and political means*, Ted Honderich ed., at pp. 23–4.

12 See Ronald Dworkin, *Taking rights seriously*, pp. 260–2.

13 For example, Benjamin DuVal, 'Free communication of ideas and the quest for truth . . .'.

14 I am indebted to Mary Hesse for very useful discussions.

15 Rationality is an enormously complex concept. I use 'rational' in the sense of 'thinking things through', where that in turn suggests *independent* thinking, rather than accepting arguments merely on blind faith. There is more to rationality than just this. Being rational also involves not having inconsistent views, and not holding views inconsistent with known facts. Moreover, rejecting known falsity is also a sign of rationality, but only when one knows *why* the rejected view is false. And that requires that we hear at least once the arguments in favour of the opposing view.

16 The opposing argument, that truth has a natural advantage, is the basis of Bagehot's 'The metaphysical basis of toleration'.

17 I rely here on points made to me by Neil Thomason.

18 An interesting exchange on this point is H. J. McCloskey, 'Liberty of expression: its grounds and limits'; and D. Munro, 'Liberty of expression: its grounds and limits'.

19 In addition to the judicial opinions cited in note 1 above, see F. Strong, 'Fifty years of "clear and present danger": from *Schenck* to *Brandenburg* – and beyond'.

20 Such suppression, although rare, appears in unexpected places. Environmental and architectural regulation may be viewed as state enforcement of particular aesthetic values. There are those, after all, who find tall buildings more pleasing to the eye than trees, and there are those who see little value in preserving Victorian reproductions of classical architecture.

21 The example suggests the relationship among language, meaning, and fact, an issue that itself has free speech implications. See my 'Language, truth, and the First Amendment: an essay in memory of Harry Canter'.

Notes to chapter 3

1 Thomas Scanlon, 'A theory of freedom of expression', p. 206.

2 See Alexander Meiklejohn, *Free speech and its relation to self-government*; Immanuel Kant, *On the old saw: that may be right in theory but it won't work in practice*, p. 72; Benedict de Spinoza, *A theologico–political treatise*, ch. XX; David Hume, 'Of the liberty of the press'.

3 [John Trenchard and Thomas Gordon], *Cato's letters: essays on liberty, civil and religious, and other important subjects*.

4 *Cf.* D. D. Raphael, *Problems of political philosophy*, pp. 179–84.
5 In this respect there is a tension between recognition of a so-called 'right' to free speech and a system based on the principles of parliamentary supremacy. This tension is even greater when juries, representing the views of 'the public', determine the scope of that right. 'Freedom of discussion is, then, in England little else than the right to write or say anything which a jury, consisting of twelve shopkeepers, think it expedient should be said or written'. A. V. Dicey, *Introduction to the study of the law of the Constitution*, p. 246.
6 This relationship between social interests and individual interests is developed most fully in Roscoe Pound, *Jurisprudence*, vol. 3, pp. 63–4, 313–17.
7 See Karl Popper, *The open society and its enemies*, vol. 1, pp. 123–4, 266.
8 For a sophisticated version of the argument from democracy in terms of this 'checking' function, see Vincent Blasi, 'The checking value in First Amendment theory'.
9 Meiklejohn's later works expanded the scope of his principle to include many subjects not strictly political. 'The First Amendment is an absolute'. Thomas Emerson has maintained that the argument from democracy 'embraces the right to participate in the building of the whole culture, and includes freedom of expression in religion, literature, art, science, and all areas of human learning and knowledge'. *The system of freedom of expression*, p. 7. And Harry Kalven noted that '[T]he invitation to follow a dialectic progression from public official to government policy to matters in the public domain, like art, seems to me to be overwhelming'. 'The New York Times Case . . .', p. 221. This progression is resisted by Robert Bork, who would confine the argument to the strictly political. 'Neutral principles and some First Amendment problems'.
10 *Free speech and its relation to self-government*, p. 16.
11 *Odes*, book III, ode iii. This phrase was quoted by Thomas Jefferson in a letter to James Madison of December 20, 1787. See Edmond Cahn, 'The firstness of the First Amendment', p. 476.

Notes to chapter 4

1 *Jurisprudence*, vol. 3, pp. 63–7, 313–17.
2 See Ronald Dworkin, *Taking rights seriously*, pp. 90–6, 188–97.
3 See Thomas Emerson, 'Toward a general theory of the First Amendment', pp. 879–81.
4 See Joel Feinberg, *Social philosophy*, pp. 4–19.
5 J. L. Austin called 'expressing' an 'odious word'. *How to do things with words*, p. 75.
6 Clearly there are many instances in which self-expressive non-verbal conduct may have a communicative component as well. Examples would be wearing an armband or wearing bizarre clothing. I am not saying that this kind of conduct is *eo ipso* outside the scope of the Free

Speech Principle. Rather, I am arguing only that what protection is available under the Free Speech Principle is derived solely from the communicative component. I will deal further with this issue in chapter 7.

7 In this respect Mill's argument for liberty of thought and discussion can be seen as merely an instance of his argument for a more general freedom of choice and diversity. But then he is not making an argument for an independent principle of freedom of speech.

Notes to chapter 5

1 Liberalism is amorphous either because it represents no more than a family resemblance among a number of different doctrines (see Richard Flathman, *The practice of rights*, p. 43), or because attempts at locating the 'essence' of liberalism (see Ronald Dworkin, 'Liberalism', in *Public and private morality*) operate at a level of extremely high abstraction. I have explored the distinction between liberalism as individuality and the doctrine of freedom of speech in 'Pornography and the First Amendment'.

2 I do not want to get into the free will/determinism issue here. But it seems clear that a rejection of determinism is implicit in any intelligible version of liberalism. Indeed, a rejection of determinism may even be presupposed by most other personal or political philosophies as well. See Isaiah Berlin, 'Introduction', in *Four essays on liberty*, pp. ix–lxiii.

3 In addition to the previously cited essay, 'Liberalism', see *Taking rights seriously*, pp. 240–78. For applications to freedom of speech, see also his 'Introduction', in *The philosophy of law*, pp. 14–16, and 'The rights of Myron Farber', *The New York Review of Books*, October 26, 1978. (My response and Dworkin's reply are in *The New York Review of Books*, December 7, 1978.)

4 I do not mean here that equality may not be important in the *application* of a Free Speech Principle. If there is such a principle, it necessarily implies some degree of equality among speakers and a limitation on the extent to which ideas may be considered unequal. See Kenneth Karst, 'Equality as a central principle in the First Amendment'. But this does not mean that equality *supports* a Free Speech Principle.

5 It seems clear to me that Dworkin used the precise terminology 'expressions of adherence' rather than 'advocacy', 'encouragement' or 'incitement' in an attempt to avoid this very problem. Even if it can be argued that this distinction puts the words into his 'liberty as independence' category rather than the 'liberty as licence' category, the speech aspect is so diluted that he is saying little if anything about freedom of speech. That may have been his intention, but I doubt if most readers will see it that way.

6 *Taking rights seriously*, pp. 275–6.

7 This topic has been of interest throughout the history of the philoso-

phy of science. Recent works include L. J. Cohen, 'Guessing'; J. H. Lesher, 'On the role of guesswork in science'.

8 Locke was among the first to recognize the practical as well as moral obstacles to interference with belief, as distinguished from practices or expression. 'The care of souls cannot belong to the civil magistrate, because his power consists only in outward force: but true and saving religion consists in the inward persuasion of the mind, without which nothing can be acceptable to God. And such is the nature of the understanding, that it cannot be compelled to the belief of any thing by outward force'. *Letter concerning toleration, in Works,* vol. 6, pp. 8, 11–12.

Dicey also noted that what some call 'freedom of thought' is more accurately described as the 'right to the free expression of opinion'. A. V. Dicey, *Introduction to the study of the law of the Constitution,* p. 239.

9 'A theory of freedom of expression'. Scanlon has more recently expressed doubts about the validity of his own argument. 'Freedom of expression and categories of expression', pp. 530–7. Despite Scanlon's own doubts, some of which parallel arguments I make in this book, the original argument is sufficiently illuminating to justify extended treatment here.

10 *American Communications Association v. Douds,* 339 U.S. 382 (1950), at p. 421.

11 'Rawls' Theory of justice', *University of Pennsylvania Law Review,* pp. 1041–4.

12 Is it so clear that those in the Original Position would not do so? This seems perhaps the greatest weakness in the contractarian characterization of the argument, but it is a weakness in the Rawlsian position generally and perhaps in all social contract theories.

13 Chapter XX, where this argument is predominant, is entitled *'Ostenditur in libra republica unicuique et sentire quae velit, et quae sentiat dicere licere'.* (That in a free state everyone may think what he pleases, and say what he thinks.)

14 'Two concepts of interests: some reflections on the Supreme Court's balancing test', pp. 767–9.

Notes to chapter 6

1 I use 'utility' and 'utilitarian' in somewhat non-technical senses, to refer to practicality, or usefulness, or pragmatic considerations in general. I do not here equate utilitarian considerations with appeals solely to happiness or pleasure. Perhaps 'consequentialism' might be a better word (see Bernard Williams, *Morality,* pp. 96–7), but I want to stress the difference between the practical considerations in this chapter and the more theoretical consequentialist arguments discussed in chapter 2 and chapter 3.

2 E.g., H. J. McCloskey, 'Liberty of expression: its grounds and limits', pp. 229–30.

3 *American Communications Association* v. *Douds,* 339 U.S. 382 (1950), at p. 442. See also H. J. Laski, *The grammar of politics,* p. 120.

4 'Against the principle that truth is strong and (given the chance) will prevail, must be set Gresham's Law, that bad money drives out good, which has some application in matters of culture and which predicts that it will not necessarily be the most interesting ideas or the most valuable works of art that survive in competition – above all, in commercial competition.' *Report of the committee on obscenity and film censorship,* Bernard Williams, chairman (London: HMSO, 1979, Cmnd 7772), p. 55. The Williams Committee's entire discussion of freedom of speech (pp. 53–60 of the Report) is both interesting and important, especially for its rejection of some of the traditional platitudes about freedom of speech.

5 'What standards for broadcasting?', *Measure,* Vol. 1 (1950), pp. 211–12.

6 My thinking on this point has been clarified by the helpful comments of Hyman Gross to a paper I delivered to the seminar on Probability and Justice in the Department of Philosophy at Cambridge University.

7 An interesting contrast is provided by the following: 'A brother who lived across the street from me came over one day and asked me what communism was. "There must be something good about it," he said, "because the man is always trying to convince us that it's bad." ' Angela Davis, *Angela Davis: an autobiography,* p. 222.

8 The King to Oxford sent a troop of horse,
For Tories own no argument but force:
With equal skill to Cambridge books he sent,
For Whigs admit no force but argument.
Sir William Brown, from *Nichols literary anecdotes,* ii, p. 330.

9 *The practice and theory of Bolshevism,* p. 98.

10 'Communication and freedom of expression', *Scientific American,* p. 163.

11 A good example is in Laski, *The grammar of politics,* p. 121.

12 Before people thought seriously about the 'tyranny of the majority', rights were perceived more as rights of the mass of the people against a single despot or a small oligarchy. Even individual rights were those exercised by an individual *qua* member of the body politic and not *qua* individual. Given this view of rights, it is not surprising that the acceptance of the jury for cases of libel, as in Fox's Act of 1843 and as in America somewhat earlier, was thought to be an enormous advance for freedom of speech.

To some extent this follows Dworkin, who has pointed out that if a right is a right against the majority, then it is absurd to allow the majority to determine the extent or strength of that right. I am not talking here about what could be called institutional self-interest, but rather simple personal self-interest.

It has also been suggested by Thomas Emerson and by Justice William Douglas of the United States Supreme Court that the desire to eliminate disagreement is especially strong in authoritarian personalities. I do not have the expertise to evaluate that assertion, but if it is true then it may be that the same attributes of character that lead to the desire to censor also lead people to aspire to positions of leadership in society. That is, those who achieve high office may already have censorship-prone personalities.

13 This example was provided by Neil Thomason.
14 *Abrams* v. *United States*, 250 U.S. 616 (1919), at p. 630.
15 Quoted in T. Tanner, 'Licence and licensing: to the presse or to the spunge', p. 11.
16 'Limits to the free expression of opinion', p. 192.
17 See R. M. Hare, 'Principles'; G. Trianosky, 'Rule-utilitarianism and the slippery slope'.
18 Trianosky, at p. 421.
19 See John Rawls, 'Two concepts of rules'.

Notes to chapter 7

1 When an act is covered by a right, it is in one sense protected *to some extent*. But I use 'protection' in the sense of resultant permission or legal ability to engage in the act. Thus an act can be covered but not protected. If the justification for a restriction is sufficiently powerful, a person can in one sense of 'right' have a right to engage in the act, but in another sense 'have no right' to engage in that act. This is so because the right in the first sense still exists even when it is not sufficiently strong to produce actual permission or legal ability in the face of a strong justification for restriction. It is therefore misleading to talk of this kind of right as a *'prima facie'* right, because it never disappears. When I have a right, in the sense in which I am using the word 'right', I can require a strong justification. The right is not my right to do x, it is my right to require a strong justification before I can be prevented from doing x. That right, as long as x is covered, *never* disappears.

2 An attempt to formulate political rules (or principles) is similar to an attempt to formulate legal rules (or principles). Thus, many of the distinctive features of legal definition (see H. L. A. Hart, *Definition & theory in jurisprudence*) are applicaple, *mutatis mutandis*, to definition in political theory.

3 As Edmund Burke noted, our inability to locate the precise point at which day ends and night begins does not detract from the utility of the distinction between day and night.

4 'Free' is one of those words, like 'real', 'direct', and 'proper', whose sense is derived primarily from contrast with their opposite. Because we start by specifying the sense in which we mean the opposite, in this case 'unfree', it is the opposite that 'wears the trousers'. J. L. Austin, *Sense and sensibilia*, ed. G. J. Warnock (Oxford: Clarendon Press, 1962), p. 15.

5 Some illustrative American cases dealing with what is misleadingly called 'symbolic speech' are *Stromberg* v. *California,* 283 U.S. 359 (1931) (red flag); *Tinker* v. *Des Moines Independent School District,* 393 U.S. 503 (1969) (armband); *Spence* v. *Washington,* 418 U.S. 405 (1974) (flag burnings).

6 *Davis* v. *Norman,* 555 F.2d 189 (8th Cir. 1977).

7 We should not forget that Wittgenstein (and Austin as well) were often concerned with the scope of the subject matter of philosophy as a discipline. Much of what they said about the sufficiency of ordinary language should be interpreted as 'sufficient for embodying all philosophically interesting distinctions' rather than as 'sufficient for all purposes'.

8 'The meaning of a word', in *Philosophical papers,* p. 37. Whether Austin believed this is something else again. See also Friedrich Waismann, 'Analytic–synthetic (part 5)'.

9 The 'least restrictive alternative' doctrine is well-entrenched in American free speech theory. See [Student Note], 'Less drastic means and the First Amendment', *Yale Law Journal,* Vol. 78 (1969), pp. 464–74. The leading case is *Shelton* v. *Tucker,* 364 U.S. 479 (1960).

10 There is a parallel between my use of action *directed at* communication and Charles Fried's use of *intention* in determining the rightness or wrongness of conduct. *Right and wrong,* pp. 20–27.

The focus on the aim or purpose of the regulation is explored in greater depth in Laurence Tribe, *American constitutional law,* pp. 580–605; John Hart Ely, 'Flag desecration: a case study in the roles of categorization and balancing in First Amendment analysis'; Thomas Scanlon, 'A theory of freedom of expression'; *United States* v. *O'Brien,* 391 U.S. 367 (1968).

11 *Bigelow* v. *Virginia,* 421 U.S. 809 (1975); *Virginia State Board of Pharmacy* v. *Virginia Consumer Council,* 425 U.S. 748 (1976); *Bates* v. *State Bar of Arizona,* 433 U.S. 350 (1977); *Linmark* v. *Township of Willingboro,* 431 U.S. 85 (1977).

12 See Willmoore Kendall, 'The "open society" and its fallacies'; Joseph Tussman, *Government and the mind.*

13 See Thomas Scanlon, 'Freedom of expression and categories of expression'.

14 My implicit distinction between primary and derivative rights under a particular political principle follows Dworkin's distinction between constitutive political positions and derivative political positions. 'Liberalism', pp. 116–17.

15 See Vincent Blasi, 'The checking value in First Amendment theory'.

16 American readers should replace *Crossroads* with *Day of our lives, As the world turns,* or any other soap opera.

17 For further elaboration of the importance of private discussion of public issues, see my ' "Private" speech and the "private" forum: *Givhan* v. *Western Line School District',* *The Supreme Court Review* (1979), pp. 217–49.

18 If some particular protection is to be allowed to the press, it can take several forms. I will not deal here with particular forms of protection, except to say that what is at issue is protection of the press as an institution, rather than protection of particular writings that appear in the press. For example, under the Swedish protection of the press, journalists have a privilege that protects them from having to provide information to public authorities, even as to pending criminal investigations. The theory of such protection is that only if journalists can deal in confidence with their sources, only if they have a privilege not unlike that normally given to lawyers and priests, will the process of investigation be effective. Such a reporters' privilege has been rejected by courts in both Great Britain and the United States, but is available by statute in a number of American states. Somewhat analogous is the Newspaper Preservation Act in the United States, which recognizes the particular importance of newspapers by granting a limited immunity from the merger restrictions of the American antitrust (free competition) laws. It would be pointless to give additional examples here. The point is that if freedom of the press is indeed a distinct principle, and not just one form of freedom of speech, then it is inevitable that members of the press will be protected even before anything actually is printed.

19 Some may argue that anything so clearly political is not art at all. The issue of what is 'art' is not the subject of this book, but any dichotomy between artistic expression and political communication would support the argument made in the text.

Notes to chapter 8

1 See also Montesquieu's discussion of 'freedom to do whatever the law permits'. *The spirit of the laws*, book XI, ch. iii.

2 See H. L. A. Hart, *The concept of law*, p. 39.

3 What counts as governmental control is debatable, but not germane to the point under discussion.

4 Ronald Dworkin, *Taking rights seriously*, p. 94, n.1.

5 *Right and wrong*, pp. 110–12.

6 I am indebted to Ian White for this example.

7 See, for example, Jerome Barron, 'Access to the press – a new First Amendment right'; Thomas Emerson, *The system of freedom of expression*, p. 671.

8 Isaiah Berlin, 'Two concepts of liberty', in *Four essays on liberty*, pp. 118–72.

9 In American law, the scarcity of broadcast frequencies has been the justification for restrictions on the broadcast media that would not be otherwise permissible. See *Red Lion Broadcasting Company* v. *FCC*, 395 U.S. 367 (1969). Yet there is something odd about assuming that government regulation is the appropriate response to the problem of allocating scarce resources, at least in a free market economy. See William

Van Alstyne, 'The Möbius strip of the First Amendment: perspectives on *Red Lion*', pp. 539–76.

10 Here again I follow John Rawls, 'Two concepts of rules'.

11 Brian Barry, *Political argument*, p. 141.

Notes to chapter 9

1 I am intentionally blinking the question of what is to count as a harm. It is not that this question is not interesting or not important. On the contrary, it is one of the central questions of political philosophy. But the only point that is germane here is that speech can cause the kinds of effects that would count as a harm under almost any theory.

2 I recognize that by utilizing an attenuated concept of individual rights it could be argued that individual rights are at stake in wartime because rights may be lost in the event of defeat by a conquering power. But such a view of rights makes it possible to cast any governmental action in terms of individual rights, rendering the very notion of a right a nullity.

3 The extreme example is a newspaper report that the defendant has confessed, but the confession is then ruled inadmissible in court for reasons unrelated to its validity as an admission of guilt. I doubt there is one person in a million, myself included, who could sit as a juror and totally disregard the knowledge of the confession.

4 See L. Frantz, 'The First Amendment in the balance'.

5 I am assuming that a determination of obscenity is something more than an ascriptive conclusion. Compare H. L. A. Hart, 'The ascription of responsibilities and rights'. Hart has since repudiated that view of legal language. H. L. A. Hart, *Punishment and responsibility*, p. v.

6 This statistical model of the criminal process is unduly and perhaps mistakenly simple. A full evaluation of probabilities in the criminal process would have to incorporate the underlying *a priori* probability of guilt among those who are brought to trial, whereas this model assumes that those on trial are as likely to be innocent as guilty. But for my purposes this crude model is sufficient.

7 See Harry Kalven, 'The New York Times case . . .', p. 213. The same view is implicit in Kalven's observation that 'classic free speech theory is really a defense of the risk of permitting a *false* doctrine to circulate . . .' 'A commemorative case note: *Scopes* v. *State*', p. 516.

8 This is not to say that we should not search for ways of accommodating both interests if possible. Sequestering jurors, for example, is one way of preserving a fair trial while allowing unlimited publicity.

9 This formulation is an amalgam of the original 'clear and present danger' phrase employed by Holmes with Brandeis' gloss that the danger must be of significant size.

10 I am not suggesting here that harm is the only valid object of governmental action. I have expressed it so merely to simplify the example.

11 See Ronald Dworkin, *Taking rights seriously*, p. 33.

12 See J. M. Finnis, 'Some professorial fallacies about rights', p. 387.

13 *The role of the Supreme Court in American government*, pp. 47–8.

14 *New York Times Co.* v. *United States*, 403 U.S. 713 (1971).

15 The expansion of the original meaning of 'censorship' to include subsequent punishment has given rise to the neologism 'pre-censorship' to refer to prior restraint.

Notes to chapter 10

1 If we want to say that some select group has special competence superior to that of the public at large, then who picks the select group? Another select group? But who picks them?

2 'Free speech and its relation to self-government', in *Political freedom: the constitutional powers of the people* (New York: Oxford University Press, 1965), p. 87. See also George Anastaplo, 'Human nature and the First Amendment'.

3 Unfortunately, the ratio is more like ten-to-one or a hundred-to-one.

4 *The open society and its enemies*, vol. 1, pp. 265–6. See also Evan F. M. Durbin, *The politics of democratic socialism*, pp. 275–9.

   The discussion here is taken from a paper I presented at the Biennial Conference of the Royal Institute of Philosophy, 15 September 1979, and appears in full in *Values in conflict*, ed. B. Leiser, pp. 228–37.

5 See John Rawls, *A theory of justice*, pp. 216–21.

6 "The interest, which [free speech] guards, and which gives it its importance, presupposes that there are no orthodoxies – religious, political, economic, or scientific – which are immune from debate or dispute. Back of that is the assumption – *itself an orthodoxy, and the one permissible exception* – that truth will be most likely to emerge, if no limitations are imposed. . . .' *International Brotherhood of Electrical Workers* v. *NLRB*, 181 F.2d 34 (2d Cir. 1950), at p. 40 (L. Hand, J.) (emphasis supplied).

Notes to chapter 11

1 In English law falsity is not part of the definition of defamation, but truth is an affirmative defence available to the publisher. In American law the defamed plaintiff must prove falsity.

2 Mill and Milton did, however, recognize the value of falsity in fostering a deeper understanding of truth. Extending this to plain factual error, however, seems attenuated.

3 See Joel Feinberg, 'Limits to the free expression of opinion', in *Philosophy of law*, p. 194.

Notes to chapter 12

1 For fuller explications, see Joel Feinberg, *The idea of the obscene*; Kurt Baier, 'Response: the liberal approach to pornography'.

2 There *can* be obscene objects or articles.

3 On formalism, see H. L. A. Hart, *The concept of law*, p. 126.

4 The arguments in this section parallel those I made in 'Speech and "speech" – obscenity and "obscenity": an exercise in the interpretation of constitutional language'; 'Response: pornography and the First Amendment'.

5 See *Report of the committee on obscenity and film censorship*, Bernard Williams, chairman (London: HMSO, 1979, Cmnd 7772); D. A. J. Richards, 'Free speech and obscenity law: toward a moral theory of the First Amendment'.

6 This is the recommendation of the Williams Committee, and has been endorsed by the United States Supreme Court in *Young* v. *American Mini Theatres, Inc.*, 427 U.S. 50 (1976).

7 Strong opposition to pornography has surfaced recently in the feminist movement. The concerns have focused on the way in which pornography can increase the likelihood of violence against women, and on the way in which sexually explicit material almost invariably presents a highly degrading image of women. These concerns are undoubtedly legitimate, but, to the extent that the opposition is directed at a wide variety of clearly communicative publications, the concerns would have to meet the high burden of justification implicit in the Free Speech Principle.

Notes to chapter 13

1 See John Rawls, *A theory of justice*, pp. 217–18.

2 'Every idea is an incitement'. Holmes, J., dissenting in *Gitlow* v. *New York*, 268 U.S. 652 (1925), at p. 673.

3 I am excluding those speech acts that *are* illegal activities in the performative sense, such as making a bet, or saying 'I do' when I am already married.

4 Holmes' views on intent and effect were well in place by the time he started to deal with the issue of free speech. See Yosal Rogat, 'The judge as spectator', *University of Chicago Law Review*, Vol. 31 (1964), pp. 213–56.

5 A law-breaker is, after all, making the claim that *his* law supersedes that of society.

6 See Ronald Dworkin, *Taking rights seriously*, pp. 197–203.

7 Thus we have Learned Hand's test of 'the gravity of the "evil", discounted by its improbability'. *United States* v. *Dennis*, 183 F.2d 201 (2d Cir. 1950), at p. 212.

8 *United States* v. *Progressive, Inc.*, 467 F. Supp. 990 (W. D. Wisc. 1979).

Notes to chapter 14

1 See Charles Reich, 'Making free speech audible'.

2 A common tactic in pre-trial discovery of documents is to give the requesting party too much, rather than too little. Imagine trying to locate,

without any guidance, one vital document in four rooms of file cabinets.

3 See Laurence Tribe, *American constitutional law*, pp. 580–605.

4 L. Frantz, 'The First Amendment in the balance', p. 1439.

5 See [Student Note], 'Less drastic means and the First Amendment', *Yale Law Journal*, Vol. 78 (1969), pp. 464–74.

Consolidated bibliography

Amdur, Robert, 'Scanlon on freedom of expression', *Philosophy and public affairs* **9** (1980), 287.

Anastaplo, George, 'Human nature and the First Amendment', *University of Pittsburgh Law Review* **40** (1979), 661.

Attwooll, Elspeth, 'Liberties, rights and powers', in *Perspectives in jurisprudence*, E. Attwooll, ed. (Glasgow: University of Glasgow Press, 1977), 79.

Auerbach, Carl, 'The Communist Control Act of 1954: a proposed legal–political theory of free speech', *University of Chicago Law Review* **23** (1956), 173.

Austin, J. L., *How to do things with words,* J. O. Urmson & M. Sibsà, eds. (Cambridge: Harvard University Press, 1975).

'The meaning of a word', in *Philosophical papers* (Oxford: Clarendon Press, 1961), 23.

Sense and sensibilia, G. J. Warnock, ed. (Oxford: Clarendon Press, 1962).

Bagehot, Walter, 'The metaphysical basis of toleration', in *Literary studies,* R. H. Hutton, ed. (London, 1884), 422.

Baier, Kurt, 'Response: the liberal approach to pornography', *University of Pittsburgh Law Review* **40** (1979), 619.

Baker, Edwin, 'Commercial speech: a problem in the theory of freedom', *Iowa Law Review* **62** (1976), 1.

'Scope of the First Amendment freedom of speech', *UCLA Law Review* **25** (1978), 964.

Barron, Jerome, 'Access to the press – a new First Amendment right', *Harvard Law Review* **80** (1967), 1641.

Barry, Brian, *The liberal theory of justice* (Oxford: Clarendon Press, 1973).

Political argument (London: Routledge and Kegan Paul, 1965).

Belaief, Gail, 'Freedom and liberty', *Journal of Value Inquiry* **13** (1979), 127.

Berger, Fred, ed., *Freedom of expression* (Belmont, California: Wadsworth, 1980).

Berger, Fred, 'Pornography, sex, and censorship', *Social Theory and Practice* **4** (1977), 183.

Berlin, Isaiah, *Against the current: essays in the history of ideas,* Henry Hardy, ed. (London: Hogarth Press, 1979).

Concepts and categories: philosophical essays, Henry Hardy, ed. (London: Hogarth Press, 1978).

Consolidated bibliography

Four essays on liberty (Oxford: Oxford University Press, 1969).

BeVier, Lillian, 'The First Amendment and political speech: an inquiry into the substance and limits of principle', *Stanford Law Review* **30** (1978), 299.

Blasi, Vincent, 'The checking value in First Amendment theory', *American Bar Foundation Research Journal* (1977), 521.

'Prior restraints on demonstrations', *Michigan Law Review* **68** (1970), 1482.

Bollinger, Lee, 'Freedom of the press and public access: toward a theory of partial regulation of the mass media', *Michigan Law Review* **75** (1976), 1.

Bork, Robert, 'Neutral principles and some First Amendment problems', *Indiana Law Journal* **47** (1971), 1.

Brennan, William, 'The Supreme Court and the Meiklejohn interpretation of the First Amendment', *Harvard Law Review* **79** (1965), 1.

Buchanan, Allen, 'Autonomy and categories of expression: a reply to Professor Scanlon', *University of Pittsburgh Law Review* **40** (1979), 551.

'Revisability and rational choice', *Canadian Journal of Philosophy* **5** (1975), 395.

Cahn, Edmond, 'The firstness of the First Amendment', *Yale Law Journal* **65** (1956), 464.

Canavan, Francis, 'Freedom of speech and press: for what purpose?', *American Journal of Jurisprudence* **16** (1971), 95.

'John Milton and freedom of expression', *Interpretation* **7** (1978), 50.

Cass, Ronald, 'First Amendment access to government facilities', *Virginia Law Review* **65** (1979), 1287.

Chafee, Zecheriah, *Freedom of speech* (London: Allen & Unwin, 1920).

Free speech in the United States (Cambridge: Harvard University Press, 1941).

Chevigny, Paul, 'Philosophy of language and free expression', *New York University Law Review* **55** (1980), 157.

Cohen, L. J., 'Guessing', *Proceedings of the Aristotelian Society* (New Series) **74** (1973–74), 189.

Cowling, Maurice, *Mill and liberalism* (Cambridge: Cambridge University Press, 1963).

Cox, Archibald, *The role of the Supreme Court in American Government* (New York: Oxford University Press, 1976).

Crawford, Charles, 'Can disputes over censorship be resolved?', *Ethics* **78** (1968), 93.

Davis, Angela, *Angela Davis: an autobiography* (London: Arrow Books Limited, 1976).

Dhavan, Rajeev and Davies, Christie, eds, *Censorship and Obscenity* (London: Martin Robertson, 1978).

Dicey, A. V., *Introduction to the study of the law of the Constitution*, E. C. S. Wade, ed. (London: Macmillan, 1964).

Durbin, Evan F. M., *The politics of democratic socialism* (London: G. Routledge, 1940).

DuVal, Benjamin, 'Free communication of ideas and the quest for truth: toward a teleological approach to First Amendment adjudication', *George Washington Law Review* **41** (1972), 161.

Dworkin, Ronald, 'Introduction', in *The philosophy of law*, R. M. Dworkin, ed. (Oxford: Oxford University Press, 1977), 1.

'Is the press losing the First Amendment?', *New York Review of Books* (December 4, 1980), 49.

'Liberalism', in *Public and private morality*, Stuart Hampshire, ed. (Cambridge: Cambridge University Press, 1978), 113.

'The rights of Myron Farber', *New York Review of Books* (October 26, 1978), with exchange (December 7, 1978).

Taking rights seriously (London: Duckworth, 1977).

Ely, John Hart, 'Flag desecration: a case study in the roles of categorization and balancing in First Amendment analysis', *Harvard Law Review* **88** (1975), 1482.

Emerson, Thomas, 'Communication and freedom of expression', *Scientific American* (September, 1972), 163.

'The doctrine of prior restraint', *Law and Contemporary Problems* **20** (1955), 648.

The system of freedom of expression (New York: Vintage Books, 1970).

'Toward a general theory of the First Amendment', *Yale Law Journal* **72** (1963), 877.

Feinberg, Joel, *The idea of the obscene* (Lindley Lecture) (Lawrence, Kansas: University of Kansas Press, 1979).

'Limits to the free expression of opinion', in *Philosophy of law*, second edition, J. Feinberg and H. Gross, eds (Encino, California: Dickenson, 1980), 191.

'Pornography and the criminal law', *University of Pittsburgh Law Review* **40** (1979), 567.

'Rawls and intuitionism', in *Reading Rawls: critical studies of A Theory of Justice*, N. Daniels, ed. (Oxford: Basil Blackwell, 1975), 108.

Social philosophy (Englewood Cliffs, New Jersey: Prentice-Hall, 1973).

Finnis, John, ' "Reason and passion": the constitutional dialectic of free speech and obscenity', *University of Pennsylvania Law Review* **116** (1967), 222.

'Scepticism, self-refutation, and the good of truth', in *Law, morality, and society: essays in honour of H. L. A. Hart*, P. M. S. Hacker and J. Raz, eds (Oxford: Clarendon Press, 1977), 247.

'Some professorial fallacies about rights', *Adelaide Law Review* **4** (1972), 377.

Flathman, Richard, *The practice of rights* (Cambridge: Cambridge University Press, 1976).

Frank, Jerome, *Courts on trial* (Princeton: Princeton University Press, 1949).

Frantz, Laurent, 'The First Amendment in the balance', *Yale Law Journal* **71** (1962), 1424.

Freund, Paul, 'The great disorder of speech', *The American Scholar* **44** (1975), 541.

'The Supreme Court and civil liberties', *Vanderbilt Law Review* 4 (1951), 533.

Fried, Charles, *Right and wrong* (Cambridge: Harvard University Press, 1978).

'Two concepts of interests: some reflections on the Supreme Court's balancing test', *Harvard Law Review* 76 (1963), 755.

Fuchs, Alan, 'Further steps toward a general theory of freedom of expression', *William and Mary Law Review* 18 (1976), 347.

Fuller, Lon, 'Freedom – a suggested analysis', *Harvard Law Review* 68 (1955), 1305.

Garvey, John, 'Freedom and choice in constitutional law', *Harvard Law Review* 94 (1981), 1756.

Gewirth, Alan, *Reason and morality* (Chicago: University of Chicago Press, 1978).

Glass, Marvin, 'Anti-racism and unlimited freedom of speech', *Canadian Journal of Philosophy* 8 (1978), 559.

Greenawalt, Kent, 'Speech and crime', *American Bar Foundation Research Journal* (1980), 645.

Gunther, Gerald, 'Learned Hand and the origins of modern First Amendment doctrine: some fragments of history', *Stanford Law Review* 27 (1975), 719.

Haley, William, 'What standards for broadcasting?', *Measure* 1 (1950), 211.

Hare, R. M., 'Principles', *Proceedings of the Aristotelian Society* (new series) 73 (1973), 1.

Harrison, Geoffrey, 'Relativism and tolerance', in *Philosophy, politics and society (fifth series)*, P. Laslett and J. Fishkin, eds (Oxford: Basil Blackwell, 1979), 273.

Hart, H. L. A., "The ascription of responsibilities and rights', in *Logic and language (first series)*, A. G. N. Flew, ed. (Oxford: Basil Blackwell, 1951), 145.

The concept of law (Oxford: Clarendon Press, 1961).

Definition and theory in jurisprudence (Oxford : Clarendon Press, 1953).

Punishment and responsibility (Oxford: Clarendon Press, 1968).

Haslett, D. W., 'The general theory of rights', *Social Theory and Practice* 5 (1980), 427.

Hayek, F. A., *The constitution of liberty* (London: Routledge & Kegan Paul, 1960).

Henkin, Louis, 'Foreword: on drawing lines', *Harvard Law Review* 82 (1968), 63.

'Morals and the Constitution: the sin of obscenity', *Columbia Law Review* 63 (1963), 391.

Holbrook, David, ed., *The case against pornography* (London: Tom Stacey Ltd., 1972).

Holmes, Oliver Wendell, 'The path of the law', *Harvard Law Review* 10 (1897), 457.

Hudson, Stephen and Husak, Douglas, 'Legal rights: how useful is Hohfeldian analysis', *Philosophical Studies* 37 (1980), 45.

Hughes, Douglas A., ed., *Perspectives on pornography* (New York: Macmillan, 1970).

Hume, David, 'Of the liberty of the press', in *Essays, moral, political and literary* (Oxford, 1963).

Hyneman, Charles, 'Free speech at what price?', *American Political Science Review* **57** (1962), 847.

Ingber, Stanley, 'Defamation: a conflict between reason and decency', *Virginia Law Review* **65** (1979), 785.

Ingram, Peter, 'Principle and practice in censorship', *Social Theory and Practice* **4** (1977), 315.

Kalven, Harry, 'A commemorative case note: *Scopes* v. *State*', *University of Chicago Law Review* **27** (1960), 505.

'The metaphysics of the law of obscenity', *The Supreme Court Review* (1960), 1.

'The New York Times case: a note on the "Central meaning of the First Amendment" ', *The Supreme Court Review* (1964), 191.

Kant, Immanuel, *On the old saw: that may be right in theory but it won't work in practice*, E. B. Ashton, trans. (Philadelphia: University of Pennsylvania Press, 1974).

Karst, Kenneth, 'Equality as a central principle in the First Amendment', *University of Chicago Law Review* **43** (1975), 20.

'The freedom of intimate association', *Yale Law Journal* **89** (1980), 624.

Kendall, Willmoore, 'The "open society" and its fallacies', *American Political Science Review* **54** (1960), 972.

Ladenson, Robert, 'Freedom of the press: a jurisprudential inquiry', *Social Theory and Practice* **6** (1980), 163.

Laski, Harold J., *A grammar of politics* (London: Allen & Unwin, 1938).

Lerner, Max, *The mind and faith of Justice Holmes* (New York: Modern Library, 1954).

Lesher, J. H., 'On the role of guesswork in science', *Studies in History and Philosophy of Science* **9** (1978), 19.

Linde, Hans, ' "Clear and present danger" reexamined: dissonance in the Brandenburg Concerto', *Stanford Law Review* **22** (1970), 1163.

Locke, John, *A letter concerning toleration*, J. W. Gough, ed. (Oxford: Basil Blackwell, 1948).

Lyons, David, 'Human rights and the general welfare', *Philosophy and Public Affairs* **6** (1977), 113.

'Rights, claimants, and beneficiaries', *American Philosophical Quarterly* **6** (1969), 173.

'The correlativity of rights and duties', *Noûs* **22** (1970), 45.

MacCallum, Gerald, 'Negative and positive freedom', *Philosophical Review* **76** (1967), 312.

Magee, Brian, *Popper* (London: Fontana, 1973).

Marcus, Ruth Barcan, 'Moral dilemmas and consistency', *Journal of Philosophy* **77** (1980), 121.

Marshall, Geoffrey, *Constitutional theory* (Oxford: Clarendon Press, 1971).

Martin, Rex and Nickel, James, 'Recent work on the concept of rights', *American Philosophical Quarterly* **17** (1980), 165.

McCloskey, H. J., 'Liberty of expression: its grounds and limits', *Inquiry* **13** (1970), 219.

Meiklejohn, Alexander, 'The balancing of self-preservation against political freedom', *California Law Review* **49** (1961), 4.

'The First Amendment is an absolute', *The Supreme Court Review* (1961), 245.

Free speech and its relation to self-government, in *Political freedom: the constitutional powers of the people* (New York: Oxford University Press, 1965).

Melden, A. I., *Rights and persons* (Oxford: Basil Blackwell, 1977).

Mill, John Stuart, *On liberty,* D. Spitz, ed. (New York: W. W. Norton, 1975).

Milton, John, *Areopagitica,* J. C. Suffolk, ed. (London: University Tutorial Press, 1968).

Moore, John Bruce, 'On philosophizing about freedom of speech', *Southwestern Journal of Philosophy* **6** (1975), 47.

Morawski, Stefan, 'Censorship versus art: typological reflections', *Praxis* **10** (1974), 154.

Morrow, Frank, 'Speech, expression, and the constitution', *Ethics* **85** (1975), 235.

Munro, D. H., 'Liberty of expression: its grounds and limits', *Inquiry* **13** (1970), 238.

Nimmer, Melville, 'The meaning of symbolic speech under the First Amendment', *UCLA Law Review* **21** (1973), 29.

'The right to speak from *Times* to *Time:* First Amendment theory applied to libel and misapplied to privacy', *California Law Review* **56** (1968), 935.

Norris, Stephen, 'Being free to speak and speaking freely', in *Social ends and political means,* T. Honderich, ed. (London: Routledge and Kegan Paul, 1976), 13.

Nozick, Robert, *Anarchy, state, and utopia* (New York: Basic Books, 1974).

Perry, Thomas, 'Reply in defense of Hohfeld', *Philosophical Studies* **37** (1980), 203.

Pollock, Frederick, 'The theory of persecution', in *Essays in jurisprudence and ethics* (London, 1882), 144.

Popper, Karl, *The open society and its enemies,* fifth edition (London: Routledge and Kegan Paul, 1966).

Pound, Roscoe, *Jurisprudence* (St. Paul, Minnesota: West Publishing Company, 1959).

Quine, Willard v. O., *Word and object* (Cambridge: Massachusetts Institute of Technology, 1960).

Raphael, D. D., *Problems of political philosophy* (London: Macmillan, 1976).

Rawls, John, *A theory of justice* (Cambridge: Harvard University Press, 1971).

'Two concepts of rules', *Philosophical Review* **64** (1955), 3.

Reich, Charles, 'Making free speech audible', *The Nation* (February, 1965), 138.

Report of the committee on obscenity and film censorship, Bernard Williams, chairman (London: HMSO, 1979, Cmnd 7772).

Richards, David A. J., 'Free speech and obscenity law: toward a moral theory of the First Amendment', *University of Pennsylvania Law Review* **123** (1974), 45.

The moral criticism of law (Encino, California: Dickenson, 1977).

A theory of reasons for action (Oxford: Clarendon Press, 1971).

Rogat, Yosal, 'The judge as spectator', *University of Chicago Law Review* **31** (1964), 213.

Russell, Bertrand, *The practice and theory of Bolshevism* (London: Macmillan, 1949).

Scanlon, Thomas, 'Freedom of expression and categories of expression', *University of Pittsburgh Law Review* **40** (1979), 519.

'Rawls' theory of justice', *University of Pennsylvania Law Review* **121** (1973), 1020.

'A theory of freedom of expression', *Philosophy and Public Affairs* **1** (1972), 204.

Schauer, Frederick, 'Can rights be abused?', *Philosophical Quarterly* **31** (1981), 225–30.

'Categories and the First Amendment: a play in three acts', *Vanderbilt Law Review* **34** (1981), 265–307.

'Fear, risk, and the First Amendment: unraveling the "chilling effect" ', *Boston University Law Review* **58** (1978), 685.

'Free speech and the paradox of tolerance', in *Values in conflict,* B. Leiser, ed. (New York, Macmillan, 1981), 228.

'Language, truth, and the First Amendment: an essay in memory of Harry Canter', *Virginia Law Review* **64** (1978), 263.

'Response: pornography and the First Amendment', *University of Pittsburgh Law Review* **40** (1979), 605.

' "Private" speech and the "private" forum: *Givhan* v. *Western Line School District'*, *The Supreme Court Review* (1979), 217.

'Social foundations of the law of defamation: a comparative analysis', *Journal of Media Law and Practice* **1** (1980), 3.

'Speech and "speech" – obscenity and "obscenity": an exercise in the interpretation of constitutional language', *Georgetown Law Journal* **67** (1979), 899.

Schram, Glenn, 'The First Amendment and the educative function of law', *American Journal of Jurisprudence* **20** (1975), 38.

Shiffrin, Steven, 'Defamatory non-media speech and First Amendment methodology', *UCLA Law Review* **25** (1978), 915.

Simon, Yves, 'A comment on censorship', *International Philosophical Quarterly* **17** (1977), 33.

Spinoza, Benedict de, *A theologico-political treatise,* R. H. M. Elwes, trans. (New York: Dover Publications, 1951).

Consolidated bibliography

Stephen, James Fitzjames, *Liberty, equality, fraternity*, R. J. White, ed. (Cambridge: Cambridge University Press, 1967).

Stone, Geoffrey, 'Fora Americana: speech in public places', *The Supreme Court Review* (1974), 233.

'Restriction of speech because of its content: the peculiar case of subject-matter restrictions', *University of Chicago Law Review* **46** (1978), 81.

Strong, Frank, 'Fifty years of "clear and present danger": from *Schenck* to *Brandenburg* – and beyond', *The Supreme Court Review* (1969), 41.

[Student Note], 'Less drastic means and the First Amendment', *Yale Law Journal* **78** (1969), 464.

Tanner, Tony, 'Licence and licensing: to the presse or to the spunge', *Journal of the History of Ideas* **38** (1977), 5.

Tinder, Glenn, 'Freedom of expression: the strange imperative', *Yale Review* **69** (1980), 162.

[Trenchard, John and Thomas Gordon], *Cato's letters: essays on liberty, civil and religious, and other important subjects* (London, 1755).

Trianosky, Gregory, 'Rule-utilitarianism and the slippery slope', *Journal of Philosophy* **75** (1978), 414.

Tribe, Laurence, *American constitutional law* (Mineola, New York: Foundation Press, 1978).

Tussman, Joseph, *Government and the mind* (New York: Oxford University Press, 1977).

Van Alstyne, William, 'The Möbius strip of the First amendment: perspectives on *Red Lion*', *South Carolina Law Review* **29** (1978), 539.

Waismann, Friedrich, 'Analytic–synthetic (part 5)', *Analysis* **13** (1952), 1.

Wellington, Harry, 'On freedom of expression', *Yale Law Journal* **88** (1979), 1105.

Williams, Bernard, 'Conflicts of values', in *The Idea of Freedom*, Alan Ryan, ed. (Oxford: Oxford University Press, 1979), 221.

'Ethical consistency', in *Problems of the self* (Cambridge: Cambridge University Press, 1973), 166.

Morality (Cambridge: Cambridge University Press, 1972).

Williams, Glanville, 'The concept of legal liberty', in *Essays in legal philosophy*, R. S. Summers, ed. (Oxford: Basil Blackwell, 1970), 121.

Wittgenstein, Ludwig, *Philosophical investigations*, G. E. M. Anscombe, trans., third edition (Oxford: Basil Blackwell, 1967).

Younger, Irving, 'The idea of sanctuary', *Gonzaga Law Review* **14** (1979), 761.

Index

Index

Cohen, L. J., 213 n7
coherence, 207 n1
commercial speech, 103, 158-60
communication, 13, 103, 109-11; and
choice, 55-7; combined with action,
99-101; and communicative intent,
96-101; distinguished from expression, 50-2, 92-5; forums for, 120-8;
freedom of, 53-6, 92-5; functions of,
44, 92-5; non-linguistic, 95-101, 111;
and self-fulfillment, 53-6
competence, popular, 41, 154-8, 219 n1
Comte, Auguste, 30
conduct, distinguished from communication, 99-101, 103, 182-3, 197-8
consensus; desire for, 82-3; as test of
truth, *see under* truth
conspiracy, 92, 189
contempt, 44
content, regulation on basis of, 101,
117-19
coverage of rights, *see under* rights *and*
Free Speech Principle
Cowling, Maurice, 34, 157
Cox, Archibald, 147
Crawford, Charles, 112

Davies, Christie, 188
Davis, Angela, 214 n7
de Tocqueville, Alexis, 37, 45
defamation, 137, 143, 167-77; 214 n12;
in American law, 43-4, 171-3, 219 n1;
as causing harm, 10, 28, 167; in English law, 44, 149, 169, 172-3, 219 n1;
as exception to Free Speech Principle,
32, 89, 167; and political speech, 43-4,
89, 143, 173-4; and public figures, 143,
174-5; and statements of opinion,
169-73
deliberation, 38, 95, 108
democracy, 71; argument from, 35-46,
47, 95, 103, 107-8, 148, 154, 173;
definition of, 36-7, 78; and equality,
41-2; and national security, 189-91;
and political speech, 35; and popular
sovereignty, 35-6
demonstrations, 99, 201-6
Dhavan, Rajeev, 188
Dicey, A. V., 211 n5, 213 n8
dignity, 41, 61-4, 95
disobedience to law, *see* civil disobedience
diversity, 12, 48, 57, 60; argument from,
66-7
Douglas, William O., 214 n12
Dreiser, Theodore, 110, 178
Durbin, Evan F. M., 219 n4

DuVal, Benjamin, 210 n13
Dworkin, Ronald, 46, 62, 68, 207 n1, 207
n2, 210 n12, 211 n2, 212 n1, 212 n3,
212 n5, 214 n12, 216 n14, 217 n4, 218
n11, 220 n6; on rights, 129-30, 207 n4;
on free speech, 64-5

educative function of government,
155-8
electronic media, 107-8, 113, 126-7, 158,
217 n9
Ely, John Hart, 216 n10
Emerson, Thomas, 78-9, 153, 211 n9,
211 n3, 214 n12, 217 n7
emotive speech, 104-5
Enlightenment, Age of, 26-7
epistemology, *see* certainty, error, fallibilism, falsity, knowledge, truth
equality; and democracy, 37, 41-2; and
dignity 62-3; and regulation of content, 212 n4
error (*see also* falsity), 24; acceptance of,
by public, 74-5; in application of Free
Speech Principle, 81-5, 170-3, 186-8;
argument from, 19, 25; discovery of,
15, 19, 25, 154; displacement of, by
truth, 15; in judicial proceedings,
136-42, 170-3; margin for, in free
speech rules, 98-9, 102, 136-42, 170-3,
186-8; relative harm of types of,
136-42, 170-3; of underinclusion or
overinclusion, 137-42, 171, 186-8;
value of, 73-5, 219 n2
ethics, 19, 21-2, 30-1
European Convention on Human
Rights, 50, 161
expression (*see also* freedom of expression), 50-2, 92, 110-11
extortion, 13, 89, 92, 102-3

fact; distinguished from value, 18-19,
21; and defamation, 169-70; statements of, 18-19, 21, 32-3
fair trial and free press, 23, 133-4, 140,
150, 218 n3, 218 n8
fallibilism, 16, 22, 24, 25, 28-9, 66, 106,
161
fallibility; of governments, 34, 44, 83,
86, 156-8; of majorities, 44-6; of
people, 22, 24-5, 34, 83, 148
falsifiability, 21, 25
falsity, 22-3; attractiveness of, 24, 28,
74-5; and defamation, 169-71, 219 n1;
discovery of, 19, 27; harm of, 22, 28;
power of, 26-8, 74-5; toleration of, 28;
value of, 17, 73-5, 219 n2

232

Index

Index

Haley, William, 75
Hall, Radclyffe, 178
Hand, Learned, 15, 209 n1, 219 n6, 220 n7
Hare, R. M., 215 n17
harm, 46, 191-2, 218 n1; as caused by speech, 10-12, 24, 28, 58, 62-4, 141, 167; as prerequisite for exercise of state power, 7, 11, 218 n10; to reputation, 28, 167
Harrison, Geoffrey, 14
Hart, H. L. A., 208 n11, 215 n2, 217 n2, 218 n5, 220 n3
Haslett, D. W., 208 n5
Hayek, F. A., 57
Henkin, Louis, 112, 188
Hesse, Mary, 210 n14
Hobbes, Thomas, 157
Hohfeld, Wesley, 123
Holbrook, David, 188
Holmes, Oliver Wendell, Jr., 15, 34, 44, 82, 157, 191-2, 197-8, 209 n1, 220 n2, 220 n4; and clear and present danger, 30, 218 n9; and marketplace of ideas, 15, 20, 209 n6; scepticism of, 20, 209 n7
Horace, 45
Hudson, Stephen, 130
Hughes, Douglas, 188
Hume, David, 36, 210 n2
humiliation, speech as causing, 10, 176
Husak, Douglas, 130
Hyneman, Charles, 86

incitement, 189, 192-4
individualism, 12, 41, 60
individuals, interests of, 47-8, 61, 71
Ingber, Stanley, 177
Ingram, Peter, 86
injunctions, 114, 150
interests, social and individual, 41-7
intuitionism, 207 n1

Jackson, Robert, 74
Jefferson, Thomas, 26, 211 n11
Joyce, James, 178

Kalven, Harry, 188, 211 n9, 218 n7
Kant, Immanuel, 36, 68-9, 210 n2
Karst, Kenneth, 59, 212 n4
Kendall, Willmoore, 34, 216 n12
Kipling, Rudyard, 110
knowledge (see also certainty, truth), 17, 19; advance of, 27-9; categories of, 30-3, 39; distinguished from certainty, 18; importance of, 17; moral, 21;

search for, 19-29; theories of, 18-19, 22

Ladenson, Robert, 112
language, 110; descriptive, 18-19; development of, 54, 99; ordinary, 12-13, 99, 208 n11, 208 n12; performative, 102, 220 n3; prescriptive, 19; as primary mode of communication, 96; of rights, 12-14, 146-7; rules of, 99; and slippery slope arguments, 83; technical, 12-13; vulgar or offensive, see profanity
Laski, Harold J., 214 n3, 214 n11
learnability, 84-5
least restrictive alternative, 100, 205-6, 216 n9
Lerner, Max, 209 n6
Lesher, J. H., 213 n7
Levellers, 106
Lewis, Sinclair, 110
libel, see defamation
liberalism, 36, 47-8, 60-1, 212 n1
libertarian theory, 11
liberty (see also freedom); abuse of, 145-7; distinguished from freedom, 113, 129; in general, 5-7, 11, 58, 60, 94; as including free speech, 5-7, 52, 58, 60, 94; and individualism, 47, 60; positive and negative, 113-16, 125-30
licensing, 15, 113-14, 149
Linde, Hans, 199
line-drawing, 83-5, 98
listeners, rights or interests of, 42, 49, 95, 104, 106
Locke, John, 14, 26, 70, 106, 213 n8
Longfellow, Henry Wadsworth, 110
Lyons, David, 130, 208 n5

MacCallum, Gerald, 114, 130
McCloskey, H. J., 210 n18, 214 n2
Machiavelli, Nicolo, 77, 160
Madison, James, 211 n11
magazines, 106-7, 113, 126
Magee, Bryan, 209 n4
Magna Carta, 39
marches, see parades
Marcus, Ruth Barcan, 207 n1
marketplace of ideas, 15-17, 19-21, 34, 126, 209 n6
Marshall, Geoffrey, 21, 24
Martin, Rex, 208 n7
Marxism, 37, 155
mass media (see also electronic media, magazines, newspapers), 106-9, 122-30, 158-9, 202
mass meetings, 108

234

Index

Index

public officials (*cont.*)
35-6, 43-5, 89, 95, 107; fallibility of,
34; and law of defamation, 171-5; as
rulers, 43-4; self-interest of, 43-4, 81-2
public policy, criticism of, 42, 45, 79, 95,
105, 107, 140, 190-7
public speech, *see under* speech
purpose of state in suppressing, *see*
under suppression

Quine, Willard v. O., 90

race relations, effect of speech on, 10,
23, 28, 29
radio, *see* electronic media
Raphael, D. D., 211 n4
rationality, 20-4, 70, 78; assumption of,
25-7, 30, 33, 74-5, 77; meaning of, 21,
25, 210 n15; in public at large, 26-7,
33, 41, 155; in scientific inquiry, 25;
in times of emergency, 30, 198-9
Rawls, John, 23, 58, 69, 207 n1, 207 n2,
213 n12, 215 n19, 218 n10, 219 n5, 220
n1
Reich, Charles, 220 n1
relativism, 62
religion and religious toleration, 14, 31,
106, 110
reputation, speech as harming, 10, 28,
167-75
Richards, David A. J., 59, 207 n1, 207
n2, 220 n5
Richards, I. A., 90
rights, 7-10; as absolute, 8-9, 90, 134-6,
208 n5; abuse of, 145-7; against government, 60, 211 n5; conflicts among,
132-45; coverage of, 89-92; created by
government, 111; derivate, 106; distinction between coverage and protection of, 89-92, 134-5, 147, 215 n1;
distinguished from interests, 56; distinguished from privileges, 116-17,
Hohfeldian analysis of, 123-5; individual, 47, 53-6, 218 n2; justification
for restricting, 9, 89-90; language of,
12-14, 146-7; natural, 49-59, 71; positive and negative justifications for,
80; as prescriptive, 90; prima facie, 9,
208 n7, 215 n1; protection of, 89-92;
relation between scope and strength
of, 134-5; as side constraints or
trumps, 7-10, 56, 207 n4; structure of,
7-10, 56, 89-92, 126-7, 145-7
riot, incitement to, 10
Rogat, Yosal, 220 n4
Russell, Bertrand, 36, 78

safety-valve, speech as, *see* catharsis
Scanlon, Thomas, 35, 68-72, 95, 160,
196, 207 n4, 210 n1, 213 n9, 216 n10,
216 n13
scepticism; epistemological, 16, 18, 20,
31, 32, 74, 162, 209 n5; of governmental ability, 80-6, 156-7
Schauer, Frederick, 46, 112
Schram, Glenn, 163
science, philosophy of, 66
scientific inquiry, 25
sedition, 81, 137, 143-4, 189, 192-3
self-censorship, 170-1
self-development, *see* self-realization
self-expression (*see also under* expression *and* freedom of expression), 50-2,
92-3, 110, 211 n6
self-fulfillment, 48-50, 53-9, 60
self-government, *see* democracy
self-realization, 48-50, 53-9
self-regarding acts, 10-11, 64, 68
self-respect, *see* dignity
Shiffrin, Steven, 46
Shostakovich, Dmitri, 109
side constraint; Free Speech Principle
as, 7-9, 56, 63; rights as, 7-9, 56, 207
n5
Simon, Yves, 34
slander, *see* defamation
slippery-slope arguments, 83-5
Smith, Adam, 16
Smith, W. Eugene, 109
social contract, 69-71
Socrates, 67
sovereignty (*see also* democracy), and
determination of political truth,
39-40; individual, 68-70; paradox of,
40-4; of people, 35-9, 194-5; powers
of, 40, 45; and right to be wrong, 37,
40
speakers, rights or interests of, 42, 49,
95, 104-6; motives of, 158-68
Speakers' Corner, 102, 114-15, 126, 201
speech (*see also* communication, expression, Free Speech Principle, freedom of speech); amplified, 99; as
causing harm, 8, 10-12, 24, 28, 58, 64,
132, 140, 167-8; commercial or corporate, 103, 158-60; as communication,
92-5; consequences of, 7-12, 64; critical of law or government, 140;
defined, 13, 89-112; distinctiveness
of, 82-3; distinguished from action,
24, 103, 182-3, 197-8; emotive, 104-5;
excess, 202; factual, 32; joined with
conduct, 99-101; normative, 31; offensive, 28; ordinary and technical